B. R. AMBEDKAR

Manchester University Press

The Pluto Educational Trust is proud to support the Global Icons series. Books published in this series will celebrate and honour individuals whose thought, activism and enduring work 'changed the world'. The Global Icons series will publish books in honour of Walter Rodney, who wrote and struggled for the freedom of black and colonised peoples. Our goal is to publish Icons from across the Global South, and from African American communities, who have become historical figures through thought or action that helped to transform their societies and the wider world. For more information see www.plutoeducationaltrust.org

B. R. AMBEDKAR

THE MAN WHO GAVE HOPE TO INDIA'S DISPOSSESSED

SHASHI THAROOR

MANCHESTER UNIVERSITY PRESS

This edition published by Manchester University Press
Oxford Road, Manchester M13 9PL

By arrangement with Aleph Book Company, New Delhi

www.manchesteruniversitypress.co.uk

www.alephbookcompany.com

British Library Cataloguing-in-Publication Data
A catalogue record for this book is available from the
British Library

ISBN   978 1 5261 7358 4   hardback

First published 2023

Printed in Great Britain
by Bell & Bain Ltd, Glasgow

MIX
Paper | Supporting
responsible forestry
FSC
www.fsc.org   FSC® C007785

*To the people of India
to whom Ambedkar gave so much
that we are yet to fully appreciate*

ALSO BY SHASHI THAROOR

NON-FICTION

Pride, Prejudice, and Punditry: The Essential Shashi Tharoor

*The Battle of Belonging: On Nationalism, Patriotism, and
What It Means to Be Indian*

Tharoorosaurus

The New World Disorder and the Indian Imperative (with Samir Saran)

The Hindu Way: An Introduction to Hinduism

The Paradoxical Prime Minister: Narendra Modi and His India

Why I Am a Hindu

An Era of Darkness: The British Empire in India

India Shastra: Reflections on the Nation in Our Time

India: The Future Is Now (ed.)

Pax Indica: India and the World of the 21st Century

Shadows Across the Playing Field: 60 Years of India-Pakistan Cricket
(with Shahryar Khan)

India (with Ferrante Ferranti)

*The Elephant, the Tiger, and the Cell Phone:
Reflections on India in the 21st Century*

Bookless in Baghdad

Nehru: The Invention of India

Kerala: God's Own Country (with M. F. Husain)

India: From Midnight to the Millennium and Beyond

Reasons of State

FICTION

Riot

The Five Dollar Smile and Other Stories

Show Business

The Great Indian Novel

'We possess the wealth of words. With weapons of words we will fight; words are the breath of our life, we will distribute the wealth of words among the people.'

—Sant Tukaram, 1608–1650

Contents

List of Plates

Preface

The first questions I am often asked about this book are 'Why Ambedkar? Why now?' It is tempting to reply, 'Read the book and find out', but I have preferred to respond by informing my questioners of two facts of which even most Indians are unaware. First, there is no Indian of whom more statues have been erected across the length and breadth of India than Ambedkar, barring, perhaps, Mahatma Gandhi. Second, when, in 2012, two respected television channels conducted a poll to name the Greatest Indian, over 20 million voters participated and resoundingly picked Ambedkar, ahead of Gandhi, Nehru, Patel and other giants of contemporary Indian history.

Arguably, there is no more important figure in contemporary India, after Mahatma Gandhi, than Dr Ambedkar: in addition to the ubiquitous statues of him, there are also more observances of his life and legacy than anyone else's. His posthumous stature has grown enormously: a controversial figure in his own lifetime, who lost more elections than he won and attracted both opprobrium and admiration in equal measure, he is almost beyond criticism today. All Indian political parties seek to lay claim to his legacy. Yet he is not as well known to general readers globally as he deserves to be. There is a vast amount of material, much of it generated by the man himself, whose copious output is estimated at some 17,500-odd pages. But a concise distillation is harder to find. A short, accessible biography for the non-specialist reader, that summarizes all the important events of his life and critically analyses his impact on India and beyond, seeks thus to fill an important gap.

It is difficult today to imagine the scale of what Dr Babasaheb Bhimji Rao Ambedkar accomplished. To be born into an 'untouchable' family in 1891, and that too as the fourteenth and last child of a poor Mahar subedar, or non-commissioned officer, in an Army cantonment, would normally have guaranteed a life of neglect, poverty, discrimination and obscurity. Not only did Ambedkar rise above the circumstances of his birth, but he achieved a level of success that would have been spectacular for a child of privilege. One of the first 'untouchables' ever to enter an Indian college, he became a professor (at the prestigious Sydenham College) and a principal (of no less an institution than Bombay's Government Law College, in those days considered the top law college in the country). One of the earliest Indian students in the United States, he earned multiple doctorates from Columbia University and the University of London, earning advanced qualifications in economics, politics and law. An heir to millennia of discrimination, he was admitted to the bar in London and became 'India's James Madison' as the chair of the Constitution Drafting Committee. The descendant of illiterates, he wrote a remarkable number of books, whose content and range testify to an eclectic mind and a sharp, if provocative, intellect. An insignificant infant scrabbling in the dust of Mhow in 1891 became the first law minister of a free India in 1947, in the most impressive cabinet ever assembled in New Delhi.

When he died in 1956, aged only 65, Ambedkar had accumulated a set of distinctions few have matched: he had successfully challenged millennia-old discrimination against Dalits (formerly 'untouchables' or 'depressed classes'), instituted the world's oldest and farthest-reaching affirmative action programme for his people and entrenched it in the Constitution, promoted liberal constitutionalism in a traditionally illiberal society, managed a balance between individual agency for India's citizens and collective affirmation action for its most marginalized communities, and articulated the most cogent and enduring case for the principles and practices of democracy in a country emerging from imperial rule. Only one distinction remained: India's highest civilian honour, the Bharat Ratna. When this was finally awarded in 1990, the only question raised by commentators was why it had taken so long.

Ambedkar's was, therefore, a monumental life. And his towering achievements were made despite suffering and enduring humiliations that might have been enough to crush the spirit of a lesser man, or turn him into a destructive force. Denied permission to sit at a desk or chair like his other classmates and obliged to learn his lessons from a gunny sack on the floor which no one would touch, and thrashed for daring to open a water tap at school when he was thirsty (since his touch was deemed polluting), Ambedkar still achieved academic excellence, winning scholarships for higher studies abroad and earning multiple doctorates in an era when upper-caste men wrote 'B.A. (Failed)' after their names to show they had got that far. Returning to the service of the maharaja who had sponsored his studies abroad, he found no one in the city willing to rent an abode to an 'untouchable', resorted to deception, was found out and thrown into the street. Sitting in a park at night with his papers and certificates strewn around him, he wept bitterly and quit the prestigious job he had earned on merit. Rising from such humiliations to become the most consequential political and social reformer of a glittering generation of freedom-fighters was Ambedkar's triumph.

And yet many feel posterity has yet to get the measure of the man. 'History,' wrote the novelist Arundhati Roy, 'has been unkind to Ambedkar. First, it contained him, and then it glorified him. It has made him India's Leader of the Untouchables, the King of the Ghetto. It has hidden away his writings. It has stripped away the radical intellect and the searing insolence.'

It is, indeed, largely true that whereas some of those who seek to stand on Ambedkar's shoulders today acknowledge his role in fighting discrimination against Dalits, and others honour his Constitution-making, they do not engage with the totality of his political and economic vision. Ambedkar's concerns and doubts about Indian democracy and his leftist view of political economy and labour rights are usually conveniently overlooked by his professed admirers. They prefer instead to do exactly what he warned against—to worship him as an idol, an act of 'bhakti' rather than the critical engagement he might have welcomed.

Reviewing Ambedkar's colossal achievements requires us to neither restrict him to his role as the great emancipator of India's Dalits, nor to glorify him as a saint above criticism, but rather to embrace his life and his ideas as a whole—the activism and the politics, the triumphs and the failures that marked his extraordinary impact on India's public consciousness. This book therefore offers a reinterpretation of his life and legacy that seeks to strike a balance: it would be a pity if the life of this extraordinary Indian were reduced to one issue—his championship of the Dalit cause—just as much as it would be wrong to gloss over his path-breaking role in that monumental endeavour. Readers of this book are invited to appreciate Ambedkar's contribution as a constitutionalist and a builder of democracy in addition to his role as a social iconoclast, and are encouraged to engage with Ambedkar's ideas and his battles for the principles for which he stood.

These include his fundamental critique of Hindu society and its practice of the caste system, or *varnashrama dharma*, whose 'annihilation' he called for in terms that alarmed those who wanted to overcome untouchability without disturbing the existing social order; his conversion to Buddhism in the last year of his life, and his exhortation to others to follow his example; his emphasis on 'constitutional morality' as a means of sinking liberal roots into an illiberal society; his revival of the idea of 'fraternity', not merely in its French Revolutionary sense but as an authentic Indian idea traceable to the Buddha and the early Buddhist *sanghas*; and his astonishing intellectual fecundity in taking on issues as diverse as provincial taxation in British India, the challenges and advantages of dividing India into linguistically organised states, and the case for Pakistan. It also acknowledges his occasionally intemperate language, his ungraciousness to Mahatma Gandhi, whom he saw as his nemesis, and his unwillingness to suffer fools gladly or make the concessions and compromises so necessary to get along in a largely hostile world.

It is important to realize that Ambedkar was not only an economist of the highest quality—Amartya Sen, India's only Nobel Prize-winning economist, was to hail him as the 'father' of his own economics—and a legal scholar of rare distinction, but also a pioneering social anthropologist, whose 1916 paper on caste at a conference in Columbia was arguably the first serious academic study of the origins and practice of the caste system in India. Ambedkar was also modern India's first male feminist: his speeches and legislative initiatives on women's rights nearly ninety years ago would be considered progressive even today in India. As a legal thinker, his emphasis on individual agency and his understanding of the true meaning of 'effective representation' in a democracy are key to the constitutional system that has been established and entrenched over the last three-quarters of a century. As a social reformer, Ambedkar's emphasis on education as the passport to social advancement and economic empowerment for 'subalterns' continues to resonate in today's India. The very idea of Indianness, so brilliantly articulated by Jawaharlal Nehru and his acolytes, was infused with an extra dimension when viewed through Ambedkar's lens of social justice for those who had been oppressed and marginalized for millennia.

Finally, in the tension between Mahatma Gandhi's vision of India and Ambedkar's, it is fair to say that it is the latter's vision that endures, codified in the Constitution of the republic. And that vision is his finest legacy. In the perennial tension between communitarian privileges and individual rights, Ambedkar stood squarely on the side of the individual. In the battle between timeless traditions and modern conceptions of social justice, Ambedkar tilted the scales decisively toward the latter. In the contestation between the wielders of power and the drafters of law, Ambedkar carved a triumphant place for enabling change through democracy and legislation. In a fractured and divided Hindu society he gave the Dalits a sense of collective pride and individual self-respect. In so doing, he transformed the lives of millions yet unborn, heaving an ancient civilization into the modern era through the force of his intellect and the power of his pen.

This book does not claim to be a comprehensive account of a remarkable, complex and well-documented life. But it is arguably the most concise work to delineate the overall contours of his experiences, his contributions and his impact. There will undoubtedly be other versions of Ambedkar's life to be written that may illuminate in greater detail one or more aspects of his biography. If this volume fulfils the curiosity of the general reader, it will have served its purpose; and if it whets the appetite of some sufficiently to prompt them to explore such aspects in greater detail in other works, it will also have served another purpose.

Ambedkar's life and legacy is far too consequential for Indians, and those interested in India, not to be aware of it. This book endeavours to serve as a contribution to building that awareness.

Shashi Tharoor
December 2022

A Note from the Author

Three caveats.

The biography of a man who is principally noted for his words rather than his actions inevitably suffers from a deficiency of incidents and a surfeit of ideas. There is undoubtedly drama and suffering in Ambedkar's life, but far more consequential is the weight of his writings, speeches, and interventions in the public debates of his time. In opting to reflect this reality, the biographer is obliged to acknowledge that this sometimes makes for a curiously bloodless tale. That the son of an untouchable subedar, scrabbling in the dust in the cantonment town of Mhow, rose to earn two prestigious doctorates and, by sheer dint of his intellectual worth, courage of conviction, and brilliance of articulation became one of the foremost figures among a generation of giants is drama enough for this writer. But the reader is fairly warned: this is the story of the rise of a man of ideas, illustrated with extensive quotations from his writings and speeches, and not of a man of physical adventure.

The second caveat relates to the use of some descriptions in the narrative. In the early chapters, and elsewhere in the book, the word 'untouchable' is freely used, even though it is a pejorative term that has long since fallen into discredit. The problem is that at the time being referred to, the word 'Dalit', the currently accepted term for the community in question, was not generally in use, and even Dr Ambedkar himself often used the term untouchables. The community—also referred to as the 'Depressed Classes'—became known after 1935 as the Scheduled Castes, and that term slips into the discourse as the narrative moves on. But the reader is asked in advance to excuse the author for reflecting the language of the times. No offence is intended.

And, finally, a third, inescapable, caveat: in my extensive reading of Dalit writings and commentary on the life and teachings of Ambedkar, I have become acutely conscious of the fact that some will object to this book on the basic ground that I am not a Dalit. I am entirely aware that the analysis of an 'objective' author, however well-read or well-informed, cannot match the insights gleaned from the personal experience of discrimination and marginalization. I will not protest, as I once did, that I have grown up oblivious of caste, because I have since been schooled to accept that even caste-blindness is a reflection of privilege, and that no Dalit can ever escape being conscious of her caste, as I was brought up to be unaware initially of my own. In the end I can only say that I have approached the subject of this short biography with respect for the man, admiration for his accomplishments, knowledge of the history, and awareness of the context. It is up to the reader to judge whether the result of my efforts is good enough.

BOOK ONE

LIFE

ONE

Laying the Foundations

1891–1923

The nine-year-old boy and his two companions, a brother and a cousin, were excited. The boy's father, who was working in another town, had invited them to spend their summer vacation with him in Koregaon.[1] The boys dressed in their best finery for the occasion, donning tailored jackets and brocade caps. They were thrilled to be travelling by train for the first time.

They had written to their father with details of their train's arrival at 5 p.m., but the message never reached him and they found no one waiting for them when they arrived. After waiting for a while, they asked people on the platform what they could do. Questions arose: who were these boys? They soon revealed they were Mahars, members of an untouchable community. Suddenly, no one was willing to be helpful. After an hour and a half of waiting helplessly, they tried to engage a cart to transport them to their father's place, several hours away by road from the train station. There were several carts sitting idle but none available to them to rent. Finally one cart was found, but the cartman was unwilling to drive the cart for fear of being 'polluted'.

In the end the boys had to agree to pay double the fare

---

[1]Vasant Moon (ed.), *Dr. Babasaheb Ambedkar: Writings and Speeches*, Vol. 12, Bombay: Education Department, Government of Maharashtra, 1993, pp. 661–91.

and drive the cart themselves, with the driver walking alongside. Many petty indignities were inflicted upon them on the long journey: people along the route refused to serve them water because of their caste, they could not let their guard down for fear that the cartman might do them harm, and they stayed anxiously awake at an overnight rest stop, segregated from others, terrified of what terrors might be lurking in the dark. The boys' excitement at their holiday trip had given way to an overwhelming sense of humiliation at their inhumane treatment for no reason but their caste identity. The nine-year-old boy on whom this incident had a profound influence was called Bhim.

Babasaheb Bhimrao Ramji Ambedkar, MA, MSc., PhD, DSc, DLitt, Bar-at-Law, was born on 14 April 1891 into a family of Mahars, a community from the Konkan area of the Bombay Presidency (a province of India during the Raj that largely comprised parts of the present-day states of Maharashtra, Gujarat, and Karnataka). The Mahars had historically been deemed untouchable in the prevailing highly stratified caste system.

To be born an untouchable in nineteenth-century India was to be consigned to the depths of human degradation.[2] Ghettoized by other communities, refused permission to draw water from a communal well or to bathe in the same ponds or rivers as caste Hindus, members of the community were regarded as outcastes whose mere shadow, let alone touch, was deemed polluting by their social 'betters' in the Hindu caste system. They were confined to the most abject of tasks—manual scavenging, the cleaning of toilets and sewers, the disposal of human and animal waste, the skinning of dead animals, and so on. Most of them never saw the inside of a school, except to sweep its floors. Caste Hindus neither accepted food or water from their hands, nor served them: the mere exchange

---

[2] Dhananjay Keer, *Dr. Ambedkar: Life and Mission*, Bombay: Popular Prakashan, 1971, pp. 1–2.

of food or water with one of them was deemed polluting. Illiterate, malnourished, abused, and despised, members of the community were, for the most part, condemned from birth to a life of misery, malnutrition, exclusion, and penury.

As with everything in India, there were variations within this general picture. Some untouchable sub-castes fared marginally better than others.[3] Their roles had evolved through history in different ways at different places and they received opportunities that elevated their status slightly above others. Ambedkar's Mahar sub-caste was one such.

The Mahars were traditionally relegated to various menial jobs and mainly served as Veskars or watchmen,[4] though Ambedkar's family played a more significant role in their ancestral village, Ambavade, in Ratnagiri district, where its members served as palanquin-bearers for the idol of the temple goddess. Some found work as labourers in the textile mills of Bombay and Nagpur.

But the Mahars also had a proud martial tradition, serving as soldiers in the guerrilla armies of the Marathas, and the British were quick to recognize this, pressing them into service in the ranks of the East India Company and subsequently of the British Indian Army.[5] (One interpretation of the word Mahar is that it is derived from 'Maha-Ari', or 'the great enemy', an etymology that reflects the Mahar combination of a belligerent spirit and a fighting temperament.) The Mahar Regiment duly acquired some distinction as fierce and heroic fighters. Both Ambedkar's father, Ramji Maloji Sakpal, born in 1848, and his grandfather, Maloji Sakpal, before him, served in the regiment, as did his mother Bhimabai's ancestors, and thus it was that

---

[3] Ibid., p. 2.
[4] Traude Pillai-Vetschera as cited in Christophe Jaffrelot, *Dr. Ambedkar and Untouchability: Analysing and Fighting Caste*, London: C. Hurst & Company, 2005, pp. 20–21.
[5] 'Indian Army's Mahar regiment: Home to two army chiefs and a Param Vir Chakra', *The Print*, 3 January 2018.

he was born in the British cantonment of Mhow, on 14 April 1891, the last child of his parents.

Ramji Sakpal was getting on in age by then and retired from the army as a subedar in 1893, when little Bhim was just two. The large family could not subsist on his meagre pension and Ramji took up a job the following year as a PWD storekeeper in the district town of Satara. Bhim, a somewhat rowdy infant, with a taste for a fight and an unwillingness to admit defeat in any situation he found himself in, was enrolled at the age of five at a local school in Dapoli, in Ratnagiri district. (The enrolment was not unusual even for an untouchable soldier's child, since education was compulsory for the children of the military. Indeed, not only Bhim's father, but also the women of his family were literate.)[6] As a young boy in Satara, according to his biographer, Dhananjay Keer, Bhim was 'pugnacious, resourceful and fearless.... Taking up a classmate's challenge to walk in the rain without an umbrella, he had come to class in wet clothes.'[7] He lost his mother when he was barely six years old; she died exhausted after giving birth to fourteen children, of whom just five—three sons, Balaram, Anandrao, and Bhim, and two daughters, Manjula and Tulsi—survived infancy.

As an untouchable, Bhim was segregated at school from the other students, made to sit in a corner of the classroom on a gunny sack—which they had to bring from home and take back at the end of the day, since the school peon, who belonged to a 'higher' caste, would not touch it[8]—and given scant attention by some teachers. But despite such indignities, he showed a precocious talent for learning. His father, a strict disciplinarian who believed in the virtues of schooling, took personal charge of his children's education and ensured that,

---

[6] Jaffrelot, *Dr. Ambedkar and Untouchability*, p. 26.
[7] Chandan Gowda, 'Ambedkar's childhood', *Bangalore Mirror*, 15 April 2016.
[8] Danish Sud, 'The Fascinating story of Dr. BR Ambedkar', *Times of India*, 17 October 2020.

despite their mistreatment, they attended school, supplementing their formal instruction with lessons of his own. He believed that the quiet predawn hours were the best time to study, and woke his children accordingly. Before examinations, Ambedkar recalled, he would be woken up at 2 a.m.[9] to prepare for them.

In 1901, Ramji took a job at Koregaon, leaving his children in the care of an aunt who proved quite incapable of looking after them. The children had to cook and fend for themselves. Bhim spoke of how they subsisted largely on rice pulav since 'we found [it] to be the easiest dish to prepare, requiring nothing more than mixing rice and mutton'.[10] The young boy learned early to be self-sufficient.

The incident of the journey to Koregaon, with which we began this chapter, and of which he later spoke feelingly, was one of many examples of discrimination that Bhim had to suffer. The discrimination continued at school, though Bhim proved a good student and performed well in his examinations: 'I could not sit in the midst of my classmates according to my rank [in class performance], but [had] to sit in a corner by myself. ... I was to have a separate piece of gunny cloth for me to squat on in the classroom, and the servant employed to clean the school would not touch the gunny cloth used by me. I was required to carry the gunny cloth home in the evening, and bring it back the next day.'[11] Similarly, he was not permitted to touch the water tap when thirsty, since his touch would 'defile' it; he had to wait for the school peon to open the tap for him, and if the peon was not available, he had to leave his thirst unquenched. It is said that once, when Bhim was found quietly drinking water from a public tap, he was beaten up for his presumption. 'No peon, no water,'[12] he

---

[9] Sunil Khilnani, *Incarnations: A History of India in 50 Lives*, New Delhi: Penguin Random House, 2017, p. 540.
[10] Moon, *Dr. Babasaheb Ambedkar*, Vol. 12, pp. 661–65.
[11] Ibid.
[12] Ibid.

later recounted bitterly. Also no washerman would wash the clothes of an untouchable, and no barber would cut their hair.

These humiliations understandably rankled, but there was the occasional kindness as well from a pair of Brahmin teachers at school—Mr Pendse, who saw the child shivering after being caught in a downpour and had him taken to his own home to be dried off and given a fresh set of clothes, and Krishna Keshav Ambedkar,[13] who quietly shared his lunch with Bhim every day. Bhim had been enrolled in school under the name of Bhiva Sakpal, Bhiva being his childhood nickname and Sakpal his father's surname, but this otherwise negligent but kind-hearted teacher changed his name in the school register to Ambedkar—a name derived from the name of his own and Bhim's ancestral village, Ambavade. Upper-caste Maharashtrians routinely adopted the practice of taking their surnames from their places of origin; untouchables did not. Mr Ambedkar decided young Bhim was worthy of bearing his own name,[14] a decision the latter willingly embraced.

In 1901, Ramji Sakpal decided to marry again, a decision that did not go down well with his youngest son. Ten-year-old Bhim vowed to be independent of his father's new household and seriously explored plans to look for work at one of the cotton mills in Satara, which employed young boys. Fortunately, better sense prevailed and he decided to focus on his studies instead, to acquire the qualifications that would enable him to make his way in the world.

The family moved to Bombay where they lived in a one-room tenement in a chawl. Living conditions were challenging: chawls were typically two- to four-storeyed buildings with one-room apartments, and the residents shared communal bathrooms.

---

[13] Some texts name him as Mahadev. I have gone by Krishna Keshav Ambedkar. See Akshay Chavan, 'Dr Ambedkar: Against all Odds', *Live History India*, 6 December 2018.

[14] 'B. R. Ambedkar—Profile', Indian National Congress official website.

Ramji's meagre pension could only support the education of one son, so the brightest, Bhim, was enrolled in the prestigious Elphinstone College's High School,[15] the only member of his community at that institution, his father borrowing money to pay for his schoolbooks. Even there he could not escape reminders of his untouchability: on one occasion, when the teacher summoned him to the blackboard to solve a problem, an uproar ensued as the other students raced to get to the blackboard ahead of him. It turned out that they kept their tiffin-boxes behind the blackboard and were terrified that Bhim would pollute their food with his presence. They pushed their tiffin boxes aside before he could reach the blackboard.[16] Bhim excelled at his studies but discrimination persisted even there: he wished to study Sanskrit[17] but was denied permission[18] by the authorities to do so since he was an untouchable, and he had to study Persian instead. But his capacity for learning was undiminished by such experiences. When he matriculated in 1907, at the age of sixteen, he had scored the highest marks in the school in Persian.

Matriculation was no small feat: Bhim Ambedkar was the first of his community to achieve this distinction. The British had invested very little in developing educational facilities for Indians and there were few schools and colleges in the country; even most upper-caste children did not pursue their studies that far. For an untouchable to do so was virtually unheard of, and Bhim's graduating from high school occasioned a public felicitation.[19] His progress in his studies also led to his marriage

---

[15] Keer, *Dr. Ambedkar*, p. 19.

[16] Ibid., pp. 17–18

[17] Lower-caste Hindus studying Sanskrit was a far cry especially since according to Ambedkar's official biographer, Dhananjay Keer, even the maharaja of Satara had to take lessons at night. Keer, *Dr. Ambedkar*, p. 5.

[18] Kancha Ilaiah, 'Why Ambedkar supported Sanskrit as national language: A response to Murli Manohar Joshi', *News Minute*, 27 April 2016.

[19] The event was presided over by S. K. Bole, a famous social reformer of the time. Keer, *Dr. Ambedkar*, p. 19.

being arranged, as was the custom of the times, in 1905, to a nine-year-old Mahar girl, Rami, renamed Ramabai.[20]

Marriage did not dissuade Bhim from his determination to pursue further studies, and he enrolled at Elphinstone College. But by the time he had passed his intermediate examinations, he received the bad news: the family simply could no longer afford to pay for his education. He would not be able to complete his degree.

At this point another well-wisher intervened. As a high-schooler, Bhim had greatly impressed the Marathi scholar and social reformer, K. A. Keluskar, who came across him reading diligently in a garden that Keluskar also used to frequent.[21] Keluskar used to lend Bhim books from his own library and presented him one of his own, a life of Gautama Buddha, that was to have a profound and lasting impact on the young man. Keluskar had heard that the maharaja of Baroda, Sir Sayaji Rao Gaekwad,[22] had, at a public meeting in Bombay, declared his willingness to help any worthy untouchable student pursue higher studies. He called on the maharaja and asked him to support Bhim. The maharaja summoned the young man for an interview and, impressed with his answers to the questions he was posed, granted him a scholarship of ₹25 a month, a princely sum in those days.[23]

The maharaja's munificence was enough not only to support Bhim's college studies but to allow the family to move to better lodgings, in a two-room apartment rather than one—the second

---

[20] NDTV News Desk, 'Who Was Ramabai Ambedkar? Some Lesser-Known Facts About BR Ambedkar's Wife', *NDTV*, 27 May 2022.

[21] Yogesh Maitreya, 'Ambedkar: A Spartan Warrior who Made Knowledge and Justice his Weapon', *Indian Cultural Forum*, 14 April 2020.

[22] Gaekwad was an iconic figure, fabled for his open acts of defiance of British authority, including turning his back on the King-Emperor at the Delhi Durbar of 1911. Alastair Lawson, 'Indian maharajah's daring act of anti-colonial dissent', BBC, 10 December 2011.

[23] Though some accounts claim the sum was ₹50, ₹25 is the figure reported by the first two Ambedkar biographers, Dhananjay Keer and M. L. Shahare.

room reserved exclusively for the brilliant young scholar to study undisturbed. In 1912, when Bhim was twenty-one and his wife sixteen, a son, Yashwant, was born to the young couple. A year later, Bhim graduated with a bachelor's degree—this in a country where many of his upper-caste compatriots had the habit of adding 'BA (Failed)' after their names as a mark of distinction for having got that far!

The maharaja promptly commissioned the fresh graduate as a lieutenant in Baroda's armed forces, but within weeks of taking up his duties, Bhim received a telegram informing him that his father was gravely ill. He resigned and rushed back to Bombay just in time to meet Ramji Sakpal for the last time. It is said that Ramji's dying gesture was to place his hand on Bhim's back as a blessing, imparting to his son his indomitable spirit and will to conquer adversity. Ramji Sakpal passed away,[24] to Bhim's immense grief, on 2 February 1913, aged sixty-five—the very age till which his son was destined to live.

Although Bhim had had to resign his commission in Baroda to return home to his father's deathbed, in June 1913, he was able to win another scholarship from the maharaja, this time to study in the United States, of £11.50 per month for three years, in exchange for a commitment to serve Baroda State on his return for a ten-year period.[25] 'It was a unique opportunity that was presented to Ambedkar,' notes Christophe Jaffrelot. 'It was due to his intelligence and capacity for hard work, but his good fortune owed much to the Maratha princely elite: non-Brahmin solidarity was to be a decisive factor in his career.'[26] He left behind his large extended family to survive on the earnings of his labourer brother, Anandrao, and sailed for the US.

In the third week of July 1913, Ambedkar arrived in New

[24] Keer, *Dr. Ambedkar*, p. 24.
[25] Ibid., p. 25.
[26] Jaffrelot, *Dr. Ambedkar and Untouchability*, p. 27.

York to study at Columbia University.[27] The United States had long been seen as a beacon of freedom in the world, and Bhim was aware of the struggle of black Americans for honour and dignity in their homeland, a struggle that in some ways mirrored that of India's untouchables. He was determined to make the most of the opportunity that being at Columbia presented him.

Eschewing most of the temptations and diversions available to young men in the Big Apple—and sending a portion of his stipend home to Bombay, to help sustain his family in his absence—Ambedkar proceeded to devote himself ferociously to his studies eighteen hours a day.[28] (At the start he briefly indulged himself in badminton, ice skating, and visiting the theatre, but that phase did not last long before his conscience drove him back to his books.) He roomed with a remarkable Parsi from Bombay, Naval Bhathena,[29] a businessman-to-be who was free from caste prejudice and who took an immense liking to the brilliant student. Ambedkar took courses in political science, moral philosophy, economics, anthropology, and sociology and authored a master's thesis on 'Commerce in Ancient India', winning an MA in 1915. Continuing his pursuit of a doctorate, Ambedkar studied Indian finance in depth and authored a thesis on the 'National Dividend of India'.

He did make the time to prepare and present a paper on a subject he was beginning to devote more thought to: 'Castes in India, their Genesis, Mechanisms and Development'. Addressing an anthropology seminar[30] in May 1916 on this theme, he

---

[27] 'In the 1910's, Off to Columbia, On to London, Columbia University', Columbia University official website.

[28] So profound was the impact of this study routine on the students of Veermata Jijabai Technological Institute that they organized an eighteen-hour study marathon to commemorate Ambedkar's 126th birth anniversary. Shreya Ramachandran, '18-hour study marathon commemorates Ambedkar's legacy', *The Hindu*, 10 April 2017.

[29] Urvish Kothari, 'Parsis in Baroda berated Ambedkar for his caste. But Naval Bhathena changed everything', *The Print*, 6 December 2019.

[30] B. R. Ambedkar, 'Castes in India: Their Mechanism, Genesis and

formulated a critique of the evils of caste that would form the beginning of his lifelong intellectual and political engagement with an issue that touched him viscerally. (He also demonstrated a gift for engaging metaphor, explaining to his American audience that 'Hinduism is like a multi-storied building in which each floor is occupied by a caste, but there is no staircase which links the different floors. One lives and dies on the floor on which one is born.'[31]) During this period he encountered the famous nationalist Lala Lajpat Rai, who was on a lecture tour of the US on behalf of the Indian Home Rule League to drum up support for India's freedom. Ambedkar attended the Lala's meetings and raised the issue of the nationalists' neglect of untouchability. The latter's response—that such issues could be resolved once freedom was won—did not please the younger man, who thereupon ended his involvement with the Home Rule League.

Ambedkar's doctoral thesis was completed and submitted in June 1916. Critical as it was of the British colonial bureaucracy's exactions, it impressed Columbia, which awarded him his PhD amid high praise. The thesis was later expanded and published as Ambedkar's first book, *The Evolution of Imperial Provincial Finance in India*.[32] It marked the beginning of his growing reputation for rigorous intellect, detailed research, and a prodigious appetite for work borne out in his rapid and prolific output.

Rather than return to serve his bond in Baroda, Ambedkar sought and obtained the blessings of the indulgent maharaja

---

Development', paper read at an anthropological seminar of Alexander Goldenweiser in New York on 9 May 1916, *Indian Antiquary,* May 1917, Vol. 61, reprinted in Moon, *Dr. Babasaheb Ambedkar,* Vol. 1, 1979.

[31] As quoted by Ananya Vajpeyi in 'B. R. Ambedkar: The Life of the Mind and a Life in Politics', Library of Congress, 2 December 2014, [Video] Retrieved from the Library of Congress, https://www.loc.gov/item/webcast-6653/.

[32] B. R. Ambedkar, 'The Evolution of Imperial Provincial Finance in British India: A Study in the Provincial Decentralisation of Imperial Finance', available on indianculture.gov.in.

to continue his studies in London on yet another scholarship. Arriving in London in October 1916, Ambedkar enrolled himself at the London School of Economics for postdoctoral studies and simultaneously registered at Gray's Inn to qualify for the bar. There was no limit to his yearning to expand the range of his intellect and enhance his academic qualifications.

But this time Ambedkar ran into resistance. The dewan of the state of Baroda was somewhat less indulgent of the gifted student than his maharaja, and ordered Ambedkar to return to fulfil his undertaking of serving the state for ten years. Though he had spent only six months in London when the order came, and World War I was raging, Ambedkar had no choice but to comply. Never one to give up easily, he won special permission from the University of London to retain his admission status on a deferred basis (albeit for a period of four years rather than ten) and to be allowed to resume his studies within that period. He was hopeful he would earn a renewed opportunity to complete his studies at LSE. Thus armed, he set out for India by ship, booking his luggage on a cargo steamer. His ship made the dangerous journey safely, but the steamer carrying his luggage, which consisted of his entire precious collection of books, and the manuscript of his thesis, was torpedoed by the Germans en route and sank without trace. Ambedkar, who always found in books the enveloping acceptance and the sense of equality of access that had been denied to him in his own life, mourned their loss bitterly.[33]

By this time, his intellect had been shaped by a variety of influences. There was Sant Kabir, the fifteenth-century mystic sage and poet, who had been revered by his father and himself, and whose original and insightful verses young Bhim had learned in childhood. These included the famous doha, 'Manus

---

[33] Krishnamurty Jayasankar, 'Ambedkar's Educational Odyssey, 1913–1927', *Journal of Social Inclusion Studies*, New Delhi: Institute of Human Development, February 2020.

hona kathin haya tou sadhu kahanse hoya?'—it's difficult enough to be a man, how will you become a sage?[34]—which reinforced Ambedkar's scepticism towards holy men. (It is said his disinclination to acknowledge Gandhi as a 'Mahatma' and his insistence on referring to him only as 'Mr Gandhi' sprang from this couplet. As he later wrote: 'Mahatmas have come and Mahatmas have gone. But the Untouchables have remained Untouchables.'[35]) There were the teachings of the Marathi saint, Sant Tukaram, which his father recited and propounded at home in Bhim's childhood; Ambedkar could quote many of Tukaram's verses by heart. To these Bhim added the intellectual influences emerging from his education—Keluskar and his admiration for Buddhism; Edwin R. A. Seligman at Columbia, whose classes on public finance the young Ambedkar devoured, and who introduced him to the London School of Economics; the labour and human rights expert James T. Shotwell, the progressive historian James Harvey Robinson, and, above all, the philosopher John Dewey, all also at Columbia, whose methods of enquiry, activist epistemology, faith in democratic institutions as enablers of change and the idea of a realist school of politics, both inspired Bhim and taught him the importance of pragmatism; the jurist and social reformer Mahadev Govind Ranade, who had battled for the uplift of the untouchables and whose ideas of social democracy found resonance with the young Bhim; and Harold Laski at LSE, whose emphasis on a moral order as the underpinning of democracy and idealist socialism became hallmarks of Ambedkar's own vision. These were all people he met and interacted with. Ambedkar also read widely and showed a particular fascination for the ideas of Bertrand Russell, whose book *Principles of Social*

[34] Ishita Aditya Ray, 'An Appraisal of Influence of Eminent Personalities on Ambedkar's Political Thought during the Early Twentieth Century', *Historical Research Letter*, IISTE.org, Vol. 2, 2012.
[35] Moon, *Dr. Babasaheb Ambedkar*, Vol. 3, p. 67, quoted in Sagarika Ghose, 'The Dalit in India', *Social Research*, Spring 2003, Vol. 70, No. 1, pp. 83–109.

Reconstruction he reviewed; Edmund Burke, whose ideas of morality in politics appealed to the young Indian; John Stuart Mill, whose insistence on freedom of thought, speech, and action became part of Ambedkar's basic credo; Booker T. Washington, the black American intellectual whose life taught him the value of education as the principal tool of empowerment; and Antonio Gramsci, whose approach towards the empowerment of the subaltern has remarkable parallels with Ambedkar's. Both Gramsci and Ambedkar found inspiration in Marxism, were critical of religion, yet considered religion culturally and politically relevant; both infused their solid emphasis on scholarship and research with intense feelings derived from their lived experiences; both focused on the 'inclusion of the excluded' through active leadership and consciousness-raising by intellectuals; and both saw the challenge of uplifting the subaltern as a problem for the whole of society and not for the victims alone.[36]

Bookless as a result of German torpedoes, but with a razor-sharp mind shaped by years of intellectual stimulation, Ambedkar arrived in Baroda in September 1917. He received a warm welcome from the maharaja, who expressed a desire to name him finance minister of the state before long, in recognition of his advanced qualifications as an economist. As an initial appointment, however, he was named military secretary to the maharaja. But after four years of enjoying the freedoms of New York, Ambedkar was repelled by the social discrimination to which he was subject in Baroda. Even the peons refused to serve him so much as a glass of water, claiming it would pollute them to do so, and threw official papers on his desk in order

---

[36] There is a fascinating comparison of the ideas of Gramsci and Ambedkar in Cosimo Zene (ed.), *The Political Philosophies of Antonio Gramsci and B. R. Ambedkar*, Abingdon, New York: Routledge, 2013, p. 23.

to avoid physical contact by handing them directly to him. Worse, he failed to find a single landlord willing to rent him accommodation, despite his status.[37] Ambedkar turned in despair and frustration to the dewan and the maharaja, and found them unable to help him. The maharaja himself was enlightened and progressive, but his officials, staff, and even servants were not, and did not stir themselves on behalf of someone they considered a presumptuous untouchable. His application for a state bungalow was referred from official to official but not acted upon with any urgency.

'My five years of staying in Europe and America had completely wiped out of my mind any consciousness that I was an untouchable, and that an untouchable wherever he went in India was a problem to himself and to others,'[38] Ambedkar recounted later. In a dilemma about where to stay, Ambedkar found himself at a Parsi-owned inn that was only open to members of the Parsi community. With no other option, and perhaps recalling how his friend Naval Bhathena had embraced him without prejudice, he decided to bribe the receptionist and have his name entered in the register as a Parsi. The deception, however, failed. On the eleventh day of his stay, some local Parsis found out Ambedkar's caste and, sticks in hand, stormed the inn. Ambedkar has described the dramatic scene in front of his room: '[They] fired a volley of questions. "Who are you? Why did you come here? How dare you take a Parsi name? You scoundrel! You have polluted the Parsi inn...." They issued an ultimatum. They must not find me in the inn in the evening. I must pack off. They held out dire consequences, and left.'[39] Ambedkar left and spent the night in a park nearby, unable to sleep. He sat under a tree with his suitcase, bedding, and all his certificates and books strewn

---

[37] Moon, *Dr. Babasaheb Ambedkar*, Vol. 12, pp. 661–91.
[38] Ibid.
[39] Ibid.

around him on the ground. Despite his Columbia degree, this was what life in Baroda had reduced him to.

'Throughout the day I searched for a house to live in but miserably failed to get any place to hide my head. I approached my friends but all turned me down on some plea or the other, expressing their inability to accommodate me. I was utterly disappointed and exhausted. What to do next? I just could not decide. Frustrated and exhausted, I quietly sat down at one place, with tears flowing out of my eyes. Seeing no hope of getting a house, and no alternative but to quit, I tendered my resignation,' he recalled.[40] Ambedkar then left for Bombay, arguing that these conditions made it impossible for him to fulfil his bond to the state. The maharaja did not hold him to his obligations, and, in November 1917, Ambedkar found himself back in Bombay, a bitter and disillusioned man. He was twenty-six, a father, and unemployed.

A year of hardship and privation ensued as he explored ways and means of making a living for his growing family, which consisted of his own wife and children as well as his brother's. Anandrao, worn out by his labours in the factory he worked in, died young in 1914, and the older Balaram, a musician and clerk, at the age of fifty-four in 1927. Bhimrao had to support Anandrao's widow and son: his nephew, Mukundrao would remain a concern for the rest of his life. Five children were also born to Ramabai and Bhim between 1912 and 1924. Ambedkar worked as a private tutor, and tried to put his economic expertise to service as an accountant, for modest reward. He even established an investment consulting business, but it failed when his clients learned that he was an untouchable. Finally, Ambedkar found employment as professor of economics at Sydenham College in November 1918. Though

---

[40] Hari Narake, N. G. Kamble, Dr M. L. Kasare, and Ashok Godghate (eds.), *Babasaheb Ambedkar: Writings and Speeches*, Vol. 17, Part III, Bombay: Education Department, Government of Maharashtra, 1979, p. 110.

it was a temporary appointment, this was a prestigious post for a scholar and paid him adequately. He was popular with his students, but his fellow professors refused to share their water jug with him,[41] an enduring reminder of the privations he would consistently have to overcome.

As a young professor from the untouchable community, Ambedkar was invited to testify before the Southborough Committee, which was preparing the Government of India Act, 1919, with a view to introducing some limited elements of self-government to India. At his hearing, Ambedkar argued that untouchables and other disadvantaged religious communities required special protections in India's highly stratified society. Ambedkar believed that reserved seats for untouchables within the Hindu fold, subject to election mainly by 'touchable' voters, would produce not true representatives of the community, but candidates acceptable to the upper castes—servants who knew how to please their masters. He therefore recommended the creation of separate electorates and reservations for the untouchable community in any political arrangements that might be made.

In his testimony, Ambedkar argued that untouchables were as separate a social group from caste Hindus as Muslims, Christians, and Sikhs were:

> The right of representation and the right to hold office under the State are the two most important rights that make up citizenship. But the untouchability of the untouchables puts these rights far beyond their reach. In a few places they do not even possess such insignificant rights as personal liberty and personal security, and equality before law is not always assured to them. These are the interests of the Untouchables. And as can be easily seen they can be represented by the Untouchables alone. They are distinctively their own interests and none else

---

[41] Akshay Chavan, 'Against All Odds', *Live History India*, 6 December 2018.

can truly voice them.... Hence it is evident that we must find the Untouchables to represent their grievances which are their interests and, secondly, we must find them in such numbers as will constitute a force sufficient to claim redress.[42]

Despite his growing visibility and the fact that he was earning a decent salary for the first time, Ambedkar continued living a frugal life in the old two-room tenement his family had occupied since his intermediate days. His aim was to save enough money to return to London before the four-year grace period he had negotiated ran out.

Once again, an enlightened maharaja came to his rescue. This was the maharaja of Kolhapur, Shahu Maharaj, a ruler committed to the abolition of caste discrimination, who made it a point to appoint untouchables to his administration and dine with them publicly, something unheard of at the time. Shahu Maharaj took a liking to the impressive Ambedkar and financed him to start a fortnightly newspaper, *Mook Nayak* (Leader of the Silent—'silent' being one of Ambedkar's terms at the time for the untouchables), which began to appear in print from January 1920. As a serving professor, Ambedkar could not formally assume the editorship of the publication, but it was for all practical purposes a vehicle for his views, and he used it to rage against the evils of the caste system and other social iniquities that blighted India. In the first issue of *Mook Nayak*, he advocated the need for a forum 'to deliberate on the injustices let loose or likely to be imposed on us and other depressed people and to think of their future development and appropriate strategies towards it critically'.[43] But when he returned to London, the publication could not be sustained and it folded in less than a year.

---

[42] Moon, *Dr. Babasaheb Ambedkar,* Vol. 1, p. 256.
[43] Valerian Rodrigues, 'Introduction', in V. Rodrigues (ed.), *The Essential Writings of B. R. Ambedkar,* Delhi: Oxford University Press, 2002, p. 9.

On 21 March 1920, Ambedkar presided over a conference of the untouchables at Mangaon in Kolhapur state, which was attended by the ruler, Shahu Maharaj, himself. Speaking at the conference, the maharaja declared of the twenty-nine-year-old: 'You have found your saviour in Ambedkar. I am confident that he will break your shackles. Not only that, a time will come when, so whispers my conscience, Ambedkar will shine as a front-rank leader of all-India fame and appeal.'[44]

Buoyed by this praise, Ambedkar attended the first All-India Conference of the Untouchables in May 1920 at Nagpur as an active participant.[45] The conference was the first time that Ambedkar's skills and presence of mind as a debater were on display and he acquitted himself well, defeating a proposal by a prominent leader of the community, Karmaveer Shinde, that the representatives of the untouchables must be elected by the members of the Legislative Council. Ambedkar argued convincingly that untouchables deserved to choose their own representatives, and his eloquence carried the day. The conference was Ambedkar's first victory in public life and his first opportunity to demonstrate to his own community his abilities as a prospective leader.

By July 1920, Ambedkar had saved enough money to plan his return to London. The maharaja of Kolhapur—whose admiration for his protégé once led him to drop in unexpectedly at the young man's residence, to the consternation of all, including Ambedkar who had to hurriedly dress properly to receive him—came through with a decent stipend of ₹1,500 and a magnanimous letter of recommendation to the LSE, infused with the Maratha monarch's anti-Brahmin solidarity:

[Mr Ambedkar] will explain [to] you the difference between the Backward Castes and the Brahmin bureaucracy. Also

---

[44] Keer, *Dr. Ambedkar*, p. 42.
[45] Ibid.

he will tell you what suffering one who tries to sympathise has to undergo at the hands of the bureaucrat Brahmins who claim to have democratic ideas, wish to raise the backward castes but who really crave nothing better than an oligarchy for themselves. He intends to lay before you, the enlightened public of England, the viewpoint of non-Brahmin Hindus who are unanimous in the opinion that in asking for Home Rule, the real object of the Brahmins has been to regain and establish their long lost power.[46]

And Ambedkar's old college roommate at Columbia, Naval Bhathena, offered him a loan of ₹5,000 to complete the required amount. Ambedkar promptly set out for London to resume his studies at LSE and simultaneously master the legal qualifications required to qualify for the bar.

Life in post-war London for the young Indian student was harsh. Ambedkar stayed at a boarding house run by a stern and miserly landlady whose minimalist offerings of food were barely enough for the young man to keep body and soul together. Waking at 6 a.m., he would spend his days at libraries, from their opening hours to closing time, devouring books. Since he could not afford to supplement his meals, Ambedkar made do with what little was available; he also walked long distances since he did not have enough money to spare for bus or train fare. Once again, he had to borrow money from Naval Bhathena, to whom Ambedkar wrote:

Believe me, I extremely regret to see you bothered on my account. I fully realise that the worries which I have thrown on you are more than even the thickest of friends can bear. I only hope that my constant asking for something or other does not break your back, and alienate

---

[46] Shahu Maharaj was a truly remarkable individual. For more details of his courageous and colourful life, see Anjali Krishnan, 'The King Who Fought The Caste System & Shaped Dr Ambedkar's Education', *Better India*.

you from me, *the only and dear friend of mine.*[47] [emphasis added].

While Ambedkar was struggling to find a decent meal in London, in Bombay Ramabai faced a daily challenge to feed her children. The couple's struggles were chronicled in their letters. Ramabai neglected herself to somehow feed her children on the daily wages of her brother and sister (which were barely enough to survive on). A starving Ambedkar wrote to her:

London, 25 November 1921

Dear Ramu,

Namaste

Received your letter. I was pained to know that Gangadhar [Ambedkar's son] is ill. Have faith in yourself. Worry would lead to nothing. I am happy to learn that your studies are continuing. I am trying to arrange some money. I am also on the verge of starvation here. I have nothing to send to you but I am trying to arrange something. If it takes time or if you are left with nothing, sell off your jewellery to run the household. I will get new ornaments made for you. How are the studies of Yashwant and Mukund [his nephew] going? You have not written anything about it.

My health is fine. Don't worry. I am pursuing my studies. I know nothing about Sakhu and Manjula. When you get the money, buy one sari each for Manjula and Laxmi. How is Shankar doing? How is Gajra?

Best to everyone

Bhimarao[48]

---

[47] Keer, *Dr. Ambedkar*, p. 46.
[48] Siddharth, 'Ramabai's sacrifices turned Bhima into Dr Ambedkar', *Forward Press*, 6 February 2020.

Far from enjoying the start of the Roaring Twenties, Ambedkar spent most of his hours reading and studying at the London Museum Library. He struck up a friendship with Frances Fitzgerald,[49] daughter of his second landlady, who worked at the India Office and assisted him with his research, and with whom he would correspond for a quarter of a century—though he insisted there was no emotional relationship between them. Ambedkar also presented a paper to the LSE Students Union which was deemed revolutionary in content and earned him something of a reputation as a radical. By June 1921, he had completed his thesis on 'Provincial Decentralization of Imperial Finance in India' and been awarded the degree of Master of Science. By October 1922 he had added another thesis to his output, this time for the University of London, entitled 'The Problem of the Rupee'.[50]

Ambedkar was fast emerging as one of the foremost Indian economic thinkers of his generation, but in the process was unable to keep up with the legal literature he had to master to qualify for the bar and chose not to appear for the bar examinations. Instead, in his hunger for education, he sought and won admission to the University of Bonn.[51] But no sooner had he moved to begin his studies in Germany than he was summoned back to London—his thesis had occasioned an uproar among the faculty because of the savagery of its attacks on British fiscal policy, and he was ordered to rewrite it before his degree could be awarded. Ambedkar had no choice but to give up Bonn, but he had no money to continue living in London either, and his family in India was in difficult straits. So, in March 1923, he returned to Bombay to rewrite his thesis there. He moderated the tone of his criticism, and tempered his

[49] Nilanjana S. Roy, 'The Ambedkar letters', *Business Standard*, 14 June 2013.
[50] Keer, *Dr. Ambedkar*, pp. 49–50.
[51] Maren Bellwinkel-Schempp, 'Ambedkar Studies at Heidelberg', University of Columbia official website.

language, but refused to alter the conclusions of his thesis. The redrafted manuscript was shipped off to London in November. This time it was accepted, and Dr Ambedkar now had a second doctorate, this time a Doctor of Science from the University of London. Ambedkar's insights into how British imperial policy manipulated the value of the rupee against the British pound to serve British interests, to the detriment of the Indian economy, and the people of India, remain unchallenged and have become the standard for understanding the role of the rupee in the finances of the British Raj. His thesis was published by the prestigious publishing house of P. S. King & Son in December 1923 and had a significant impact on Indian policy discourse. His next book, *The Evolution of Provincial Finance in British India,* published in 1925, demonstrated how British fiscal policy had impoverished India through punitive taxation, including a land tax that hurt agriculture and punitive customs and internal excise duties that damaged industrial growth.[52] Ambedkar's analysis made the nationalist case that the British government was running India in the interests of British manufacturers.

Ambedkar had by now established himself as one of India's most qualified economists (the Nobel laureate Amartya Sen would go on to call him 'the father of my economics'), and a man of rare learning and acumen, with a string of degrees few (if any) in India could boast and a mastery of several academic disciplines. Ambedkar made it a point to wear Western clothes at all times, and a suit and tie at every formal or even semi-formal occasion. This flew in the face of the prevailing Indian nationalist preference for Indian clothes made of homespun khadi, and was an early act of individualist rebellion. His attire signified his rejection even of the new nationalist orthodoxy: he refused to be defined and limited by his birth identity, which prescribed what clothes he could

---

[52] K. N. Kadam, *Dr. Babasaheb Ambedkar and the Significance of his Movement: A Chronology*, Bombay: Popular Prakashan, 1991, p. 81.

wear. Though some have seen the Western suit and tie as merely reflecting his identification with the heritage of the world, which he had acquired through his education abroad, to my mind it also signified his rejection of the trappings, sartorial as well as social, that relegated his people to the margins of traditional Indian society.[53]

But he had undergone considerable hardships to get to his present position of scholarly eminence, and moreover owed money to his friend Naval Bhathena (who had supplemented his original loan several times more to bail Ambedkar out of financial difficulties) and had to earn a proper income to support his family. Rather than teach economics for a living, Ambedkar decided he could make a larger income as a barrister; after all, he had studied law in London, even though he had not been called to the bar. On that basis he was eligible to obtain a sanad or licence to practise law in Bombay, but only on the payment of a hefty fee that he could not afford. Once again, Naval Bhathena came to the rescue, providing the required sum, and Ambedkar began his practice as a barrister in Bombay in June 1923.[54]

For an untouchable to succeed as a lawyer in Bombay was no easy task. It was not easy even for Indians of higher castes, since there was a widespread perception that major cases needed to be argued by British lawyers—the judiciary was overwhelmingly white European in composition and inclined to favour European lawyers. A handful of Indians had made a significant mark and amassed considerable renown and wealth as lawyers, but they were all of more privileged backgrounds

---

[53] See, for instance, Supriya Nair, 'The Ambedkar Suit and Dalit Identity', *Voice of Fashion*, 22 April 2019; and '"Gandhi shedding clothes not revolutionary, but Ambedkar wearing three-piece suit is"', *The Hindu*, 25 April 2012.

[54] A comprehensive list of some important cases may be found in Shashank Shekhar Singh, 'Remembering Babasaheb Ambedkar the lawyer', *Bar and Bench*, 14 April 2020.

and castes.[55] Upper-caste Indian solicitors were disinclined to offer cases to an untouchable barrister, or even to deal with one. The very few cases that initially came Ambedkar's way were, therefore, of very poor people and small litigants who offered extremely modest fees or sought his help pro bono. Worse still, such cases confined Ambedkar to arguing in the subordinate courts, whereas his erudition and command of the English language were in every respect worthy of pursuing arguments at the High Court. Such treatment might have broken a lesser man, but Ambedkar had developed an iron will over the years. He believed in himself, and was confident his time would come.

---

[55] These included such eminences as Motilal Nehru, C. Rajagopalachari, Lala Lajpat Rai, Bal Gangadhar Tilak, Chitta Ranjan Das, Bhulabhai Desai, Rajendra Prasad, Saifuddin Kitchlew, and Mohammed Ali Jinnah, none of whom belonged to the Depressed Classes.

TWO

Mounting the Podium

1923–1930

Strikingly, the son of the conservative nationalist Bal Gangadharpant Tilak became an Ambedkar ally. Shridharpant Tilak actively participated in Ambedkar's social and public activities, for instance speaking at the Conference of Depressed Class Students in Poona in October 1927, over which Ambedkar presided. He was a regular visitor to Ambedkar in Bombay, and was also hospitable to Ambedkar and members of his community in defiance of his own community's prejudices. After the Poona conference, Shridharpant hosted a tea party in Ambedkar's honour at his residence, Gaikwad Wada. He also invited a choir of untouchable boy singers to dine at his home, defying the Brahmin trustees of the Kesari-Maratha Trust, who disapproved of his gesture. Cocking a snook at the orthodoxy, Shridharpant Tilak put up a board outside his residence (named for his father as 'Lokmanya Nivas') announcing that it was home to the 'Chaturvarnya Vidhwansak Samiti' (Chaturvarna Annihilation Committee). No such committee existed; but Shridharpant Tilak was advertising his convictions and allegiances, which brought upon him the wrath of his relatives and the local Brahmin community. Shridharpant came under tremendous pressure to recant; various humiliations were heaped on him and he was even abused in *Kesari*, the newspaper that had been founded by his father. The liberal Shridharpant's and his equally reformist brother Rambhau Tilak's quarrel with the trustees of the Kesari-Maratha Trust became ugly, with legal cases being filed in court that dragged on for seven years. (The Tilak brothers had even wanted to hire Ambedkar as their lawyer, but he declined.) In the end, the unbearable pressure from the orthodox Brahmin community and the conservative Kesari-Maratha Trust—Shridharpant referred to them as 'a gang of rascals'—proved too much, and the young Tilak took his own life on 25 May 1928 by jumping under the Bombay–Poona express train. He wrote a final letter addressed to Ambedkar:

> Before the letter reaches your hand, the news of [my] leaving the world would have [reached] your ears. In order to advance the work of your 'Samaj-Samata-Sangh' educated and social reformist youth need to be attracted to the movement. I am extremely delighted to see your persistent efforts in this and I am confident that God will bless you with success. If the Maharashtrian youth take this cause, then the problem of untouchability will be resolved in merely 5 years. To convey the grievances of my depressed classes brothers to God Krishna, I am going ahead. Please convey my regards to friends.
>
> With regards,
>
> Sincerely.
>
> Yours truly,
> Shridhar Balwant Tilak

Ambedkar mourned Shridharpant's death: 'I was expecting great amount of karma from Shridharpant,' he wrote in an editorial.[1]

_ﾟ_

---

[1] Suraj Yengde, *Caste Matters*, New Delhi: Penguin Random House, 2019.

Ambedkar began his law practice in 1923. At the time, India was in ferment. The Montagu–Chelmsford reforms[2] had brought in elements of modest self-government to India, offering a limited number of educated and property-owning Indians opportunities to influence government policies. The Khilafat Movement and Mahatma Gandhi's call for non-cooperation had roused the masses, and the Depressed Classes—as the untouchables were more politely being called—were not exempt from the ferment. Gandhi himself had called for abolishing the mistreatment of the Depressed Classes and unifying Hindu society beyond the barriers of caste. In August 1923, the Bombay Legislative Council passed a resolution recommending that public facilities, including wells, schools, dispensaries, and dharamshalas maintained out of public funds, be open to the Depressed Classes. The Bombay government accepted the recommendation and issued instructions for its implementation in September. Change was in the air.

Movements against untouchability had been active throughout India since the nineteenth century, fighting for education, temple entry, access to public facilities like water tanks, the right to a livelihood beyond scavenging (including being given land for agriculture), and the removal of restrictions on their use of roads and public transport. In these agitations, the Depressed Classes had received support from various social reform organizations, Christian missionaries, and, in Maharashtra, the Satyashodhak Samaj, founded by the pioneering anti-caste activist, Jyotirao Phule, in 1873.[3]

---

[2] 'Montagu–Chelmsford Report', Making Britain, Open University official website.

[3] Phule dedicated his book *Slavery* (1873) 'to the good people of the United States as a token of admiration for their sublime and selfless dedication and their sense of sacrifice with regard to the cause of slavery of the Negroes; and with the fervent desire that my fellow countrymen follow the noble example in the emancipation of their Shudra brothers from the fetters of Brahminical slavery'. Jyotirao Phule, *Slavery: Collected Works of Mahatma Jotirao Phule*, Vol. 1, Bombay: Government of Maharashtra, 1991, p. xxvii.

But progress in bringing about meaningful change had been negligible.

On 9 March 1924, Ambedkar called a public meeting at Bombay's Damodar Hall to set up an organization, the Bahishkrit Hitakirini Sabha[4] (Assembly for the Rights of the Excluded, also known as the Depressed Classes Institute), to fight for the rights of the Depressed Classes and to speak on their behalf to the authorities. The sabha also aimed to advance education and culture, as well as to set up libraries, schools, and similar institutions.[5] The founding motto of the sabha was 'Educate, Organise and Agitate'. Interestingly, the sabha was established with prominent upper-caste figures occupying its formal leadership positions and thirty-three-year-old Ambedkar serving as chair of its managing committee. The Gujarati Brahmin judge, Dr C. H. Setalvad, served as the sabha's president, the Jewish mayor of Bombay, Meyer Nissim, and the Parsi scholar and linguist, G. K. Nariman, were vice presidents, and prominent Brahmins and Marathas like G. N. Sahasrabuddhe, Dr R. P. Paranjpye, Dr V. P. Chavan, and B. G. Kher served in leadership slots. However, the management of the sabha was under the control of its chairman, Ambedkar, its secretary, S. N. Shivtarkar, a Dalit of the Chambhar (leather-worker) caste, and the treasurer, N. T. Jadhav, who like Ambedkar was a Mahar. This arrangement was very much Ambedkar's doing and in keeping with his vision: he believed firmly that the problems of the Depressed Classes were not their concern alone, but required Hindu leaders of other castes and sympathetic Indians of other communities to commit themselves to a complete restructuring of Hindu society. But control and day-to-day work responsibilities remained with the Dalit community.

This was an important difference from the other social

---

[4] Keer, *Dr. Ambedkar*, p. 55.
[5] Team Ambedkarite Today, 'Bahishkrit Hitakarini Sabha', *Ambedkarite Today*.

movements set up to reform Hindu society, notably Mahatma
Gandhi's own efforts to enhance Hindu consciousness of the
wrongs of untouchability and to work for the social uplift of
the community, which he articulated regularly in his newspaper,
Harijan. In Bombay, Justice Ranade had started a Social
Conference[6] in a similarly reformist spirit, and the Hindutva
ideologue, Vinayak Damodar Savarkar, released in 1924 from
detention in the Andamans and interned in Ratnagiri, had
established a Hindu Sangathan, one of whose core objectives
was the eradication of untouchability. But these were all
organizations of the upper castes, conceived by upper-caste
leaders that sought to change upper-caste behaviour. Ambedkar
wanted an organization of the untouchables demanding, and
fighting for, their own rights, in partnership with sympathetic
and enlightened upper-caste figures.

Ambedkar saw the reformists as treating the symptoms
rather than the disease; he felt their approach would at best
bring about superficial change and involve gestures like dining
publicly with members of the Depressed Classes, without
fundamentally altering their condition. By 1924, he was clear
that root-and-branch change was required: the legal abolition
of untouchability by an act of a free Indian legislature, access
to public facilities like wells and temples, the opening up of
the priesthood to non-Brahmins, and the institution of Hindu
religious practices and rituals that would not discriminate
against those belonging to the Depressed Classes. This was
the direction in which he sought to lead the community, with
the uncompromising determination that had already marked
his life thus far.

Equally he felt the need to goad his own people into adopting
the proactive approach he wished them to take. In his speech

---

[6] Charles Herman Heimsath, 'VIII. Mahadev Govind Ranade and the National
Social Conference', *Indian Nationalism and Hindu Social Reform*, Princeton:
Princeton University Press, 2015, pp. 176–204.

to the sabha, he was blunt to the point of unpleasantness:

> My heart breaks to see the pitiable sight of your faces and
> to hear your sad voices. You have been groaning from time
> immemorial and yet you are not ashamed to hug your
> helplessness as an inevitability. Why did you not perish in
> the prenatal stage instead? Why do you worsen and sadden
> the picture of the sorrows, poverty, slavery and burdens of
> the world with your deplorable and detestable miserable
> life? You had better die and relieve this world if you cannot
> rise to a new life and if you cannot rejuvenate yourselves.
> As a matter of fact, it is your birthright to get food, shelter
> and clothing in this land in equal proportion with every
> individual high or low. If you believe in a respectable life,
> you must believe in self-help, which is the best help![7]

The sabha started its activities immediately, creating a hostel for
untouchable students in Sholapur (aided by a grant from the
municipality), so that they would not need to deal with hostile
upper-caste landlords, setting up a reading room and a hockey
club in Bombay, launching a monthly magazine called *Saraswati
Vilas*,[8] and inculcating a love for learning among young people.
But Ambedkar's own activities went beyond such acts of social
service; the sabha, for him, became a platform to arouse the
consciousness of his people about the injustices to which
they were subject, and to get them to demand their rights. He
travelled from village to town to conduct public meetings of the
community across the Bombay Presidency and Goa. In Nipani in
1925,[9] he attended and addressed the first Provincial Depressed
Classes Conference, of which he was one of the moving spirits.
He convened and presided over a conference of the community

---

[7] Keer, *Dr. Ambedkar*, p. 60.
[8] Ravi Ranjan and M. K. Singh, *Dr. Bhimrao Ambedkar*, New Delhi: K. K.
Publications, 2021, p. 96.
[9] Keer, *Dr. Ambedkar*, p. 65.

at Malwan the same year. In his address to the Bombay Province Bahishkrut Parishad (Conference of the Excluded) held in Belgaon district on 11 April 1925, Ambedkar told his people, 'only if you fight intensively will you regain your manuski (basic human dignity)'.[10]

While Ambedkar was clearly emerging as a leading voice of the Depressed Classes, he took care to preserve his status as an authority on finance, submitting a paper on India's currency and the gold-exchange standard to the Royal Commission set up to look at India's finances, which interviewed him on his views in December 1925. He also published a booklet on the exchange rate between the pound and the rupee, making the case that the rupee was overvalued to the detriment of the Indian producer. This was important; he felt he needed to earn and retain people's respect for his academic attainments, all the more to address them authoritatively on issues of social reform. However, he was unsuccessful in his application to be appointed principal of Sydenham College; the college offered him a professorship instead, which he turned down. He preferred to teach part-time, instructing students at Batliboi's Accountancy Training Institute,[11] and earning some supplementary income as a part-time examiner for Bombay University, which left him enough time for his other interests. Ambedkar was also continuing his work as a lawyer. In 1926, he won a landmark case[12] in which he successfully defended three non-Brahmin activists who had been prosecuted for defaming Brahmins in a pamphlet they had published. This was a resounding success that was widely noticed and applauded. He increasingly took on such cases pro bono, even spending his own money to

---

[10] Shailaja Paik, 'Dalit Feminist Thought', *Economic & Political Weekly*, Vol. 56, Issue No. 25, 19 June 2021.

[11] Anand Teltumbe and Suraj Yengde (eds.), *The Radical in Ambedkar: Critical Reflections*, New Delhi: Penguin Books, 2018; Keer, *Dr. Ambedkar*, p. 66; Sumit, 'A jurist with no equals', *Forward Press*, 13 July 2017.

[12] Ibid. Interestingly this case was also called the 'enemy of the country' case.

house poor litigants from the Depressed Classes who could not afford to stay in Bombay while prosecuting their cases.

His personal life was, however, marred by tragedy and ill-health. Of the five children who were born to Ramabai and him between 1912 and 1924, only his son, Yashwant, born in 1912, survived. Gangadhar, Ramesh, Indu, and Rajaratna, who followed, all passed away. His third son, Rajaratna, was the apple of Ambedkar's eye, and the proud father uncharacteristically spent many happy hours playing with him. But, when he was just over a year old, Rajaratna died of double pneumonia in 1924. Ambedkar shared his pain in a letter to his friend Dattoba Pawar in heart-wrenching words:

> We [Ramabai and Ambedkar] will not be able to get over the shock of the death of our last son soon. These hands have delivered three sons and one daughter to the cremation ground. Whenever I remember them, my heart aches. What we had thought about their future lies in ruins. Clouds of pain are hovering over our life. The death of the children has made our lives as tasteless as food without salt.... My last son was extraordinary. I am yet to see a child like that. His departure from this world has made my life like a garden full of thorns. I am so despaired and distressed that I cannot write any more. Accept salutations from your friend in deep agony.[13]

To another friend, Ambedkar wrote:

> There is no use pretending that I and my wife have recovered from the shock of my son's death and I don't think we ever shall. We have in all buried four precious children, three sons and a daughter, all sprightly,

---

[13] M. L. Shahare and Nalini Anil, *Babasaheb Dr. Ambedkar Ki Sangharsh Yatra Evam Sandesh*, New Delhi: Samyak Prakashan, 2014, p. 70; translation in Siddharth, 'Ramabai, The woman whose sacrifices turned Bhima into Dr. Ambedkar', *Forward Press*, 2 February 2020.

auspicious and handsome children.... My last boy was a
wonderful boy, the like of whom I had seldom seen. With
his passing away life to me is a garden full of weeds.[14]

The pregnancies affected Ramabai's health adversely, and
though she was a young woman, Ambedkar's wife, often forced
to starve, struggled to cope with the demands of running his
household and managing a family. As a result, both husband and
wife were in poor health much of the time.

Ambedkar's professional life, however, grew in stature and
visibility. In 1925, he was appointed to the Bombay Presidency
Committee to work with the Simon Commission, which was
visiting India to make recommendations for the country's
political evolution. This gave Ambedkar the opportunity to
formulate his own recommendations for the future Constitution
of India.[15] Little did he realize then that this would foreshadow
the crucial role he would play a quarter of a century later in
drafting independent India's Constitution.

The year 1927 marked one of the biggest steps forward in
his evolution as a political leader. Two major events occurred
in January 1927. Ambedkar addressed a public meeting at
Bhima-Koregaon,[16] site of a famous victory of the Mahar
Regiment against the Brahmin-led Peshwa army, to denounce a
new British policy barring untouchables from military service.
This became a major cause, especially since large numbers
of individuals from the community had enlisted and fought
bravely in World War I. Equally, serving in the military entitled
soldiers of the Depressed Classes to place their children in free
schools and give them the education that would be essential
for their empowerment. To deny them that opportunity by

---

[14] Keer, *Dr. Ambedkar*, p. 66.
[15] Uttam Khobragade, 'Constitution revolution engendered by Dr Ambedkar',
Times of India, 4 May 2020.
[16] Kadam, *Dr. Babasaheb Ambedkar and the Significance of his Movement*, pp.
82–83.

excluding them from military service was a retrograde step by the British. This was a theme to which Ambedkar would frequently return.

Also in January 1927, Ambedkar was nominated by the governor of Bombay to the provincial legislative council. This was an honour that significantly advanced his ability to represent the interests of the Depressed Classes in a forum that could make a tangible difference in their lives. A felicitation meeting was convened by his growing band of admirers at which a handsome purse was presented to him to assist in pursuing his endeavours. Ambedkar promptly donated the entire sum to the Bahishkrit Hitakirini Sabha.

The Bombay Legislative Council's 1923 resolution opening public facilities to the Depressed Classes had remained largely unimplemented because of the resistance of the upper castes, even though the council reiterated its contents in 1926. Ambedkar decided to take action to put the law into effect on the ground. In March 1927, Ambedkar led a major protest meeting at Mahad in Kolaba District of Bombay Presidency, where the Chawdar water tank[17] was, on paper, open to all, but in practice unavailable to the Depressed Classes. Since no Hindu landlord allowed the use of his land for the meeting site of the conference, a patch of land was obtained with great difficulty from a Muslim. Some 5,000 delegates from the Depressed Classes around the presidency attended and heard Ambedkar deliver the presidential address of the conference, urging them to stand up for their rights, to pursue education, to fight to serve in the army and the police, and to stop eating the discarded morsels of the upper castes. 'At the outset let me tell those who oppose us that we did not perish because we could not drink water from this Chawdar Tank. We now want to go to the Tank only to prove that, like others, we are also

---

[17] Ibid., p. 83.

human beings. This Conference has been called to inaugurate an era of equality in this land.'[18] Token gestures would not be enough, he added; the doors of every profession should be thrown open to the community. He lamented the government's decision to exclude them from the army:

> The military offered us unique opportunities of raising our standard of life and proving our merit and intellect.... It is nothing less than treachery on the part of the British to have closed the doors of the army to the Untouchables who had helped them establish the Indian empire while their home government was at grips with the French during the Napoleonic War.[19]

Ambedkar's speech invoked the values of the French Revolution, comparing the Mahad conference to the Etats Généraux de Versailles of 1789, which had marked the formal revolt of the Third Estate. The first resolution passed by the conference was a declaration of human rights, which repudiated the authority of the Hindu scriptures that upheld doctrines of social inequality. The conference then resolved that the ancient Hindu law book, the *Manusmriti*, which they excoriated for its justifications of caste discrimination and untouchability, and which reduced the Shudras and the outcastes to slavery, be publicly burnt. Accordingly, at 9 p.m. on 25 December 1927, the *Manusmriti* was placed on a pyre and burned—an act that shocked the Hindu community, as it was intended to.[20] Ambedkar demanded that such archaic texts be replaced by a new Hindu code to govern the life of his people. This action won him the undying enmity of Hindu traditionalists, who swore by Manu, in

---

[18] Keer, *Dr. Ambedkar*, p. 99 contains a detailed account of the Mahad meeting and Ambedkar's speech in Chapter 6.

[19] Keer, *Dr. Ambedkar*, p. 71 contains a detailed account of Ambedkar's speech in Chapter 5.

[20] Kadam, *Dr. Babasaheb Ambedkar and the Significance of his Movement*, p. 87.

particular of the nascent Hindutva movement, many of whose leaders hailed Manu as the greatest of all lawgivers.

Years later, in an interview in 1938, Ambedkar explained that the torching of the *Manusmriti* was quite intentional.

> It was a very cautious and drastic step, but was taken with a view to forcing the attention of caste Hindus. At intervals such drastic remedies are a necessity. If you do not knock at the door, none opens it. It is not that all the parts of the *Manusmriti* are condemnable, that it does not contain good principles and that Manu himself was not a sociologist and was a mere fool. We made a bonfire of it because we view it as a symbol of injustice under which we have been crushed across centuries. Because of its teachings we have been ground down under despicable poverty and so we made the dash, staked all, took our lives in our hands and performed the deed.[21]

Ambedkar then led a march to the Chawdar Tank in Mahad and became the first untouchable to draw water from it and drink, an act followed by hundreds of other delegates. As the Dalit writer Yashica Dutt explains:

> The act of Dalits drinking water from the same source as upper castes was neither simple nor ordinary. It was downright revolutionary since it directly attacked notions of purity and pollution, one of the most fundamental ideas of the caste system. Certain upper-caste Hindus at the time didn't even tolerate a Dalit's shadow on their person, much less make physical contact with them. Food and water have a sacred context in Hinduism. Regardless of what the British laws at the time allowed, Ambedkar perhaps understood the radicalness of leading Dalits to drink the same water that upper-caste people also consumed. With this seemingly

---

[21] Keer, *Dr. Ambedkar*, p. 106.

small gesture, Ambedkar defied a sacredly held caste belief
and asserted the absolute equality of Dalits.[22]

The procession then marched peacefully back to the conference
venue. But as the meeting was ending, upper-caste miscreants
organized an attack on the site; hooligans with bamboo staves
assaulted any members of the community they could find, beating
up the delegates and severely injuring twenty. Though tempers
were inflamed, Ambedkar pacified the protestors and urged
them not to resort to violence, which would serve them ill. After
succeeding in maintaining peace, Ambedkar led an enquiry into
the violence and submitted a detailed report to the police, which
led to the arrest and successful prosecution of five of the rioters.

The events at Mahad seized the imagination of the public
and were the subject of lively controversy in the newspapers.
Opinion was divided, with many luminaries of all communities
endorsing Ambedkar's satyagraha while others argued about
whether the Depressed Classes had been needlessly provocative
by marching on the water tank. Several upper-caste notables,
even in Mahad itself, supported Ambedkar, just as Sridharpant
Tilak had. The orthodox elements there, however, conducted a
'purification' ceremony at the water tank that included dipping
cow dung and cow urine into the tank as part of the rituals,
as Brahmin priests chanted mantras. (Ambedkar's views on
the very notion that cow dung was purer than the touch of a
Bahishkrit individual are mercifully not recorded.)

Amid the controversy, it became clear that the events at
Mahad in 1927 had joined the illustrious historic events of
the Vaikom Satyagraha of 1925 (for access by members of the
community to a public road in Travancore) and the unsuccessful
prosecution of an untouchable, Murgesan, in Madras in 1926
(for entering a Hindu temple), as landmark events in the

---

[22] Yashica Dutt, *Coming Out As Dalit: A Memoir*, New Delhi: Aleph Book
Company, 2019, pp. 109–10.

awakening of India's Depressed Classes to their rights and disabilities. And Ambedkar, at thirty-six, was already among their most prominent spokesmen, the best educated and one of the most articulate in English. He had clearly become, in his own right, a force to be reckoned with.

∽

In April 1927, Ambedkar launched his own fortnightly newspaper in Marathi, *Bahishkrit Bharat*,[23] as a platform for his views. The publication served both to alert his own constituency of Depressed Classes to what was happening in the country and to reach out to those among the upper castes who could be persuaded by reasoned argument of the need to promote and protect the rights of the community. Each issue carried an editorial authored by him in which Ambedkar raised penetrating questions about the regressive practices of caste discrimination and challenged their underlying illogicality. He repeatedly pointed to the inconsistency of privileged Hindus demanding equal treatment from the British while denying it to their fellow Indians, those who belonged to the Depressed Classes. He urged all those who sympathized with the cause of justice for the community to practise what they preached in their own daily lives. 'If you say your religion is our religion, then your rights and ours must be equal,' he argued. 'But is this the case? If not, on what grounds must we remain in the Hindu fold, in spite of your kicks and rebuffs?'[24]

Ambedkar was careful to stress—especially in resisting calls from some young hotheads to exclude all Brahmins from the cause—that he was not opposed to Brahmins as individual human beings but to Brahminism as an oppressive practice, and that he welcomed the support of enlightened Brahmins like

---

[23] Siddharth, '"Bahishkrit Bharat": Ambedkar's decisive challenge to Brahminism', *Forward Press*, 30 January 2020.
[24] Keer, *Dr. Ambedkar*, p. 92.

Tilak. He quoted extensively from the Bhagavad Gita and other Hindu scriptures in support of his arguments. Ambedkar was also careful to endorse Mahatma Gandhi's call for non-violence, with the caveat that though this was preferable, the need for violence could not be entirely ruled out if non-violence failed.

Even as Ambedkar was building up an impressive foundation of arguments for his political stand, reactionary forces were regrouping. In August 1927, the Mahad municipality, in defiance of the Legislative Council, revoked its earlier resolution and declared that the Chawdar Tank would no longer be open to the Depressed Classes. Outraged, Ambedkar convened a meeting at which it was resolved to once again offer satyagraha at the tank in December. This in turn led to volleys of criticism from orthodox Hindus, to which Ambedkar replied with a reminder that his people were seeking rights within the Hindu fold. They had chosen, he added in a veiled threat, not to consider conversion to another faith. The satyagraha passed off peacefully, but changed nothing: the municipality refused to allow Depressed Classes to draw water from the Chawdar Tank.

Ambedkar's next major act of an eventful year was to reach out across gender lines. After the Mahad Conference Ambedkar addressed a meeting of about 3,000 women of the community, the first meeting of its kind in modern India.[25] He exhorted them to stand up for themselves: 'Never regard yourself as an untouchable. Live a clean life. Dress yourself like the touchable ladies. Attend more to the cultivation of the mind and the spirit of self-help.... Send your children to schools.'[26] At his urging, the women left the conference having changed their style of draping their saris to match other Hindu women—a visual reflection of the principle of equality that undergirded his beliefs.

---

[25] Ayesha Sultana, 'On the Participation of Women: A Reading of Ambedkar's "The Mahad Satyagraha"', *All About Ambedkar: A Journal on Theory and Praxis*.
[26] Keer, *Dr. Ambedkar*, p. 104.

It was at this time that Ambedkar sought to broaden the base of his public appeal by making a pilgrimage to the Raigad Fort associated with the Maratha warrior-king Chhatrapati Shivaji Maharaj, the greatest hero of the Hindus of Maharashtra, whose battles against the bigoted Mughal emperor, Aurangzeb, were the stuff of legend. For Ambedkar, honouring a hero who had taken on impossible odds to fight for his people against the greatest power the world had known, the mighty Mughal empire, resonated with his own unequal battle for untouchable rights. The symbolism of his visit was not lost on his high-caste enemies, however, and even such an act was not conducted without controversy.

Early in 1928, Ambedkar was invited to preside over a meeting of the Depressed Classes that had been convened to consider a proposal to build a temple honouring their great saint, Chokhamela.[27] Ambedkar guided the discussion to a decision that the community's energies would be better directed to removing untouchability rather than constructing a temple. Ambedkar's logic was, as usual, impeccable: a separate temple would marginalize its untouchable worshippers, whereas they should continue to demand access to the same temples as other Hindus; the expenses involved in constructing and maintaining a temple building would constitute a major financial burden for the community; and, in any case, reform of untouchability had to be more utilitarian and go beyond concerns of idol worship, for which he had little patience. Ambedkar's view prevailed; the temple was not built.

Ambedkar's public life, his social activities, and his increasing political standing began to interfere with his now flourishing legal practice. Taking on cases required time that he could ill afford to spare from his multiple other engagements. He had started his legal work as a means of ensuring financial security,

---

[27] Yogesh Maitreya, 'In Chokamela's Bhakti, Past Transforms into Radical Present', *Newsclick*, 16 November 2019.

but, to his mind, this seemed a petty aim compared to his real objective, which was now nothing less than the transformation of Hindu society. His membership of the legislative council was a far more valuable platform for him to pursue this objective, to articulate his ideas through powerful interventions and to introduce bills that would give legal effect to his vision.

This was easier said than done, of course, as Ambedkar discovered when he introduced a bill in March 1928 to amend the Hereditary Offences Act, 1874,[28] under which Mahars in government service were obliged, if prevented by illness or other circumstances from fulfilling their duties, to provide a member of their family to perform the same tasks during that period, at no additional compensation. The law was based on the assumption that the Depressed Classes were relegated by birth to the performance of certain menial functions and that the fulfilment of their duties was a hereditary obligation rather than a statutory right as other employees might enjoy. In a meticulously argued, legally sound, morally impassioned speech, Ambedkar dissected the iniquitous law before the legislature and called for the abolition of its most untenable provisions. The council heard him in silence and then referred the bill in August 1928 to a select committee consisting almost entirely of upper-caste grandees, which, in the fullness of time, rejected its arguments, prompting a bitter Ambedkar to withdraw the bill in July 1929.[29] (Once, in the Bombay Legislative Council, Ambedkar was challenged by nationalists, with whom he often crossed words, to remember that he was 'a part of the whole'. He replied crisply, 'But I am not a part of the whole, I am a part apart!'[30]) He had more success, however, when he fought for maternity benefits for women labourers.

---

[28] Keer, *Dr. Ambedkar*, p. 111.
[29] Ibid., p. 114.
[30] It is stated that Vasant Moon sourced this quote after rummaging through tomes of the Bombay Legislative Assembly Debates. Raja Sekhar Vundru, 'From Marathi to English', *The Hindu*, 3 June 2013.

In April 1929, Ambedkar was invited to preside over the Ratnagiri District Conference at Chiplun. In his presidential address to the conference, Ambedkar said: 'You must abolish slavery yourselves. It is disgraceful to live at the cost of one's self-respect. Self-respect is a most vital factor in life. Without it, man is a mere cipher. To live worthily with self-respect, one has to overcome difficulties. It is out of hard and ceaseless struggle alone that one derives strength, confidence and recognition.'[31]

Ambedkar's neglect of his legal practice even as he was acquiring prominence as a lawmaker had placed a severe strain on his family finances, however, and in June 1928 he accepted the post of professor at Bombay's prestigious Government Law College.[32] This became his only source of regular income to support a family which had long borne, in stoic understanding, the burden of his remarkably single-minded focus on public issues.

In June 1928, there arrived in Bombay the Indian Statutory Commission led by Sir John Simon to look into issues relating to self-government for India, in response to the widespread agitations that had engulfed the country over the preceding decade. The betrayal by perfidious Albion of promises to grant India dominion status in return for support during World War I—support that was given generously and unstintingly by all sections of Indian opinion, and whose value is estimated, in today's money, at over £8 billion, paid for by a poor and destitute people reeling from inflation and influenza—had triggered a wave of protests from the end of the war. These, in turn, had been met by the repressive Rowlatt Acts[33] that ruthlessly suppressed free speech and harassed Indian protestors, the barbaric Jallianwala Bagh massacre of peaceful protestors in

---

[31] Keer, *Dr. Ambedkar*, p. 127.
[32] Kadam, *Dr. Babasaheb Ambedkar and the Significance of his Movement*, p. 89.
[33] Vali Nasr, 'South Asia from 1919', in *The New Cambridge History of Islam*, Francis Robinson (ed.), Cambridge: Cambridge University Press, 2010, pp. 558–90.

Amritsar in 1919 that still ranks as one of the worst atrocities
of the Raj, and mass arrests of Indian nationalists. Mahatma
Gandhi then supported the Khilafat Movement that united
Hindus and Muslims in a campaign to get the British to restore
the caliphate in Turkey, a cause which collapsed when the
rationalist Kemal Atatürk triumphed in that country's civil war,
but which served the purpose of arresting the widening schism
between adherents of the two major Indian religions, a schism
deliberately provoked by a British imperial policy of 'divide and
rule'. Gandhi's Non-cooperation Movement and advocacy of
peaceful non-violent protest had galvanized public opinion in
India, convincing the British of the need to address the country's
growing nationalist fervour through 'constitutional' means.
The Simon Commission was assigned the task of ascertaining
Indian opinion and formulating recommendations to this end.

The principal nationalist organization, the Indian National
Congress, resolved to boycott Simon, who was duly met by
black flag waving protestors everywhere he went, carrying
banners emblazoned 'Simon Go Back'. Instead, the Congress set
up a committee under the estimable lawyer Motilal Nehru to
draft an Indian Constitution in place of whatever Simon was
likely to come up with. The Nehru Report that emerged was
an impressive document, containing the first draft of an Indian
Constitution, which did a commendable job of accommodating
Muslim interests in order to end the communal divide the
British had been fomenting. But it was blamed for ignoring the
plight of the Depressed Classes, whose interests found barely
a mention, leaving Ambedkar and his sympathizers convinced
that the Hindu upper castes were indifferent to the well-being
of the untouchable underclass.

Defying the Congress boycott, Ambedkar submitted a
long memorandum, in two parts, to the Simon Commission
in May 1928, calling for provincial autonomy, adult suffrage,
and reserved seats for Muslims and the Depressed Classes, and

he testified before it in October. His defiance of the Congress boycott even led to his own students walking out of his law class in protest.[34]

Ambedkar later recounted an incident from this period that taught him the huge importance of dignity and self-respect for members of his community. In 1929, he visited a village, Chalisgaon, to look into the grievances of the untouchable community there on behalf of the Bombay government. Alighting at a nearby railway station, he was perplexed to be kept waiting for an hour despite the evident availability of many tongas there. The colony he was to visit was not very far away, but his hosts insisted he should not walk there; they wished to transport him in a tonga. Eventually he was seated alone in a tonga with a driver and the two set out. Almost immediately there was a near collision with a motor car; soon after, while negotiating a culvert, the horse-carriage struck a wall, the horse bolted, Ambedkar was thrown senseless onto the ground and the horse and carriage fell into the river. Ambedkar was in pain and had several fractures and bruises, but survived.

Upon investigation by an outraged Ambedkar, it turned out that none of the regular tongawallahs had been willing to drive an untouchable passenger, even one of Ambedkar's eminence. Finally, one carriage owner agreed to lease his vehicle to Ambedkar's hosts for a hefty fee, but refused to drive it himself: it was beneath his dignity to drive an untouchable. For Ambedkar's Mahar hosts, it was equally undignified to ask their distinguished guest to walk. So they decided to hire the vehicle; they rashly thought it would not be difficult for one of them to drive the tonga, despite never having done it before. This turned out to be an incorrect assumption. The volunteer driver, completely ignorant of the fine art of tonga-driving, lost

---

[34] Keer, *Dr. Ambedkar*, p. 116.

control of the horse and carriage, causing a near collision and then the accident. Ambedkar ruefully observed that his hosts 'forgot that the safety of the passenger was more important than the maintenance of his dignity.... To save my dignity, the Mahars of Chalisgaon had put my very life in jeopardy.'[35] It was an object lesson in the irrationality of prejudice and the importance of self-respect.

By 1930, the nationalist movement had gathered pace, with the fervour ignited by Mahatma Gandhi's Salt March to Dandi leading to widespread protests, mass imprisonment, and the killing of unarmed protestors in savage waves of imperial repression. Ambedkar, too, was active, starting a new weekly, *Janata* (People), and promoting a major agitation in the town of Nasik to permit temple entry to members of the Depressed Classes. He informed the trustees of the famed Kalaram Temple of his decision to lead his people into the temple peacefully to worship Lord Ram. An impressive 1,500 protestors, including some prominent Brahmin sympathizers, assembled in Nasik for a conference over which Ambedkar presided.[36] But when they marched in an orderly and peaceful manner to the temple they found a phalanx of security personnel, led by the Nasik district magistrate, a Briton, barring their way. The next day they returned to squat before the temple to offer peaceful satyagraha, and found that security had been reinforced in front of every gate and any protestor who so much as stood up, let alone attempted to enter, was brutally beaten down with lathis. It is to Ambedkar's credit that he kept the protest entirely peaceful, but every compromise he attempted to broker—including one whereby some of his people would be permitted to pull the temple chariot carrying the idol of Ram, along with members of the upper caste—was violated by the latter, with the full support of the district administration.

---

[35] Moon, *Dr. Babasaheb Ambedkar*, Vol. 12, p. 681.
[36] Keer, *Dr. Ambedkar*, p. 137.

With the agitation continuing, the caste Hindus were forced to keep the famous temple closed for a whole year. Ambedkar met with many distinguished upper-caste Hindus, including the industrialist and philanthropist G. D. Birla, in his efforts to find a solution, but on the whole the agitation failed to secure entry for the Depressed Classes. The temple remained closed to them till 1935.

While this was going on, the Simon Commission published its report in May 1930, recommending the creation of a central legislature of 250 Indians, to be elected by a very limited franchise of literate and property-owning Indians, divided into separate electorates for the principal communities—'divide and rule' at its most blatant. There were no special provisions for the Depressed Classes. Candidates from the community could contest in the 150 seats marked for the Hindus, provided their suitability to do so was certified by the governor of the province concerned. Ambedkar opposed this bitterly. 'Demand the right to elect our own representatives of our choice, untrammelled by any condition or limitation whatsoever. We are certainly the best judges of our interests and we must not allow even the Governor to assume the authority to determine what is good for us.'[37]

In reaction to the Simon report, the first All-India Depressed Classes Conference was convened in Nagpur in August 1930, with Dr Ambedkar presiding. His speech on the occasion reflected the best of his qualities as an advocate, infusing a visionary approach to the future of the nation with a meticulous assembling of damning detail. His indictment of British misrule and the colonial impoverishment of India was searing: 'In the first quarter of the 19th century when British Rule in India had become an established fact, there were five famines with an estimated loss of 1,000,000 lives. During the second quarter,

---

[37] Ibid., pp. 140–41.

there were six famines with a recorded loss of lives of 5,000,000. And during the last quarter of the century what do you find? Eighteen famines with an estimated mortality which reached the awful total between 15,000,000 and 26,000,000.' Chronic poverty, he averred, was a result of British rule; freedom was indispensable to create a prosperous and egalitarian society. While acknowledging that the British had brought law and order to India, he added: 'But we cannot forget that people, including the Depressed Classes, do not live on law and order; what they live on is bread and butter.'[38]

He called on the Bahishkrit, the excluded, to fight for swaraj, independence from British rule, and also for their rights to liberty, equality, and fraternity in a free India. 'But I must take this opportunity to emphasize that political power cannot be a panacea for the ills of the Depressed Classes. Their salvation lies in their social elevation. They must cleanse their evil habits. They must improve their bad ways of living. By a change of their mode of life they must be made fit for respect and friendship. They must be educated. Mere knowledge of the three R's is insufficient for the great height many of them must reach in order that the whole community may along with them rise in the general estimation. There is a great necessity to disturb their pathetic contentment and to instil into them that divine discontent which is the spring of all elevation.'[39]

He was critical of the humiliations inflicted upon the Depressed Classes by the Hindu upper castes but strongly spoke for his people's rights to be treated on a par with other Hindus, affirming that they remained an integral part of the Hindu faith. 'The movements of social reform,' he averred, 'will result in the emancipation of our people and the establishment of such a state of society in this country of ours in which one

---

[38] Ibid., p. 142.
[39] Ibid., p. 143.

man will have one value in all domains of life, political, social and economic.'[40]

The conference took a heavy toll on Ambedkar, who collapsed and fell unconscious at one point.[41] He was only thirty-nine, but he had driven himself beyond any reasonable limit. It was the first warning sign that Ambedkar was heedless of human frailty, including his own.

---

[40] M. L. Shahare, *Dr. Bhimrao Ambedkar: His Life and Work*, National Council of Educational Research and Training, 2010, p. 39.
[41] Keer, *Dr. Ambedkar: Life and Mission*, p. 144.

THREE

Scaling the Peaks

1930–1935

The stocky, bespectacled untouchable lawyer, just thirty-nine years old, rose to address the ornate Round Table Conference in London on 12 November 1930. Proceedings had been opened by the king-emperor George V himself, and were being presided over by the prime minister, Ramsay MacDonald, but Ambedkar was unfazed by the occasion. 'In speaking before this Conference, I am voicing the viewpoint of one-fifth of the total population of British India—a population as large as the population of England or France—which has been reduced to a position worse than that of a serf or a slave,' he declared bluntly. 'I want to emphasise the fact that one-fifth of the total population of British India—a population as large as the population of Britain—has been reduced to a position worse than that of serfs or slaves.'[1]

But the lawyer did not spare his hosts either. 'I maintain that the untouchables in India are also for replacing the existing Government by a Government of the people, for the people and by the people.' His argument for self-governance typically reconciled both sets of demands:

> When we compare our present position with the one which it was our lot to bear in Indian society of pre-British days, we find that, instead of marching on, we are marking time.

---

[1] Shahare, *Dr. B. R. Ambedkar*, pp. 41–42.

Before the British, we were in the loathsome condition due to our untouchability. Has the British Government done anything to remove it?... Our wrongs have remained as open sores and they have not been righted, although 150 years of British rule have rolled away.... Of what good is such a Government to anybody?... We must have a Government in which the men in power will give their undivided allegiance to the best interests of the country. We must have a Government in which men in power, knowing where obedience will end and resistance will begin, will not be afraid to amend the social and economic code of life which the dictates of justice and expediency so urgently call for.[2]

He concluded:

I am afraid it is not sufficiently realized that in the present temper of the country, no constitution will be workable which is not acceptable to the majority of the people. The time when you were to choose and India was to accept is gone, never to return. Let the consent of the people and not the accident of logic be the touchstone of your new constitution if you desire that it should be worked.[3]

The Round Table Conference of prominent Indian leaders in London at which B. R. Ambedkar had spoken so boldly and forthrightly had been called by the British government to attempt to mollify the widespread public hostility all across India to the Simon Commission and the almost universal rejection of its recommendations.[4] The conference was attended by representatives of the various Indian political parties, British officialdom and politicians, and some twenty Indian princes (to

---

[2] Keer, *Dr. Ambedkar*, pp. 150–51.
[3] Moon, *Dr. Babasaheb Ambedkar: Writings and Speeches*, Vol. 2, pp. 503–509.
[4] Making Britain, 'Round Table Conferences, 1930-32', Open University official website.

add to the fifty-three Indians of assorted shades of opinion whom
the British deemed to be appropriate representatives of a cross-
section of Indian interests).

However, the Indian National Congress, the pre-eminent
nationalist organization, with most of its leadership in jail
for having led a civil disobedience movement, boycotted
the conference, severely undermining its credibility. Two
representatives of the Depressed Classes, Dr Ambedkar and Rao
Bahadur Rettaimalai Srinivasan[5] of Madras, the latter a staunch
supporter of British rule, were invited. Ambedkar, questioned
on his decision to attend a conference the nationalist Congress
was boycotting, explained his reasoning: 'I will demand what is
rightful for my people, and I will certainly uphold the demand
for Swaraj'[6]—the position of an Indian nationalist who was
simultaneously a fighter for the rights of the Depressed Classes.

As has been noted, King George V opened the conference
and Prime Minister Ramsay MacDonald presided. The British
message was that they wished to signal their determination
to resolve the political crisis in India on terms that would be
broadly acceptable to the Indian people. To this end, the views
of all sections of opinion would need to be heard.

Ambedkar's speech on the occasion—on behalf, as he put
it, of 20 per cent of the population of the British empire in
India—both supported India's calls for self-government and,
as we have seen, his people's demands for emancipation. His
words caused a flutter both among the British, whose rule he
was so comprehensively dismissing, and the 'moderate' Hindus,
who were alarmed by his assertion of the need to alter the
existing social conditions. But Ambedkar's speech and his
overall approach at the conference served to establish him
simultaneously as a nationalist and patriot on the one hand,

---

[5] You can read more on this fascinating personality here, B. Kolappan, 'Little-
known facts about a well-known leader', *The Hindu*, 21 August 2012.
[6] Keer, *Dr. Ambedkar*, p. 145.

and as a fierce advocate of the interests of the downtrodden, on the other.

He was made a member of most of the nine subcommittees established to go into the various questions arising at the conference. Ambedkar focused particularly on the Federal Structure Committee, where he argued for a strong central government, which he considered essential to protect the rights of the Depressed Classes and promote their welfare. He made common cause[7] with Hindu Mahasabha leader Balakrishna Shivram Moonje, who issued a joint declaration with him on the commitment of the hardcore Hindu leadership to upholding the rights of the Depressed Classes. Ambedkar drafted a Declaration of Fundamental Rights that would prevail in a future independent India and Moonje endorsed them before the press. This was a significant political achievement for Ambedkar, who was simultaneously staving off British alarm at his nationalist pronouncements, seeking to avoid an irreparable breach with the conformist Srinivasan, and asserting the core demands of his community. Ambedkar was perhaps the one delegate who emerged from the collapse of the conference with his reputation enhanced.

The Round Table Conference ended in a shambles in February 1931, two months after it began, hopelessly divided on issues of electoral representation and the system of election, communal interests, and the allocation of seats for election. The absence of the Indian National Congress, which was spearheading the struggle for freedom on the ground, also cast doubt on the relevance of the proceedings. The British responded by releasing Mahatma Gandhi and other detained Congressmen, and a 'pact'[8] between the viceroy, Lord Irwin,

---

[7] Keith Meadowcroft, 'The All-India Hindu Mahasabha, untouchable politics, and "denationalising" conversions: the Moonje–Ambedkar Pact', *Journal of South Asian Studies*, 2006.

[8] Archana Subramanian, 'Striking a deal', *The Hindu*, 3 March 2016.

and the Mahatma decided that the latter would suspend his civil disobedience movement and attend a reconvened Round Table Conference later that year.

Ambedkar then called on Mahatma Gandhi in Bombay, but this first meeting, in August 1931, was not a success. When Ambedkar entered the room, it took some time for the Mahatma, who kept conversing with others, to notice him. Ambedkar wondered whether he was being deliberately insulted. Then the Mahatma spotted him. He remarked that he had gathered that Ambedkar had a number of grievances against him. But he should know that 'I have been thinking over the problems of Untouchables ever since my school days. I had to make enormous efforts to make it a part of the Congress platform. The Congress has spent not less than 20 lakhs on the uplift of the Untouchables.'[9] Ambedkar responded with his characteristic bluntness that the money had been wasted since it had provided no practical benefit for the uplift of his community. The Congress could have made rejection of untouchability a condition of membership, as it had done the wearing of homespun khaddar. But there had been no real change of heart on the part of the Hindus and that is why the Depressed Classes felt they could not rely on the Congress, but only on themselves, to resolve their plight.

The Mahatma tried to mollify Ambedkar, hailing him as 'a patriot of sterling worth' in the struggle for the homeland. 'Gandhiji, I have no homeland,' was Ambedkar's famous reply. 'No self-respecting Untouchable worth the name will be proud of this land.' He went on: 'How can I call this land my own homeland and this religion my own wherein we are treated worse than cats and dogs, wherein we cannot get water to drink?' The Round Table Conference, he added, had given recognition

---

[9] Ravi Ranjan and M. K. Singh, *Ambedkar: The Source of Life and Vision*, Delhi: K. K. Publications, 2021, p. 103. A fuller text of the entire conversation was recorded ad verbatim by Keer, *Dr. Ambedkar*, pp. 165–66.

to the political rights of the Depressed Classes. What was the Mahatma's view of this? Gandhi's reply was uncompromising: 'I am against the political separation of the Untouchables from the Hindus. That would be politically suicidal.'[10]

At about the same time, Ambedkar scored a personal triumph when the Bombay Presidency announced that it would open police recruitment to the Depressed Classes, something he had been ceaselessly calling for. And when invitations were issued to the second Round Table Conference (from 7 September to 1 December 1931), this time including pre-eminent leaders like the Mahatma himself and the Muslim League's Mohammed Ali Jinnah, Ambedkar was not only prominently included, but he was asked to wield the pen for the drafting of a potential future Constitution for India.

Unfortunately, Ambedkar's health again laid him low: fever, diarrhoea, and vomiting prevented him from leaving for London at the same time as the other delegates, and he arrived in mid-September just as discussions had begun to heat up. The Federal Structure Committee of the conference was the venue for a pair of speeches by the Mahatma and Dr Ambedkar that were a portent of things to come. The Mahatma spoke of the Indian National Congress, with its diverse and all-inclusive membership, as the sole representative of all Indian interests, classes, castes, faiths, and regions (and also of both genders, pointing to its several female presidents, something no other party could boast of). Ambedkar spoke of two themes in particular, the specific problems of the Depressed Classes and the future constitutional dispensation of free India.

On the former subject, Ambedkar refused to be patronized. He disagreed openly with the Mahatma's stand that no special provisions were required to cater to the needs of his community. When Pandit Madan Mohan Malaviya (founder

---

[10] Keer, *Dr. Ambedkar*, pp. 165–67.

of Banaras Hindu University and a prominent Congressman) remarked[11] that if the British had devoted enough resources to the eradication of illiteracy in India, there would have been no Depressed Classes to speak of, Ambedkar testily pointed out that his own extensive academic qualifications had made no difference to his being treated as an 'untouchable'. On the latter subject, he clashed with the representatives of the Indian princes in his demand for elected representatives from the princely states. The maharaja of Bikaner, Sir Ganga Singh, pointedly said that the traditional rulers could not be expected to give the nationalists a blank cheque;[12] Ambedkar responded bluntly to the effect that sovereignty resided with the people and not with their rulers, whereas the Mahatma assured the princes that the Congress had no intention of interfering in their internal affairs. (In this, Ambedkar's view was to prevail over the Mahatma's; before the decade was out the Congress had established a States People's Conference[13] to fight for the rights of the people of the princely states, with a unit in each state.)

Even though Gandhi and the Congress agreed with Ambedkar on several measures to counter caste discrimination—such as political reservations, temple entry, inter-caste dining and inter-caste marriages, eradication of untouchability, greater educational and employment opportunities—from Ambedkar's point of view it made perfect sense to stand apart from Mahatma Gandhi on the issue of the rights of the Depressed Classes. His reasoning was that had he opposed the British and sided with Gandhi, he would not have gained anything for his people from the British, while Gandhi, judging by the Congress's track record thus far, would not, in Ambedkar's view, have given his people anything more than pious blessings and hollow platitudes. Cooperation

---

[11] Keer, *Dr. Ambedkar*, pp. 173–74.
[12] Ibid., p. 172.
[13] John McLeod, *Sovereignty, Power, Control: Politics in the States of Western India, 1916-1947*, Delhi: D. K. Print World, 2007, p. 136.

with the British, in language they could understand and terms they could accept, would secure recognition for his cause and, conceivably, approval of his demands. Supporting the Mahatma and the Congress would subsume his cause within the larger Congress struggle, within which it would not be a priority. That was why, although his name was included on the Central Board of the Anti-Untouchability League, which the Mahatma had renamed the Harijan Sevak Sangh, he did not attend any of its meetings. Ambedkar wanted the organization to be largely controlled by untouchables and to focus on annihilating caste; Gandhi wanted it controlled by caste Hindus, on the grounds that untouchability was a Hindu sin and Hindus should take the lead in ending it. 'I am described as a traitor by Congressmen,' Ambedkar conceded, 'because I oppose Gandhi.'[14] But he was convinced that his stand would be vindicated.

(It must be said that Ambedkar's was not the only view from his community on this question. M. C. Rajah, prominent politician and activist from the Madras Presidency, for instance, believed strongly in the importance of organizing the Depressed Classes within mainstream Hindu society. In his view, Ambedkar's advocacy of separate electorates would simply make the community, which was already socially ostracized, 'politically untouchable' as well.)[15]

The other major issue before the Round Table Conference was the Hindu–Muslim question. While formally assigned to the Minorities Committee, the topic was in fact being discussed privately between representatives of the two major communities rather than in the open forum. Ambedkar made it clear in his own remarks that while he could not object to such discussions as might come up with an agreed solution to the vexed problems of the communal question, he would not cede to anyone else the right to speak on behalf of the Depressed Classes. He asked

---

[14] Keer, *Dr. Ambedkar*, p. 194.
[15] Quoted in Jaffrelot, *Dr. Ambedkar and Untouchability*, p. 59.

Mahatma Gandhi, who was leading the effort and constituting a committee to pursue the communal question, to include a representative of the Depressed Classes in that committee; the Mahatma agreed. The effort, however, failed, and the Mahatma announced before the conference that a principal reason for the failure was that those negotiating on the matter were not true representatives of their communities—a pointed reference to the fact that Ambedkar was a government appointee.

This comment led Ambedkar to react with asperity, and his fury was not easily assuaged. 'I have not the slightest doubt that even if the Depressed Classes of India were given the chance of electing their representative to this Conference, I would all the same find a place here.'[16] He rejected the Mahatma's claims to represent the interests of the Depressed Classes: 'We feel nobody can remove our grievances as well as we can and we cannot remove them unless we get political powers in our own hands. I am afraid the Depressed Classes have waited too long for time to work its miracle!'[17]

It took an intervention by the British prime minister to soothe frayed tempers over the issue. A tea was duly arranged between the two antagonists at 2 p.m. on 14 August 1931, at which Ambedkar graciously acknowledged the Mahatma's efforts to uplift the community, while disagreeing with him fundamentally on the way forward.[18] An uneasy truce then reigned between the two.

Politics was not the only point of difference between the two men. As an economist, Ambedkar disagreed with the Gandhian philosophy of limiting needs and restricting consumption, which he linked to a mindset of poverty. He was strongly in favour of economic growth; the problem, he argued, is not property but its unequal distribution. Similarly, he had little patience with the

---

[16] Moon, *Dr. Babasaheb Ambedkar*, Vol. 9, p. 65.
[17] Keer, *Dr. Ambedkar*, p. 151.
[18] Shahare, *Dr. Bhimrao Ambedkar*, p. 45.

Mahatma's faith in idyllic village life, which Ambedkar believed condemned the Depressed Classes to a life of degradation. Whereas Gandhi romanticized traditional village life, Ambedkar saw villages as 'cesspools' of caste oppression and social and economic backwardness.[19] The pressure of population on land, he argued, needed to be eased by industrialization, which would offer meaningful and remunerative work to surplus agrarian labour. Ambedkar saw industrialization and urbanization as the only way out for the Depressed Classes. These were mutually irreconcilable worldviews.

While the conference was in progress, a general election unseated Ramsay MacDonald, bringing the Conservatives under Stanley Baldwin[20] to power. On 5 November 1931, at a reception that followed in Buckingham Palace, Ambedkar had an opportunity to brief the king-emperor extensively on the situation of the Depressed Classes, leaving the monarch visibly moved.[21] It was clear that as long as Ambedkar was there, it would be impossible to brush the problem of untouchability under the carpet, or to leave it to well-meaning but ineffective upper-caste representatives to address the issue. His stature, already enhanced by his performance at the first Round Table Conference, was elevated even further by his role at the second.

The failure of the second Round Table Conference once again gave the British the opportunity to point to the intractable differences of opinion between Indian leaders as necessitating their continued direct control of India. The new prime minister then took it upon himself in 1932 to announce a Communal Award on behalf of his government to govern the future political representation of the various Indian communities. He decreed that there would be separate electorates for the

---

[19] S. A. Aiyar, 'Ambedkar vs Gandhi: The risks of village empowerment', *Times of India*, 9 February 2014.
[20] For more on Stanley Baldwin, see 'Stanley Baldwin (1867-1947)', BBC History.
[21] Keer, *Dr. Ambedkar*, p. 181.

various communities: while Hindus would contest for the general seats, there would be reserved lists of voters and seats for Muslims, Sikhs, Christians, and Europeans. As for the Depressed Classes, they would have a double vote, one to place their own representatives in the provincial assemblies and the other to participate in the 'general' polls that would elect Hindu legislators. They would receive 78 seats in the proposed Central Legislature.[22]

Ambedkar, speaking in the Bombay Legislative Council on a different bill, had already strongly supported the principle of communal representation:

> Sir, India is not Europe. England is not India. England does not know the caste system. We do. Consequently, the political arrangements that may suit England can never suit us. Let us recognise the fact. I want a system in which I will have not only a right to go to the ballot box but also the right to have a body of people belonging to my own class inside the House, who will not only discuss matters but take part in deciding issues. I say, therefore, that communal representation is not a vicious thing; it is not a poison; it is the best arrangement that can be made for the safety and security of the different classes in this country. I do not call it a disfiguring of the constitution.... It is a decoration of the constitution.[23]

But Indian political opinion largely saw the Communal Award as a classic example of the British 'divide and rule' strategy, and the Indian National Congress rejected it outright. Mahatma Gandhi announced that he would fast unto death until the award was withdrawn.[24] The government had no right to separate the Depressed Classes from the Hindu electorate to which they

---

[22] Ibid., p. 204.
[23] Ibid., p. 228.
[24] Ibid., p. 205.

rightfully belonged by providing separate electorates for them to elect their own representatives. Ambedkar, on the other hand, consistent with his long-expressed views, welcomed the principle of separate representation for his community, which had been oppressed for millennia. Public opinion turned anxious as the Mahatma's health began to deteriorate in Yerawada Jail, where the British had incarcerated him.

Dr Rajendra Prasad, later to preside over the Constituent Assembly and serve as the Republic's first president, led efforts to broker a compromise with Ambedkar in order to persuade the Mahatma to give up his fast. 'To save Gandhi's life,' Ambedkar stubbornly stated, 'I will not be a party to any proposals that would be against the interests of my people.' He criticized Gandhi for 'releasing reactionary and uncontrollable forces' against members of the Depressed Classes, who would undoubtedly have to face vicious reprisals if Gandhi actually succumbed to the fast. On the day before the fast began, Ambedkar had declared: 'I shall not sacrifice the rightful demands of my people just to save the life of Mahatma Gandhi.' But when the 'fast unto death' began on 20 September 1932, a number of senior leaders arranged for Ambedkar to visit the fasting Mahatma.

On 22 September, Ambedkar arrived at Yerawada to find the Mahatma in an extremely emaciated condition, lying on an iron cot under a mango tree in the prison garden, being tended to in an atmosphere of gloom. This world-renowned saintly figure, and hero to hundreds of millions, was at death's door and the eyes of the world were on whether Ambedkar would make it possible to save his life. Ambedkar spoke calmly, quietly, and in a tone of great respect to lay out his community's case before the Mahatma. The older man heard him out and responded, 'You have my fullest sympathy. I am with you, Doctor, in most of the things you say.' Then the Mahatma added, 'But you say that what concerns you most is my life?' Ambedkar nodded, adding, 'Yes, Gandhiji, in the hope that you would devote yourself solely to the cause of my people, and become our hero too.' The Mahatma was quick to respond that, in that case, Ambedkar knew what to do to save his life. 'Do it and save my life.... You are untouchable by birth and I am by adoption. We must be one and indivisible. I am prepared to give up my life to avert the break-up of the Hindu community.'[25]

Put like that, Ambedkar felt he had little choice in the matter. He agreed to explore a formula that respected Mahatma Gandhi's concerns.

Meanwhile the older man's health took a turn for the worse and he was publicly said to be nearing the end. Ambedkar returned the next day, 23 September, to prison to inform the Mahatma that he would accept a provision of 148 reserved seats for members of the Depressed Classes in the provincial assemblies and 10 per cent of all the seats in the Central Legislative Assembly for the community, to be voted for by all Hindu voters and not just the Depressed Classes. But Ambedkar wanted the issue to be put to a referendum of all adult members of the community, who should have the right to determine their own destiny. This the Mahatma could not accept: morally, he felt, it was essential for Hinduism to expiate its own sins by treating its own Depressed Classes humanely rather than having them go their own way. He suggested to Ambedkar that a referendum could be organized after five years: 'Five years or my life!' as he rather dramatically put it.[26] Ambedkar gave in and dropped the requirement of a referendum.

An agreement, soon hailed in the media as the Poona Pact,[27] was drafted and signed on 24 September by the Mahatma, Ambedkar, and a host of upper-caste Hindu leaders including

---

[25] A detailed account of the conversation may be found in Shahare, *Dr. Bhimrao Ambedkar*, pp. 51–53.

[26] Keer, *Dr. Ambedkar*, p. 214.

[27] Ibid.

Dr Prasad and C. Rajagopalachari, the Tamil Brahmin who would later serve as the only Indian governor-general of India and who had been a staunch defender of the rights of the Depressed Classes, playing a pivotal role in the Murugesan temple entry case.[28] Most saw the agreement as a historic compromise that would guarantee Depressed Classes representation while keeping the Hindus united, but some voices in the untouchable community were not mollified. They felt Ambedkar had surrendered to emotional blackmail and sold out his own people's interests under pressure from the galaxy of notables clustered around the Mahatma. As Yashica Dutt reports, 'Dalits continue to mourn the signing of the Poona Pact, and observe 24 September as a dark day when their political rights were coerced away to protect the privileges of upper-caste Hindus.'[29]

But mainstream Indian opinion stood behind him. A major public meeting in Bombay on 25 September was addressed by Hindu notables like Pandit Madan Mohan Malaviya and Sir Tej Bahadur Sapru (head of the Liberal Party), who praised Ambedkar generously while calling on all Hindus to eradicate the evil of untouchability from the country.[30] The next day, the British cabinet recommended the Poona Pact to parliament for endorsement, and Mahatma Gandhi gave up his fast. Three days later, he asked G. D. Birla, the influential Indian industrialist who was his wealthiest principal supporter, to finance (to the tune of ₹600,000, a considerable sum in those days) the establishment of an All-India Anti-Untouchability League that the Mahatma would personally spearhead.[31]

A third Round Table Conference was convened in London in November 1932. From on board his ship Ambedkar wrote to a friend of the Mahatma's, commenting on his differences

---

[28] As recounted in Tiruchanoor Case-Rajaji, Scribd.
[29] Dutt, *Coming Out As Dalit*, p. 118.
[30] Keer, *Dr. Ambedkar*, p. 215.
[31] Jaffrelot, *Dr. Ambedkar and Untouchability*, p. 67.

with Gandhi: 'The touchables and Untouchables cannot be held together by law, certainly not by any electoral law substituting joint electorate for separate electorate. The only thing that can hold them together is love.... The salvation of the Depressed Classes,' he went on, 'will come only when the caste Hindu is made to think and is forced to feel that he must alter his ways. I want a revolution in the mentality of the caste Hindus.'[32]

This would require a mass movement all over India, which would require agitation and satyagraha, such as in Malabar where temple entry had been achieved as a result of a mass popular upsurge against the prevailing iniquitous laws. Ambedkar urged caste Hindus to take the lead to bring about such change.

The British had been foolish to call the third Round Table Conference when Mahatma Gandhi was still imprisoned, which unsurprisingly led the Indian National Congress to boycott it. Though the conference met for almost two months, it proved a damp squib. Ambedkar found himself unimpressed by the attitude of the Indian Muslim delegates to social reform; they were inclined to be supportive of Hindu orthodoxy on untouchability in order to insulate their own community from the risk of reform. This was reminiscent of an episode when Ambedkar and a group of his people visiting Daulatabad Fort were upbraided by Muslims there for helping themselves to water from a public well;[33] it had come as something of a surprise for him then to see Muslims upholding untouchability. Seeing their stand here, Ambedkar expressed disappointment that India's Muslim leaders had learned nothing from the changes Atatürk had wrought in Turkey.

Meanwhile in India, the Gandhians were as good as their word, and the temple entry movement gathered momentum. In early 1933, a controversy arose around the entry of untouchables to the famed Guruvayur Temple in Kerala. The Mahatma initially

---

[32] Keer, *Dr. Ambedkar*, p. 221.
[33] Ibid., p. 246.

announced that he would fast with his foremost disciple in the region, K. Kelappan,[34] to ensure their entry but the Zamorin of Calicut, in whose domains the temple fell, remained adamant that he would not interfere with established practice. The Mahatma then suggested a referendum of Hindus in Ponnani taluka, where the temple was situated, to ascertain public opinion in the matter. To the surprise of most, 56 per cent of the Hindus voted in favour of temple entry and only 9 per cent against. But the Zamorin was unmoved.[35] At this point a Brahmin leader, Sir Ranga Iyer, introduced an Untouchability Abolition Bill[36] in the Central Legislative Assembly, and Dr P. Subbarayan did the same in the Madras Legislature. Gandhiji postponed the date of his threatened fast pending the decision of the viceroy on these bills.

At the Mahatma's invitation, soon after his return to India, Ambedkar called upon the still imprisoned leader at Yerawada. Gandhi asked Ambedkar to support the Iyer and Subbarayan bills publicly. Ambedkar responded that he could not endorse the Subbarayan text, which failed to condemn untouchability and did not go far enough, merely urging that temple entry be allowed wherever a referendum approved it. The Mahatma tried to persuade the younger man that Hinduism ought to be allowed to reform itself; his ideal was to get caste Hindus to 'expiate their sins and purify Hinduism'.[37] Temple entry was a valuable step in this direction. Ambedkar disagreed politely but firmly: it was far more important to emancipate the Depressed Classes politically, economically, and socially. Once this occurred, temple entry would follow; it was not the central issue. The real problem was the caste system, which needed to be eradicated for untouchability to end.

---

[34] Ibid., p. 217.
[35] Moon, *Dr. Babasaheb Ambedkar*, Vol. 9, p. 116.
[36] Ibid.
[37] Keer, *Dr. Ambedkar*, p. 227.

The Mahatma invited Ambedkar to express his views in a message in the first issue of a new journal he was starting, *Harijan,* which would replace his flagship *Young India.* Harijan meant 'the people of God', the term Mahatma Gandhi preferred to use for those who had hitherto been called untouchables or Depressed Classes. Ambedkar accepted the invitation and was uncompromising in his stand: 'The out-caste is a by-product of the caste system. There will be out-castes as long as there are castes. Nothing can emancipate the out-caste except purging the Hindu faith of this odious and vicious dogma.'[38] He had said much the same thing earlier:

> Some men say that they should be satisfied with the abolition of untouchability only, leaving the caste system alone. The aim of abolition of untouchability alone without trying to abolish the inequalities inherent in the caste system is a rather low [aim] ... low is a crime, let us probe the evil to its very roots and not be satisfied with [a] mere palliative to assuage our pain. If a disease is not rightly diagnosed, the remedy will be useless and the cure may be delayed. Even if we suppose that the stigma of untouchability is wiped out, what will be the status of the present-day untouchables? At the most they will be treated as Shudras. And what are the rights of the Shudras? The Smritis treat them as mere Helots and the Smritis are the guides of the caste Hindus in the matter of gradations in the caste system. Are you willing to be treated as Shudras? Are you willing to accept the position of Helots?[39]

It was this understanding that lay behind Ambedkar's lack of enthusiasm for Gandhi's approach, even though in 1933 the Mahatma embarked on a countrywide anti-untouchability tour, largely because, in historian Ramachandra Guha's words, 'he

---

[38] Ibid.
[39] Shahare, *Dr. Bhimrao Ambedkar,* pp. 31–32.

was provoked and stunned by Ambedkar's criticism'.[40] Nor was Ambedkar particularly attracted to the Mahatma's preference for working with caste Hindus to get them to see the light. Again, he had said as much elsewhere: 'That the caste system must be abolished if the Hindu society is to be reconstructed on the basis of equality, goes without saying; Untouchability has its roots in the caste system. They cannot expect the Brahmins to rise in revolt against the caste system. Also, we cannot rely upon the non-Brahmins and ask them to fight our battle. Most of these are more interested in bringing the Brahmins down rather than in raising the level of the suppressed classes. They too want a class of people on whom they can look down upon, and have the satisfaction of not being quite the under-dogs of the society. This means that we ourselves must fight our battles, relying on ourselves.'[41] At a meeting in Mazgaon, Bombay, in February 1933, he had exhorted his community to 'Learn to live in this world with self-respect. You should always cherish some ambition to do something in this world. They alone rise who strive. Some of you nurse the wrong notion that you will not rise in this world. But remember that the age of helplessness is ended. A new epoch has set in. All things are now possible because of your being able to participate in the politics and legislatures of this country.'[42]

The Mahatma replied in the next issue of *Harijan*, reiterating his faith in the Hindu caste system. 'I am a Hindu, not merely because I am born in the Hindu fold, but I am one by conviction and choice,' the Mahatma stated. 'There is no superiority or inferiority in the Hinduism of my conception. But when Dr Ambedkar wants to fight Varnashram itself, I cannot be in his camp, because I believe Varnashram to be an integral part of

---

[40] Amrita Dutta, 'RSS detested Ambedkar in his lifetime but now must praise him: Ramchandra Guha', *Indian Express*, 8 September 2018.
[41] Shahare, *Dr. Bhimrao Ambedkar*, p. 32.
[42] Keer, *Dr. Ambedkar*, p. 234.

Hinduism.'[43] That open disagreement marked the fundamental parting of the ways between the saint and the lawyer. From here on, relations between them would only get worse.

∼

In 1933, the British government issued a White Paper[44] outlining preliminary ideas for new constitutional arrangements for India that would incorporate a greater measure of self-government within the British empire. The White Paper, which was based on the discussions at the third Round Table Conference (17 November to 24 December 1932), was to be examined in depth by a Joint Committee of both houses of the British parliament, to which a representative delegation of Indians would be invited to testify. Though the proposals were almost universally condemned by the principal Indian political parties—the Congress, the Muslim League, and even the Hindu Mahasabha—the Joint Committee was duly constituted. Ambedkar was named among the seventeen Indians invited from British India, along with seven from the princely states. Before leaving for England, he consulted widely, and called on the imprisoned Mahatma to hear his views.

The discussions in England occupied the best part of seven months, from May 1933 to the end of the year. Ambedkar distinguished himself, notably in a memorable two-day exchange with Sir Winston Churchill in October.[45] While some of the Indian delegates sought to undo the provisions of the Poona Pact, Ambedkar was able to win the support of the assistant secretary of state for India to uphold it. Ambedkar stated on his return to India that it would be in the interests of the Depressed Classes to accept the proposals in the White Paper, which had essentially survived the Joint Committee's scrutiny.

Ambedkar's health had suffered from the arduous schedule

---

[43] Ibid., p. 230.
[44] Ibid., p. 235.
[45] Ibid., p. 241.

he had put himself through in the preceding few years, and he returned to India on the verge of physical and mental collapse. Fortunately, he allowed himself to be persuaded by friends to undertake a period of enforced rest at an Ayurvedic retreat in the hills. Somewhat restored, he returned to Bombay in June 1934 to resume his law practice and to teach at the Government Law College. He also began building himself a house in the area known as Hindu Colony in the Bombay suburb of Dadar. Ambedkar designed the house himself; his principal preoccupation was not the residential quarters below, but the upper floor, which was mainly intended to house his extensive collection of some 50,000 books. (Ambedkar's love for books was so intense that his biggest fear was that he would lose his eyesight and be unable to read—a deprivation so unimaginable that in that case, he averred, he would end his life.)[46] The house took more than two years to complete.[47]

Sadly, one person would not live in it. Ambedkar's long-suffering wife Ramabai, who had undergone decades of neglect, penury, and solitude as her husband pursued his career, lost her battle with ill-health on 26 May 1935, aged just thirty-seven. She died with one wish unfulfilled—to make a pilgrimage to the holy centre of Pandharpur. Ramabai's views on religion and temple worship differed from her husband's. Ambedkar's hostility to Hinduism meant that he vehemently opposed campaigning for entry into temples where his people were disrespected. Ramabai, however, insisted on praying at temples whenever possible and made independent visits to places of worship despite her husband's irritation with her devotion.

Ambedkar knew that had she undertaken the journey to Pandharpur as an untouchable she would not have been allowed into the temple but would have been asked to offer

---

[46] Ibid., pp. 474–75.
[47] Like Jefferson, Ambedkar first studied architecture and then built his home. Keer, *Dr. Ambedkar*, p. 244.

her prayers at a distance, a humiliation he did not want her to undergo. He told her to reject 'that Pandharpur which prevents its devotees from seeing the image of God'. Instead, 'by our own virtuous life, selfless service and spotless sacrifice in the cause of the down-trodden humanity we would create another Pandharpur.'[48]

In an unusual instance, Ramabai had wholeheartedly participated in Ambedkar's idiosyncratic shraddha ceremony for his deceased father. Instead of offering a meal and sweets to Brahmins after the ceremony as the ritual normally requires, Ambedkar instead offered a meal of meat and fish to forty students from his community.[49]

Ambedkar was shattered by the death of his beloved Ramu (the diminutive by which he called her). She had suffered much for him, endured his neglect and his preoccupation with public life stoically, starved to keep her family fed, borne the burdens of the years when the family could barely make ends meet, and mourned the loss of three sons and a daughter. 'She did not flinch from carrying basketfuls of cow dung on her head during periods of financial distress,' Ambedkar had written in a revealing article in *Bahishkrit Bharat* in 1928. 'And this writer could not find even half an hour in 24 hours for this extremely affectionate, amiable and venerable wife.'[50] Ambedkar ensured his wife was cremated according to traditional Hindu rituals, though wearing her favourite white sari rather than the green one tradition required. He then retired to his room and wept all night.[51] Five years later, when he published his book *Pakistan or the Partition of India*, Ambedkar dedicated it to Ramabai:

---

[48] Keer, *Dr. Ambedkar*, p. 248.
[49] Urvi Desai, 'Feminist battles within the home: Why Ambedkar's views on marriage and birth control are relevant', *The Leaflet*, 13 April 2019.
[50] Siddharth, *Bahishkrit Bharat mein Prakashit Babasaheb Dr Ambedkar ke Sampadakiye*, translation Prabhakar Gajbhiye, New Delhi: Samyak Prakashan, 2017, p. 152.
[51] Keer, *Dr. Ambedkar*, p. 249, says he wept inconsolably for a week.

Inscribed to the memory of Ramu

As a token of my appreciation of her goodness of heart, her nobility of mind and her purity of character and also for the cool fortitude and readiness to suffer along with me which she showed in those friendless days of want and worries which fell to our lot.

Ambedkar was an early feminist. His relationship with his first wife, Ramabai, founded upon friendship and debate despite disagreement, in many ways is an accurate representation of one of the most powerful feminist slogans of the twentieth century, 'The Personal Is Political'. Ambedkar's feminism within the home was certainly unusual for an Indian and practically unknown at the time for an Indian male.[52] He spoke extensively on the role of women in Indian society; he did not exclude women from his emphasis on equality, placing equal emphasis upon both caste and gender-based discrimination. Ambedkar had argued in his pioneering 1916 Columbia lecture on 'Castes in India' that endogamous marriage—marriage exclusively within the same caste and community—was the primary reason for the perpetuation of caste. His challenge to privilege and hierarchy extended to questioning the norms that extended these notions within the home. He elaborated further on the thought in a talk to a female audience at the All-India Depressed Classes Women's Conference (1942): 'Give education to your children. Instil ambitions in them... Don't be in a hurry to marry: marriage is a liability. You should not impose it upon children unless financially they are able to meet the liabilities arising from them.... Above all let each girl who marries stand up to her husband, claim to be her husband's friend and equal, and refuse

---

[52] Desai, 'Feminist battles within the home'.

to be his slave.' His courageous undermining of the sanctity of marriage in a society where great importance is given to the marital status of a woman, and his demand for women to stand as equals with men within marriage, constituted an unparalleled and audacious assertion of dignity for Indian women within their own families. In this he was a rare and pioneering male voice in a tradition of Dalit feminism ranging from Muktabai Salve in the mid-nineteenth century to Jaibai Chaudhari in the early twentieth.[53]

Ambedkar would go on to declare in 1938 to the Bombay Legislative Assembly, 'If men had to bear the pangs which women have to undergo during childbirth none of them would even consent to bear more than a single child in his life.'[54] In his work in the assembly, Ambedkar also highlighted women's limited recourse to medical assistance, and loss of lives due to inadequate affordable healthcare, an issue that is still largely unresolved. Instead of having children in rapid succession, and subsequently opting for risky abortions, Ambedkar boldly recommended birth control in the interests of the woman's health and well-being. Ambedkar sought to pass a resolution in support of government-funded birth control in the Bombay Legislative Assembly in 1938, but his resolution was defeated with eleven members voting in favour of the Bill and fifty-two members opposing it (on the grounds that it would spread immorality and cause a breakdown of the Indian family unit). His reaction can only be imagined.

Four days after Ramabai's death, Ambedkar assumed his new appointment as the first Indian principal of the prestigious Government Law College, on 1 June 1935.[55] It was a remarkable distinction for one of such humble beginnings, and it was accompanied by public speculation about his impending

---

[53] Paik, 'Dalit Feminist Thought'.
[54] Desai, 'Feminist battles within the home'.
[55] Keer, Dr. Ambedkar, p. 249.

retirement from politics. But Ambedkar still had a long way to go in public life.

~~

Reports from London in the second half of 1934 indicated that a draft Indian Constitution would be making its way through parliament and would, for the first time, give India's Depressed Classes the right to vote for their own representatives, as had been determined by provisions in the Communal Award. The Congress Party, whose leaders had just been freed from detention, however adopted a confusing stand on the Communal Award, which they neither endorsed nor denounced. The ambivalence of several Hindu leaders on the Poona Pact troubled Ambedkar greatly, but he stuck to his guns and took pains to applaud Mahatma Gandhi for his continued support to it.

When the Joint Committee's report came out, there was a new wrinkle: the proposed governance structure would include a second (upper chamber), the Legislative Council, with no guaranteed representation for the Depressed Classes. Ambedkar promptly criticized this, arguing that it would undermine the spirit of the Poona Pact.[56] He was increasingly convinced that the caste Hindus were not sincerely committed to giving the Depressed Classes their due. Reports of his dissatisfaction mounted, and by late 1935 the media were suggesting that he might announce his conversion to another religion.[57] Ambedkar had earlier publicly declared that he had no intention of abandoning the religion of his forebears, his aim being only to achieve full rights for his people within it, but the newspaper reports claimed he was on the verge of changing his stand. This alarmed some prominent Hindu leaders, who urged that the community needed to make the concessions necessary to keep Ambedkar and his followers in their fold.

---

[56] Ibid., pp. 246–47.
[57] Ibid., p. 251.

It was against this background that the Depressed Classes Conference convened at the end of October 1935. (It was called Dalit Vargiya Parishad[58] in Marathi, one of the first public uses of the term 'Dalit', a word translated either as 'the Broken People' or 'the oppressed'.) In an impassioned oration that lasted an hour and a half, Ambedkar first recounted in detail the indignities, injustices, and humiliations heaped upon his people for centuries. They had struggled to obtain the minimal civil rights obtainable within Hindu society but had consistently encountered resistance and ill-will from the upper castes. The time had therefore come, he argued, to ask themselves a question they had thus far kept in abeyance. Since their privations were all the result of the accident of being born within the Hindu fold, would they be better off converting to another religion, which would honour them as equal members of that faith? This was not a question to be answered lightly; it would require serious reflection and deliberation before a decision could be arrived at. But members of the community should give up their five-year-old satyagraha to enter the Kalaram Temple; it was not worth the effort. After all, religion existed to serve mankind, and not the other way around. And as for himself, Ambedkar said he was unfortunately born a Hindu untouchable but asserted: 'I solemnly assure you that I will not die a Hindu.'[59]

Ambedkar's speech was greeted with great enthusiasm by leaders and practitioners of other faiths, who wrote and telegraphed him to say he would be welcome in their fold: Muslims, Christians, Sikhs, and Buddhists all applauded his intention to convert and offered him the hospitality of their faiths. Mahatma Gandhi expressed his disappointment at Ambedkar's 'unfortunate' statement, stating that untouchability

---

[58] Gail Omvedt, *Ambedkar: Towards an Enlightened India*, New Delhi: Penguin Random House, 2017, p. 99.
[59] Keer, *Dr. Ambedkar*, p. 253.

was on its last legs anyway. He went on to argue that he did not approve of conversion: religion, he said, was not a cloak one could put on or discard, but an integral part of one's self. Ambedkar dismissed this argument with contempt as implying that a status conferred at birth could not be changed: 'The difference between humans and animals is that animals cannot progress. Humans can.'[60]

Other Hindu leaders pleaded with Ambedkar to reconsider, saying the Hindu faith itself would be imperilled if the Depressed Classes were to convert away from Hinduism. Ambedkar told one such leader, the prominent Hindu missionary Masurkar Maharaj—who had earned fame for reconverting 10,000 Goan Catholics to Hinduism in 1935[61]—that he would reconsider if upper-caste Hindus vowed to make a sincere effort to abolish untouchability within a specified time frame. But he added sarcastically that in the meantime Maharashtrian Brahmins should install a leader from the Depressed Classes as the Shankaracharya for one year and a hundred Chitpavan Brahmin families should fall at the feet of the new Shankaracharya.[62]

Even as he demanded a time-bound end to untouchability, Ambedkar expressed scepticism that it would happen. 'Some people think that religion is not essential to society. I do not hold this view,' Ambedkar declared to a delegation of upper-caste Hindus who had called on him in an attempt to change his mind. 'I consider the foundation of religion to be essential to the life and practices of a society. At the root of the Hindu social system lies Dharma as prescribed in the *Manusmriti*. Such being the case, I do not think it is possible to abolish inequality in Hindu society unless the existing foundation of the Smriti religion is removed and a better one laid in its place.

---

[60] Omvedt, *Ambedkar*, p. 106.
[61] Keer, *Dr Ambedkar*, p. 258.
[62] Ambedkar proposed installing K. K. Sakat, a Depressed Class leader, as the Shankaracharya; Keer, *Dr Ambedkar*, p. 258.

I, however, despair of Hindu society being able to reconstruct itself on a better foundation.'[63]

Finally, he told a Hindu delegation from Nasik, in response to their entreaties, that he was prepared to wait five years for concrete evidence of a change of heart and behaviour by upper-caste Hindus. He needed positive deeds, he said, and not mere words. His visitors were happy to leave it there.

'Lost rights are never regained,' Ambedkar observed, 'by begging and by appeals to the conscience of the usurpers, but by relentless struggle.' Reducing himself to a supplicant was the surest way to his own extinction: as he remarked, 'Goats are used for sacrificial offerings and not lions.'[64]

---

[63] Keer, *Dr. Ambedkar*, p. 259.
[64] Ibid., p. 82.

FOUR

View from the Mountaintop

1935–1946

In December 1935, the Jat-Pat-Todak Mandal, an organization dedicated to abolishing casteism by promoting and sponsoring inter-caste marriage, invited Ambedkar to the Punjab to deliver a lecture the following year. But when Ambedkar sent them a copy of his draft presidential speech in April, the organizers reacted with alarm.

'You have more than once stated in your address that you had decided to walk out of the fold of the Hindus and that that was your last address as a Hindu,' their chief, Har Bhagwan, wrote to Ambedkar.

> You have also unnecessarily attacked the morality and reasonableness of the Vedas and other religious books of the Hindus, and have at length dwelt upon the technical side of Hindu religion, which has absolutely no connection with the problem at issue.... The last portion which deals with the complete annihilation of Hindu religion and doubts the morality of the sacred books of the Hindus as well as a hint about your intention to leave the Hindu fold does not seem to me to be relevant. I would therefore most humbly request you on behalf of the people responsible for the Conference to leave out the passages referred to above.... We doubt the wisdom of making the address unnecessarily provocative and pinching.

Ambedkar refused, replying:

> I would prefer to have the Conference cancelled—I do not
> like to use vague terms—if the Mandal insisted upon having
> my address pruned to suit its circumstances. You may not
> like my decision. But I cannot give up, for the sake of the
> honour of presiding over the Conference, the liberty which
> every President must have in the preparation of the address.
> I cannot give up, for the sake of pleasing the Mandal, the
> duty which every President owes to the Conference over
> which he presides, to give it a lead which he thinks right
> and proper. The issue is one of principle, and I feel I must
> do nothing to compromise it in any way.

He went on:

> I am amazed to read that you characterize the portion of
> the speech to which your Committee objects as 'irrelevant
> and off the point'. You will allow me to say that I am a
> lawyer and I know the rules of relevancy as well as any
> member of your Committee. I most emphatically maintain
> that the portion objected to is not only most relevant but is
> also important. It is in that part of the address that I have
> discussed the ways and means of breaking up the Caste
> System. It may be that the conclusion I have arrived at as to
> the best method of destroying Caste is startling and painful.
> You are entitled to say that my analysis is wrong. But you
> cannot say that in an address which deals with the problem
> of Caste it is not open to me to discuss how Caste can be
> destroyed.

After a protracted argument, Ambedkar withdrew, saying that
they should invite someone whose speech they approved of. But
he did so with a parting shot:

> This is certainly the first time in my life to have been invited
> to preside over a Conference of Caste Hindus. I am sorry

that it has ended in a tragedy. But what can anyone expect from a relationship so tragic as the relationship between the reforming sect of Caste Hindus and the self-respecting sect of Untouchables, where the former have no desire to alienate their orthodox fellows, and the latter have no alternative but to insist upon reform being carried out? [1]

Ambedkar finally had the text published himself in May 1936, as a short book entitled *Annihilation of Caste*. It was his most far-reaching indictment of the caste system in general. It included strong attacks on orthodox Hindus and their religious leaders and 'a rebuke of Gandhi' for his ambivalence on varnashrama dharma. Gandhi wanted the 'avarnas', 'Ati-Shudras', and 'Depressed Classes' to be assimilated as equals into the caste system. Ambedkar believed this would resolve nothing in their condition; he argued that 'the outcaste is a bye-product of the caste system. There will be outcastes as long as there are castes. Nothing can emancipate the outcaste except the destruction of the caste system.' In his book, Ambedkar declared that the greatest barrier to the uplift of the Depressed Classes was Hinduism itself. As he wrote:

> In the last analysis, this means you must destroy the authority of the Shastras and the Vedas.... You must take the stand that Buddha took. You must take the stand which Guru Nanak took. You must not only discard the Shastras, you must deny their authority, as did Buddha and Nanak. You must have courage to tell the Hindus that what is wrong with them is their religion—the religion which has produced in them this notion of the sacredness of Caste.[2]

---

[1] The entire correspondence may be found at 'Prologue [How this speech came to be composed—and not delivered]', Columbia Center for Teaching and Learning (CTL).

[2] Ghanshyam Shah (ed.), *Caste and Democratic Politics in India*, New Delhi: Permanent Black, 2004, p. 103.

Ambedkar also suggested that what he was recommending would strengthen the Hindus as a community: 'From where does the Sikh or the Mohammedan derive his strength which makes him brave and fearless? I am sure it is not due to relative superiority of physical strength, diet or drill. It is due to the strength arising out of the feeling that all Sikhs will come to the rescue of a Sikh when he is in danger and that all Mohammedans will rush to save a Muslim if he is attacked. The Hindu can derive no such strength. He cannot feel assured that his fellows will come to his help. Being one and fated to be alone he remains powerless, develops timidity and cowardice and in a fight, surrenders or runs away.'[3] He added, to soften the seeming attack on Hinduism as a religion that had dismayed the organizers of his talk and prompted the withdrawal of their invitation: 'Caste has nothing to do with religion. It is a custom whose origin I do not know and do not need to know for the satisfaction of my spiritual hunger. But I do know that it is harmful both to spiritual and national growth.'[4] (He had earlier written: 'There is no doubt in my opinion that unless you change your social order you can achieve little by way of progress. You cannot mobilise the community either for defence or for offence. You cannot build anything on the foundation of caste. You cannot build up a nation, you cannot build up a morality. Anything that you will build on the foundations of caste will crack and will never be whole.'[5])

The English version of *Annihilation of Caste*, 1,500 copies, quickly sold out, and the book was soon translated into Gujarati, Hindi, Malayalam, Marathi, Punjabi, and Tamil and widely circulated. Gandhi wrote a rejoinder in *Harijan*, claiming that untouchability was not sanctified by the scriptures

---

[3] Moon, 'Annihilation of Caste', *Writings and Speeches*, Vol. I, p. 55.
[4] Ibid., p. 83.
[5] Shahare, *Dr. Bhimrao Ambedkar*, p. 114.

and not essential to Hinduism;[6] but in so doing he again defended varnashrama, the caste system, saying it did not justify any notion of superiority of one caste over another. In this rejoinder he was building upon an argument he had made in one of his earlier writings (*Young India*, 13 August 1925): 'Varnashrama, in my opinion, was not conceived in any narrow spirit. On the contrary, it gave the labourer, the Shudra, the same status as the thinker, the Brahmin.' Five years earlier, he wrote (*Young India*, 25 February 1920): 'I am one of those who do not consider caste to be a harmful institution. In its origin, caste was a wholesome custom and promoted national well-being.' In 1921, Gandhi declared in his journal *Navajivan* that, 'I believe that if Hindu Society has been able to stand, it is because it is founded on the caste system.' In his criticism of Ambedkar, having explicated his view that caste was a means of ordering professions, and did not imply superiority or even greater affluence for one caste against another, Mahatma Gandhi wrote: 'If caste and varna are convertible terms, and if varna is an integral part of the shastras which define Hinduism, I do not know how a person who rejects caste, i.e., varna, can call himself a Hindu.'[7]

Ambedkar reacted with counter-arguments that included pointing out that even Gandhi and his family did not follow their hereditary caste occupations. He also summarized the main arguments of the famous speech he had never delivered

---

[6] 'The Curse of Untouchability', in R. K. Prabhu and U. R. Rao (eds.), *The Mind of Mahatma Gandhi*, Ahmedabad: Navajivan Trust, 1960.

[7] The terms 'varna' and 'jati' are both used for 'caste', but are not, strictly speaking, identical. Varna goes back to the early days of the caste system and is a broader term dividing society into four general occupational castes: Brahmins (priests and scholars); Kshatriyas (warriors and rulers); Vaishyas (merchants and farmers); and Shudras (manual workers), with others like Dalits treated as outcastes. Jati reflects the evolution of the castes as detailed markers of professional identity derived from birth, and is applied to specific sub-castes within each broad caste as well, such as cobblers, potters, scribes, and so on. One rarely escapes one's jati identification even if one has abandoned the hereditary profession from which it is derived.

on the 'Annihilation of Caste':

> (1) That caste has ruined the Hindus; (2) that the reorganisation of Hindu society on the basis of chaturvarnya is impossible because the varnavyavastha is like a leaky pot or like a man running at the nose. It is incapable of sustaining itself by its own virtue and has an inherent tendency to degenerate into a caste system unless there is a legal sanction behind it which can be enforced against everyone transgressing his varna; (3) that the reorganisation of Hindu society on the basis of chaturvarnya would be harmful, because the effect of the varnavyavastha would be to degrade the masses by denying them opportunity to acquire knowledge and to emasculate them by denying them the right to be armed; (4) that Hindu society must be reorganised on a religious basis which would recognise the principles of liberty, equality and fraternity; (5) that in order to achieve this object the sense of religious sanctity behind caste and varna must be destroyed; (6) that the sanctity of caste and varna can be destroyed only by discarding the divine authority of the shastras.[8]

Ambedkar made it clear he saw Gandhi as a defender of the status quo, trying to put an acceptable spin on oppressive traditions. 'Gandhi,' he declared, 'is the most determined enemy of the Untouchables.' Whereas the Mahatma described Ambedkar as a man of 'original views ... who has carved out for himself a unique position in society', his praise seemed somewhat doubled-edged. 'Whatever label he wears in future, Dr Ambedkar is not the man to allow himself to be forgotten....' Calling Ambedkar the 'most uncompromising exponent' of attacks on Hinduism and 'one of the ablest' among its critics, Gandhi added ambiguously: 'He is certainly the most irreconcilable among

---

[8] B. R. Ambedkar, 'A Reply to the Mahatma', Round Table India.

them.' At one point in 1930 Mahatma Gandhi had been more generous:

> I have the highest regard for Dr. Ambedkar. He has every right to be bitter. That he does not break our heads is an act of self-restraint on his part. He is today so much saturated with suspicion that he cannot see anything else. He sees in every Hindu a determined opponent of the 'untouchables', and it is quite natural....[9]

Ambedkar was more blunt in his attacks on the Mahatma. In a 1939 lecture he put it starkly: 'To my mind there is no doubt that the Gandhi age is the dark age of India. It is an age in which people, instead of looking for their ideals in the future, are returning to antiquity.'[10] Years later, Ambedkar claimed, somewhat unfairly, that Gandhi had a habit of condemning the caste system in English while upholding it in Gujarati. Whatever the truth of his allegation, the battle lines between the two men were now clearly drawn.

The Government of India Act was passed by the British parliament in 1935.[11] It embodied the results of the various deliberations over the preceding three years, at the Round Table Conferences and in the Joint Committee, to adumbrate a Constitution for India that provided some measure of electoral democracy and self-governance. Under its provisions, elections were announced to the provincial assemblies in 1937—though with a limited electorate that, in a country of over 300 million, permitted only 30 million to vote—setting off a flurry of campaign activity by the country's various political parties.

[9] B. R. Ambedkar, 'Gandhi and His Fast', *Writings and Speeches*, Vol. V, pp. 353–54.
[10] B. R. Ambedkar, 'Federation versus Freedom', Gokhale Institute of Politics and Economics, Kale Memorial Lecture, 1939, p. 154.
[11] 'Government of India Act, 1935', Constitution of India.

Feeling that none of the established parties would offer a suitable vehicle for the interests of the Depressed Classes, Ambedkar founded his own political party, the Independent Labour Party (ILP), in August 1936. It would speak for the interests of the downtrodden—industrial workers, farmers, tenants, landless labourers—as well as demand thorough social reform to elevate the condition of the Depressed Classes. It advocated a social democratic platform, land reform, and social safety nets. Among the elements in its programme were improved sanitation in the villages and proper housing.

Ambedkar situated his ILP[12] in proximity to the Communists but distinct from them. 'History shows that where ethics and economics come in conflict, victory is always with economics,' he argued. 'Vested interests have never been known to have willingly divested themselves unless there was sufficient force to compel them.'[13] But that did not convince him about the Communists' analyses nor their methods. 'The seizure of power,' he declared, 'must be by a proletariat. The first question I ask is: Will the proletariat of India combine to bring about this revolution...? Can it be said that the proletariat of India, poor as it is, recognises no distinctions except that of the rich and poor? Can it be said that the poor in India recognise no such distinctions of caste or creed, high or low?'[14] To Ambedkar, the flaw with Indian communism was its single-minded focus on class to the exclusion of the lived reality of caste. As he explained, '[T]he caste system is not merely a division of labour. It is also a division of labourers.' Worse still, caste derived its power not from money or property but by being sanctified by religion. 'Why do millionaires in India obey

---

[12] Keer, *Dr. Ambedkar*, pp. 285–86.

[13] Aruna Roy, 'Is Unbridled Capitalism a Threat to Constitutional Democracy in India?', Dr. Ambedkar Memorial Lecture, 2015. p. 15.

[14] Jagannatham Begari (ed.), *B.R. Ambedkar and Social Transformation: Revisiting the Philosophy and Reclaiming Social Justice*, New Delhi: Routledge, 2021.

penniless Sadhus and Fakirs?... That religion is the source of power is illustrated by the history of India where the priest holds a sway over the common man often greater than the magistrate and where everything, even such things as strikes and elections, so easily take a religious turn and can so easily be given a religious twist.'[15]

The Communist leader E. M. S. Namboodiripad notoriously blamed Ambedkar for the diversion of the people's attention from the objective of full independence to the 'mundane cause of the uplift of Harijans [Untouchables]'.[16] 'Mundane cause?' For Ambedkar, that was the cause that mattered; everything else was secondary. 'In the fight for swaraj you fight with the whole nation on your side. In this, you have to fight against the whole nation—and that too, your own. But it is more important,' he concluded, 'than swaraj.' As he famously added, 'Lost rights are never won by appeals to the conscience of the usurpers, but by relentless struggle.'

After a nine-week vacation in Europe to replenish his energies, Ambedkar returned to India in January 1937 and embarked immediately upon the campaign trail, touring all districts of the Bombay Presidency in the quest for support for his party. A notable upper-caste advocate of untouchable rights, N. C. Kelkar, who had left the Congress on that issue, hailed Ambedkar as 'the Uncrowned King of the Depressed Classes'. The Congress put forward their own candidates from the community for the seats reserved for them, nominating India's first great cricketer from the Depressed Classes, Palwankar Baloo,[17] for the seat being contested by Ambedkar. Despite the vastly superior resources and organization of the Congress, fourteen of the seventeen candidates nominated by Ambedkar's

---

[15] B. R. Ambedkar, *The Annihilation of Caste*, General Press, 2020, p. 90.
[16] Nishikant Kolge, *Gandhi Against Caste*, New Delhi: Oxford University Press, 2017.
[17] Dhrubo Jyoti, 'India's first Dalit cricketer Palwankar Baloo fought against caste barriers on the field and off it', *Hindustan Times*, 16 September 2018.

party—including Ambedkar himself—were victorious in the Bombay Assembly elections in February. Ambedkar had to give up his position as principal of the Law College after a mere two years, but victory was sweet.

The icing on the cake came on 17 March 1937 when the Bombay High Court upheld the right of the Depressed Classes to draw water from the Chawdar Tank in Mahad, the site of Ambedkar's first agitation a decade earlier. 'Truth always succeeds in the end,' Ambedkar had observed when the Mahad municipality decided to revoke the Chawdar Tank's opening to the Depressed Classes. 'It is not as if drinking the water of the Chawdar Lake will make us immortal,' he observed. 'We have survived well enough all these days without drinking it. We are not going to the Chawdar Lake merely to drink its water. We are going to the Lake to assert that we too are human beings like others.'[18] In upholding the triumph of 'truth', Ambedkar, rather like Gandhi, cited ideas and examples from the Gita because, he said, it was acceptable to both the touchables and the untouchables.

According to Ambedkar, a fight, whether violent or non-violent, was just if the end sought was good and just. But the justness of an end did not change, he observed, with the means employed for its achievement; the justness of an end did not vary with the employment of different means, as a verb changes with its subject. In this he differed from Mahatma Gandhi, who taught that a just end cannot be pursued by unjust means; indeed, Gandhi insisted that the means used must always be worthy of the ends pursued. To Gandhi, a resort to violence vitiated the noble cause of freedom; to Ambedkar, the liberation of the Depressed Classes was such a transcendent goal in itself that any means could be used to achieve it.

---

[18] Siddharthya Swapan Roy, 'The Lake of Liberation', *Outlook*, 8 April 2016.

In this, he felt a certain bitterness towards the Mahatma that boiled over on the issue of the Chawdar agitation. For Ambedkar the issue was the primordial one of human equality. Men may not all be equal, he stressed, but equality was the only possible governing principle. This was the central issue of the Mahad Satyagraha, and it was one on which he wrote in his June 1945 screed 'What Congress and Gandhi Have Done to the Untouchables':

> The Untouchables were not without hope of getting the moral support of Mr Gandhi. Indeed, they had very good ground for getting it. For the weapon of satyagraha—the essence of which is to melt the heart of the opponent by suffering—was the weapon which was forged by Mr Gandhi, and who had led the Congress to practise it against the British Government for winning swaraj. Naturally the Untouchables expected full support from Mr Gandhi to their satyagraha against the Hindus, the object of which was to establish their right to take water from public wells and to enter public Hindu temples. Mr Gandhi however did not give his support to the satyagraha. Not only did he not give his support, he condemned it in strong terms.[19]

That his cause prevailed gave Ambedkar satisfaction, but confirmed his dislike for the Mahatma.

After some delay caused by the Congress's initial unwillingness to form the government, the new legislative assembly convened in July 1937. Within a month Ambedkar was clashing with the new premier, B. G. Kher, about the level of the proposed salaries and benefits being accorded to ministers; Ambedkar wanted their emoluments to take into account the prevailing social and economic conditions, which

---

[19] B. R. Ambedkar, *What the Congress and Gandhi Have Done to the Untouchables*, New Delhi: Gautam Book Centre, 1946, p. 238.

in his view merited a salary of ₹75 a month rather than the ₹500 proposed by the government.[20] In September, Ambedkar introduced a bill to abolish the khoti system of land tenure in the Konkan region of the presidency and provide rights and benefits to landless tenant farmers.[21] He also moved an amendment to another piece of legislation that used the term 'Harijan', which he found patronizing—after all, weren't all people the children of God?—and called for its deletion. 'While it seems harmless enough to call a group that is discriminated against God's children, it has deeply problematic undertones,' explains Dutt. 'By connecting Dalit suffering to divine fate, it lets upper-caste Hindus, who are the ones perpetrating the suffering, off the hook. It also indicates, quite damagingly, that the Harijans' lower caste is somehow related to their karma.'[22] The Congress majority prevailed on the issue, and Ambedkar rose to express his disappointment, arguing that the views of the Depressed Classes themselves on the issue of what they were to be called ought to have mattered more to the ruling party. With Kher defending the term, Ambedkar led other legislators from the community in a walkout of the assembly to register their protest.[23]

It is true that, at that time, Ambedkar did not have an alternative term to suggest to the government to replace the Mahatma's coinage of 'Harijan'. He had himself used, instead, the Marathi word for the 'excluded' (bahishkrit), the English terms 'untouchables' and 'Depressed Classes', and occasionally the term 'mook', the 'silent' (though given his own eloquence, it was never a term that was likely to apply credibly to him). When independent India's own Constitution was adopted in 1950, the untouchable castes were listed in a Schedule attached

---

[20] Keer, *Dr. Ambedkar*, p. 295.
[21] Ibid., pp. 296, 300.
[22] Dutt, *Coming Out As Dalit*, p. 120.
[23] Keer, *Dr. Ambedkar*, p. 302.

to the Constitution, and the Harijans were thenceforth officially referred to as the Scheduled Castes. Ambedkar's opposition to 'Harijan' continued for the rest of his life, and by the 1970s it had yielded to the term 'Dalit' (or 'oppressed') in popular and then in official use.

As an opposition legislator, Ambedkar was a fierce and uncompromising advocate of working-class and labour interests. He strongly criticized the Industrial Disputes Bill of 1937 as an instrument designed to favour the capitalists at the expense of the workers. When the Congress Party's majority ensured its passage, Ambedkar joined the Bombay Trades Union Congress in calling for a protest strike, addressing a rally which mobilized some 80,000 protestors. The successful and largely peaceful strike on 7 November 1937 (only largely, since clashes between some workers and police led to the deaths of two workers) marked an evolution in Ambedkar's standing as an advocate of workers' rights and not merely a leader of the Depressed Classes.[24]

It was during this time that Ambedkar reiterated his famous credo, 'Educate, Organise and Agitate'. He explained in a speech at Nagpur:

> You have less need of an assurance from me that I will fight for the ideal. I stand in greater need of an assurance from you. You have assured me of your love and affection. It was quite unnecessary. I want an assurance of another kind. It is an assurance of strength, unity and determination to stand for our rights, fight for our rights and never to turn back until we win our rights. You promise to do your part. I promise to do mine. With justice on our side, I do not see how we can lose our battle.[25]

---

[24] Arjun Ram Meghwal, 'B R Ambedkar laid the foundation for workers' rights, social security in India', *Indian Express*, 1 May 2020.
[25] Shahare, *Dr. Bhimrao Ambedkar*, p. 75.

Ambedkar went on with passion:

> It is a matter of joy to fight this battle. The battle is in the fullest sense spiritual. There is nothing material or sordid in it. For our struggle is for our freedom. It is a battle for the reclamation of human personality which has been suppressed and mutilated by the Hindu social system and will continue to be suppressed and mutilated if in the political struggle, the Hindus win and we lose. My final words of advice to you are, 'Educate, Organise and Agitate,' have faith in yourselves and never lose hope. I shall always be with you as I know you will be with me.

As has been noted, Ambedkar's Independent Labour Party and his own politics veered close to Marxist and Communist ideology, but the tendency of the left to see all issues in economic terms meant that for them only class mattered, not caste. Socialists assumed that the Depressed Classes were simply a landless proletariat whose problems would be ended by land redistribution, and that in a truly egalitarian society their problems would disappear as economic justice was asserted. Ambedkar tackled these assumptions in a 1936 issue of *Janata*:

> The base is not the building. On the basis of economic relations a building is erected of religious, social and political institutions. This building has just as much reality as the base. If we want to change the base, then first the building that has been constructed on it has to be knocked down. In the same way, if we want to change the economic relations of society, then first the existing social, political and other institutions will have to be destroyed.

He went on to argue that without the eradication of caste there could be no successful working-class struggle. In the process he attacked the Congress socialists led by Nehru, adding to the profound cleavage between him and all sections of that party.

1 Ambedkar along with his son Yashwant, wife Ramabai, sister-in-law Laxmibai (wife of his elder brother, Anandrao Ambedkar), nephew Mukundrao (Anandrao's son) and his favourite dog Toby

2 The First Round Table Conference, 12 November 1930

3 Ambedkar and others before signing the Poona Pact, 1932

4 Ambedkar with others welcoming British politician Sir Stafford Cripps, 1942. The Cripps Mission was sent by the British government to India in March 1942 to garner Indian support for the British war efforts in World War II

5 Ambedkar taking the oath as the first Law and Justice Minister in independent India, in August, 1947. Ambedkar served in the first Nehru ministry until he resigned on September 27, 1951

6 Ambedkar sharing a light-hearted moment with Rao Bahadur S. K. Bole, an Indian reformer, activist, barrister and Independent Labour **Party** leader from Bombay

7 Ambedkar with the Drafting Committee. While Ambedkar drafted most of the Constitution of India, his original committee consisted of six members including K. M. Munshi, Muhammed Saadulah, Alladi Krishnaswamy Iyer, Gopala Swami Ayyangar, N. Madhava Rao (replacing B. L. Mitter, who resigned due to ill health), and T. T. Krishnamachari (replacing D. P. Khaitan after his death in 1948)

8 Ambedkar after his appointment at the Government Law College in Bombay, 1935. He would go on to be appointed principal of the Government Law College, a position he held for two years

9 Ambedkar is formally initiated into the Buddhist faith at Dikshabhoomi, Nagpur, watched by thousands of followers. It was to overcome the caste system that Ambedkar decided to adopt Buddhism in 1956

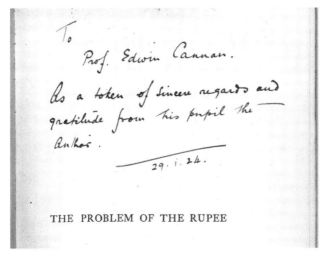

To
Prof. Edwin Cannan.

As a token of sincere regards and gratitude from his pupil the Author.

29. i. 24.

THE PROBLEM OF THE RUPEE

10 Ambedkar's signed dedication to his supervisor, 1924

भारत का हाइ कमीशन
लन्दन

THE HIGH COMMISSION OF INDIA,

LIBRARY
INDIA HOUSE,
ALDWYCH,
LONDON, W.C.2.

TELEPHONE: 01-836 8484 EXT. 115
TELEGRAMS: HICOMIND, LONDON, W.C.2.

OUR REFERENCE: LIBY/052/79 LSE

9th April, 1979

Dear Sir,

  We have received an enquiry from India addressed to our
High Commissioner, who has asked me to find out the answer, if
this is possible:-

  The date on which London University conferred the degree
of D.Sc. on Dr. B.R. Ambedkar. We know that the thesis was
entitled 'The Problem of the Rupee' and that the degree was
finally granted in June 1923. There was much controversy about
this particular thesis as it was revolutionary in character for
that period of time, and Dr. Ambedkar was asked to write some of
the work again, although I believe that in the end it was submitted
as originally prepared. Dr. Ambedkar was at the London School of Economics.

  If the exact date could be given we would be most grateful.

Yours faithfully,

R, Travis (Mr.)
Librarian

The Administrative Officer,
London School of Economics & Political Science,
Houghton Street,
Aldwych, W.C.2.

11 Letter from the High Commission of India, 1979, requesting
confirmation of the date Ambedkar completed his thesis

BHIMRAO. R. AMBEDKAR
M.A. Ph. D. D. Sc.
Barrister-at-Law.
J. P. M. L. C.

Bhimrao R. Ambedkar

RAJGRAHA
NEW DADAR
BOMBAY – 14.

8th January 1935.

Dear Mr. Lansbury,

    I am sending a statement of views on the Report
of the Joint Parliamentary Committee as it affects
the Depressed Classes. The report has caused profound
dissatisfaction among the Depressed Classes and I
trust that you will see your way to come to their
rescue ~~of the~~ by suggesting modifications of the
proposals of the J.P.C. so as to safeguard their -
interests.

        I am,

        Yours sincerely

        B R Ambedkar

To The Hon'ble Mr. George Lansbury M.P.

12 Letter from Ambedkar to George Lansbury MP, 1935, enclosing
a statement which criticized the Joint Parliamentary Committee's
report on the Indian Constitution and urging Lansbury to come 'to
the rescue' of the depressed classes, who were completely dissatisfied
with the report

13 A bust of Ambedkar at the London School of Economics, donated to the LSE by FABO (Federation of Ambedkarite and Buddhist Organisations)

14 Portrait of Ambedkar by G. S. Nagdeve, gifted to LSE by the Dr Ambedkar Memorial Committee

The British Raj's experiment in self-government largely worked for two years, but foundered on the thoughtless decision of the viceroy to declare war on Germany in September 1939 on behalf of India, without even a gesture of consultation with elected Indian leaders. The irony was that the Congress had been in the forefront of anti-fascist opinion in the country, and would probably have been easily persuaded to cooperate in the war effort against Nazism and Fascism, provided some powers were transferred to elected Indian leaders. But after this snub, the elected Congress governments resigned, a major setback for the evolution of the polity.

The resignations provided an opportunity to those parties that had been decimated by the Congress in the 1937 elections. Jinnah and the Muslim League declared the Congress resignations to be a 'Day of Deliverance'. Ambedkar was quick to join them: 'I read Mr. Jinnah's statement,' he declared, 'and I felt ashamed to have allowed him to steal a march over me and rob me of the language and the sentiment which I, more than Mr. Jinnah, was entitled to use.'[26] He went on to suggest that the Depressed Classes were considerably more oppressed by Congress policies than were Indian Muslims. Ambedkar joined Jinnah in addressing a heavily attended Day of Deliverance event in a Muslim-dominated locality of Bombay, where each outdid the other in their invective against the Congress Party. Ambedkar was a convinced supporter of the war, which he saw as a fight to save democracy.

Though the British were happy enough to replace the provincial Congress governments with obliging puppets, they also well knew that they needed to accommodate the concerns of the popular representatives of the electorate. Sir Stafford Cripps, a Labour Party leader, was sent to India to negotiate

[26] Keer, *Dr. Ambedkar*, p. 330.

with them with a view to granting India dominion status after
the war. His proposals for a loose confederation were promptly
denounced by every segment of Indian opinion, including the
Congress (Mahatma Gandhi famously called them 'a post-dated
cheque on a crashing bank'[27]) and the Muslim League (which
said it wanted a separate state for Muslims altogether), as well
as by Ambedkar, who objected to the lack of special provision
for the Depressed Classes analogous to that being envisaged
for the Muslim community.

Emboldened by the opportunities for power and pelf granted
to them by the British in exchange for collaborating with the
war effort, the Muslim League in 1940 passed the historic
Lahore Resolution, demanding the creation of a separate state
of Pakistan for India's Muslims. In his usual manner, combining
scholarly research with a penchant for polemics, Ambedkar
authored a 400-page volume titled *Thoughts on Pakistan*,
analysing Hindu–Muslim relations in the subcontinent and
examining the pros and cons of the concept of a separate state
of Pakistan, including the alternative of granting autonomy to
Muslim-majority regions, which would hopelessly weaken the
state. Ambedkar concluded that a multicultural nation was
arguably preferable, but since Muslim opinion seemed to want
a separate state in areas of Islamic cultural hegemony, the
Hindus should concede Pakistan to the Muslims. He proposed
that the provincial boundaries of Punjab and Bengal should
be redrawn to separate the Muslim and non-Muslim majority
areas—an inevitable consequence of the demand for partition.
If the Muslims objected to redrawing provincial boundaries,
they did not 'understand the nature of their own demand'.

Ambedkar's analysis was couched in political pragmatism. A
nation could be built amongst the peoples of India through a
systematic effort at amalgamation, especially given the existence

---

[27] Shyam Ratna Gupta, 'New Light on the Cripps Mission', *India Quarterly*, Vol.
28, No. 1, 1972, pp. 69–74.

of many examples of syncretism and coexistence among the communities, but if there was no will for such nation-building among the majority of Muslims, the creation of Pakistan was inevitable. Ambedkar's views were completely out of sync with mainstream non-Muslim opinion in India; yet they prefigured much of what eventually transpired a few years later.

In April 1941, Ambedkar turned fifty, to much acclaim. Grand public functions were organized in Poona and on Bombay's Chowpatty Beach to honour him. In June 1942, he was named to the Viceroy's Executive Council,[28] the highest decision-making body in the land under the British Raj—the first member of his community to have been so honoured. His acceptance of the viceroy's offer of the Labour portfolio on the council was denounced by the Congress as a sell-out. Ambedkar responded that he would be the first to renounce the position if he found himself unable to make a difference in the lives of the workers and the toiling classes of the country. Indeed, as the member responsible for labour, irrigation, and power, he was able not only to promote and defend labour rights, but also to bring in innovative techniques for water management, establishing an approach to water resource development, conservation, and distribution that has stood the test of time.[29]

In August 1942, the Congress Party declared the 'Quit India'[30] agitation, demanding that Britain leave India, in the Mahatma's phrase, 'to God or anarchy'. The British responded with repression, and a wave of arrests put all the Congress leaders, and a significant number of the party's workers, in prison. Ambedkar did not support the Quit India movement, taking to All-India Radio to express his support for the war against the Nazis as a war for the rebirth of a new social

---

[28] Shahare, *Dr. Bhimrao Ambedkar*, p. 77.
[29] Uttam Kumar Sinha, 'BR Ambedkar's Pioneering Role in Water Management', *Hindustan Times*, 16 April 2022.
[30] '1942 Quit India Movement', Making Britain, Open University.

order.[31] The victory of Nazism, he declared, would sound the death-knell for the values of liberty, equality, and fraternity; it had to be defeated for the sake of freedom.

When, in February 1943, Mahatma Gandhi undertook a twenty-one-day fast of 'self-purification' in prison,[32] the Indian members of the Executive Council came under pressure from public opinion to end their cooperation with the British, and two of them resigned. Ambedkar once again did not oblige. He felt he could use his position for the benefit of the labourers of India. Presiding over the meetings of the council's Standing Committee on Labour, he was able to push forward a number of new initiatives—to establish joint labour-management committees in all industries manufacturing goods for the war effort, to establish employment exchanges, and to grant paid holidays to industrial workers.

The Mahatma was duly released from detention on grounds of ill-health[33] and resumed his engagement with the national question, reaching out through Rajagopalachari with a conciliatory offer to the Muslim League's Jinnah. Ambedkar wrote to the Mahatma expressing support for the initiative but adding that it was not enough to settle the Hindu–Muslim question; the problems between caste Hindus and untouchables also needed to be resolved. The Mahatma wrote back to Ambedkar that he disagreed: the problems of the Harijans were of a religious and social nature, he said, that needed to be resolved within the confines of Hindu religion and society.[34] The breach between the two men had now widened to a chasm.

Meanwhile, the widower Ambedkar had family concerns: he had been a neglectful parent, and was worried about the financial future of his son and nephew. Perhaps inevitably, he

---

[31] Shahare, *Dr. Bhimrao Ambedkar*, p. 78.
[32] Anindita Basu, 'Gandhi And His Fasts', *Swarajya*, 2 October 2015.
[33] Shahare, *Dr. Bhimrao Ambedkar*, p. 79.
[34] Ibid.

turned again to the one friend he had constantly relied upon on financial matters, Naval Bhathena. He wrote to Bhathena asking him 'to draw a plan of any industry he would like to suggest for his son and nephew, so that the boys might have an honest calling as a means of living and he might die peacefully'. Ambedkar also requested Bhathena to teach his wards some stable business so that they could support themselves.[35]

As the war was winding down, the attention of the British and Indian political leaders turned once again to the burning question of India's future. In July 1942, Ambedkar had wound up the Independent Labour Party and transformed his political vehicle into the Scheduled Castes Federation. Addressing the federation in May 1945,[36] he advocated a vision of a united India in which due weightage would be given to the various minority populations to ensure that their interests could not be overridden by the Hindu majority. In his constitutional scheme, the Depressed Classes would hold the balance between the caste Hindus and the Muslims. His speech was predictably and understandably condemned by the Congress, but not taken up by the British either. When the imprisoned nationalists were released from prison and summoned for discussions by the viceroy in Simla in July 1945, Ambedkar, as a member of the viceroy's Executive Council, could not take part.

Meanwhile, as we have noted, he published a scathing attack, *What Congress and Gandhi Have Done to the Untouchables*, which won him a great deal of attention and notoriety but also some enmity. The Mahatma's American biographer, Louis Fischer, described him in a 1946 book as 'the bitterest man I met in India', adding that Ambedkar was 'anti-Gandhi, pro-Pakistan and the most pro-British Indian I encountered'.[37] With demobilized Mahars agitating for re-entry into the army,

---

[35] Keer, *Dr. Ambedkar*, p. 404.
[36] Shahare, *Dr. Bhimrao Ambedkar*, p. 80.
[37] Omvedt citing C. B. Khairmode, 1999, 8: 17 in *Ambedkar*, p. 100.

Ambedkar used his influence on the council to promote the renewed recruitment of the Depressed Classes, raising three Mahar military battalions for the first time since recruitment from the community had been stopped in 1893.

In July, the British electorate unseated Churchill and his government, bringing the Labour Party to power. Exhausted by war and shaken by a mutiny of the Royal Indian Navy, the new British government had no desire to expend the resources required to hold on indefinitely to its restive empire in India and wanted to move rapidly towards independence. In September 1945, general elections were announced in India for the following year. All parties understood that these elections would define the terms under which British rule would end. The Muslim League had taken advantage of the absence of the imprisoned Congress from the public arena to dramatically increase its membership (from 20 lakhs to 2 crores) and financial resources during the war years, and was poised to push its demand for a separate state of Pakistan. The Congress was anxious to regroup and reassert itself as the voice of the majority who stood for an inclusive and united India.

Ambedkar's chosen political vehicle was the underfunded Scheduled Castes Federation. When Cripps returned to India in March 1946 at the head of a Cabinet Mission, tasked with finding a formula for Indian independence that would be acceptable to all parties, he met with Ambedkar, who submitted a memorandum calling for safeguards for the Scheduled Castes in the new Constitution of the country. But the Cabinet Mission, preoccupied as it was with the Hindu–Muslim question, neglected to include any such provisions in its proposals. It issued a state paper calling for an Indian Federation, an interim government, and the establishment of a Constituent Assembly to finalize a new Constitution. There was no mention of the Scheduled Castes.

With the publication of the state paper, the viceroy dissolved his executive council and Ambedkar returned to Bombay in May 1946 to fight for his people. As far as the British were concerned, it was the start of the end game. For Ambedkar, the real challenge had just begun.[38]

---

[38] Shahare, *Dr. Bhimrao Ambedkar*, p. 82.

FIVE

Triumph and Disillusion

1946–1956

The legendary movie star Dilip Kumar was in Aurangabad and found himself in the same hotel where Dr Ambedkar was staying while setting up an educational institution in the city. Dilip Kumar was not just a matinee idol at the peak of his popularity, he was also a personal friend of Prime Minister Pandit Jawaharlal Nehru, who would consult him regularly on cultural matters and issues relating to cinema and the creative industry. Dilip Kumar was proud to count among his acquaintances the leaders of different political parties; he took an interest in them irrespective of their ideology, and they in turn respected him greatly for his familiarity with the important issues of the era. When he heard about Dr Ambedkar being in the same hotel, he expressed his desire to meet the creator of the Constitution and offer him a donation for the colleges he was establishing.

A meeting was duly arranged and the movie star called on the constitutionalist. But he found Ambedkar at his most difficult. While accounts of their encounter differ, most agree that the eminent lawyer gave the actor short shrift, treating him dismissively. One version has the great man starting the conversation by attacking the film industry: he believed it was one where there were men and women who were not 'good people and had no morals and values'. Before Dr Ambedkar could go any further, Dilip Kumar interrupted him, turning on the considerable charm at his command to explain to Ambedkar that he was misinformed and had a 'wrong picture' about the film industry. The story goes that Ambedkar was not so easily mollified, recounting a long list of unsavoury cases which he said proved to him that the film industry was not an admirable enterprise. Unable to get a word in, Dilip Kumar walked out. A somewhat more prosaic version of the story also exists. According to this, Ambedkar lectured the friends who had tried to arrange the meeting, 'I do not want donations from actors, industrialists or businessmen.' When told of this response, Dilip Kumar is said to have remarked, 'Dr Ambedkar is like my father. I fully appreciate his views.'[1]

In the more dramatic version of this episode, Dr Ambedkar's friends, who had arranged the meeting, told him that he should not have behaved with Dilip Kumar this way, because the actor had come to him not just to pay homage but to offer a generous donation towards his causes. This occasioned a testy Ambedkar retort: He would never, he told his friends, change his opinions, decisions, and values for money. The two men never met again.[2]

I have chosen to recount both versions of this story because both illustrate a trait of Dr Ambedkar—his determination to do things his way at any cost, even at the risk of losing well-wishers and financial support. There were more important setbacks than the unsuccessful meeting with Dilip Kumar in Ambedkar's life at this time. The Scheduled Castes Federation fared poorly in the elections of 1946; all but two of its candidates (one each in Madras and Punjab) lost, and Ambedkar himself was defeated by a Congressman.[3] Of the total 151 constituencies reserved for the Scheduled Castes the Congress won 141. The religious

---

[1] Shahare, *Dr. Bhimrao Ambedkar*, pp. 85–86.
[2] 'When Dilip Kumar met Dr. BhimRao Ambedkar', *Bollyy.com*, 11 January 2021.
[3] Keer, *Dr. Ambedkar*, pp. 487–88.

polarization brought about by the demand for Pakistan meant
that the League captured nearly all the Muslim seats, while
Congress swept the general constituencies. The Hindu–Muslim
question had clearly trumped other issues, caste and class
included, in the voters' priorities.

However, in what would be the last decade of his life, there
were highs as well. His professional standing undiminished,
Ambedkar spent part of 1946 establishing two institutions
of higher learning in pursuit of his own ideals—Siddharth
College of Arts in Bombay (named after the Buddha) and
Milind College in Aurangabad (named for an ancient King,
Milinda, who is revered by Buddhists). It was these institutions
that the great movie star had wished to support. Their names
indicated his growing interest in, and affinity for, the Buddhist
faith, to which he had first been introduced by his old mentor,
Professor Keluskar.[4] Both institutions received some funding
from the government. Ambedkar established them under the
aegis of the People's Education Society, whose objective, to this
day, is 'not merely to give education but to give education in
such a manner as to promote intellectual, moral and social
democracy'.[5] It is a measure of his devotion to these institutions
that he eventually donated his magnificent library of over
50,000 books to Siddharth College, for a price less than half
of what the industrialist G. D. Birla had been willing to pay
to acquire the lot.[6]

Despite his reputation as a staunch advocate of the rights
of the Depressed Classes—particularly to education—Ambedkar
insisted that both colleges would be open to students of all
communities, and staffed by teachers drawn from all castes and
creeds. Merit, he insisted, was the only worthwhile criterion to
ensure quality education. As a result, both institutions rapidly

---

[4] Shahare, *Dr. Bhimrao Ambedkar*, p. 9.
[5] Official website of Siddharth College of Arts, Science and Commerce, Mumbai.
[6] Keer, *Dr. Ambedkar*, p. 475.

developed a reputation for excellence and attracted students from good schools, while providing an educational haven to students from the Depressed Classes. Many of their alumni rose to positions of great prominence and would go on to declare that without Dr Ambedkar they would never have had the opportunity to do so.

Stories are told of Ambedkar's personal involvement in the establishment, construction, and functioning of both colleges. Ambedkar was tireless in his efforts to pursue a wide variety of undertakings, devoting himself with single-minded determination to their fulfilment. As an institution-builder, the social organizations and political parties he established and led had tended not to last very long, as his restless energies drove him to the next institution. But his two colleges have survived as lasting monuments to his idealism and aspiration.

In August 1946, an interim government was established in India to run the country in the lead-up to independence, headed by the Congress Party's Jawaharlal Nehru.[7] There was only one minister from the Scheduled Castes, Babu Jagjivan Ram of the Congress. Instigated by his supporters and well-wishers, Ambedkar travelled to England in October to meet with the prime minister and high officials to press the case for more representation for his community.[8] He was unsuccessful in persuading them of the need to change the arrangements—the British felt the Scheduled Caste Federation's poor performance in the recent elections did not warrant any additional representation for it—and he returned empty-handed in November. He was just in time for the inaugural session of the new Constituent Assembly that was to prepare a Constitution for independent India. Though he had been defeated in Bombay, Ambedkar had been elected to the Constituent Assembly from Bengal, where the Muslim League-dominated assembly had supported his election.

[7] Shahare, *Dr. Bhimrao Ambedkar*, pp. 90–91.
[8] Keer, *Dr. Ambedkar*, p. 385.

The country was bitterly divided. The Muslim League, which had swept the Muslim seats in the general elections, and interpreted its victory as a mandate for the creation of a separate state of Pakistan, paralysed the interim government with its non-cooperation with the Congress ministers, and boycotted the Constituent Assembly. When it opened, with Dr Rajendra Prasad presiding, on 9 December 1946, Prime Minister Jawaharlal Nehru delivered a stirring speech and moved a resolution enshrining the objectives of the assembly and its proposed Constitution. At this point, the unaffiliated liberal leader, Dr M. R. Jayakar, who had supported Ambedkar in many of the latter's battles for justice in the past, rose to propose that debate be suspended until the Muslim League and the Indian princely states had also joined the work of the assembly.[9] Since neither seemed to be in prospect in the foreseeable future, Jayakar's suggestion was received amid much consternation. Prasad then turned to another unaffiliated member, Ambedkar, for his views.

'I know today we are divided politically, socially and economically,' Ambedkar told the assembled notables, the greatest Indians of the era. 'We are in warring camps and I am probably one of the leaders of a warring camp. But with all this, I am convinced that given time and circumstances, nothing in the world will prevent this country from becoming one. And, with all our castes and creeds, I have not the slightest hesitation in saying that we shall in the future be a united people. I have no hesitation in saying that notwithstanding the agitation of the League for the partition of India, some day enough light will dawn upon the Muslims themselves and they too will think that a United India is better for everybody.'[10] He turned to the Congress Party, which had seemed determined to push on, despite the absence of the Muslim League. 'The question

---

[9] Shahare, *Dr. Bhimrao Ambedkar*, p. 91.
[10] Ibid.

I am asking is, is it prudent for you to do it? Is it wise to do it? Power is one thing and wisdom and prudence quite a different thing. In deciding the destinies of the people, the dignities of the leaders or men or parties ought to count for nothing. Let us prove by our conduct that we have not only the power but also the wisdom to carry with us all sections of the country and to make them march on that road which is bound to lead us to unity.'[11]

Ambedkar's speech carried the day and the assembly decided to suspend its debates till January, in the hope of incorporating all sections of opinion within its deliberations. Meanwhile, the country was descending into chaos and violence, as Hindus and Muslims began assaults upon each other, and each day recorded gruesome incidents of violence, killing, and arson. Amid the rioting and general breakdown of law and order, the Congress leadership conceded the League's demand for the Partition of the country. The Constituent Assembly, in turn, resumed its work, with the League's absence no longer a relevant consideration. In April 1947, the Assembly adopted its report on Fundamental Rights and the doughty Congress leader Sardar Patel moved a resolution completely abolishing untouchability in any form.[12] Ambedkar was present at this moment that marked the fulfilment of his lifelong campaign for justice for his people.

With the passage of the Indian Independence Act by the British parliament,[13] the country was to be partitioned, and the Constituent Assembly became, in effect, the parliament of the soon-to-be-independent India. Ambedkar had been elected from undivided Bengal, and the partition of that state cost him his seat, requiring him to be re-elected to the Constituent Assembly. Dr Jayakar had resigned in dismay at the break-up

---

[11] Ibid.
[12] Ibid., p. 92.
[13] Ibid.

of the country and Ambedkar sought election to the seat he had vacated. The Bombay Legislative Assembly, dominated by the Congress Party, duly obliged and Ambedkar returned to the Assembly as a member.

Meanwhile, at the end of July 1947, Prime Minister Nehru had to name the first cabinet of independent India and wanted it to embrace the widest possible range of Indian opinion. Despite the long history of antagonism between the Congress Party and Ambedkar, Nehru invited him to join the cabinet as law minister. Ambedkar agreed.[14] The perennial outsider, who had proudly worn the label of the 'excluded', was now 'included', at the centre of power in a newly free country.

That was not all. A month later, Ambedkar was named chairman of the Drafting Committee of the Constituent Assembly, at the head of a distinguished galaxy of legal eminences, no fewer than five of whom had been knighted by the king-emperor for their distinguished services to the legal profession. He would be the principal author of the new Constitution—India's James Madison. It was an extraordinary tribute to the son of a Mahar subedar from Mhow, and it marked the ultimate acknowledgement by his peers of Ambedkar's incontestable place in the national firmament.[15]

The prolific Ambedkar also wrote a pair of major books at this time. The first, in 1947, entitled *Who Were the Shudras?*,[16] attempted to explain the creation of the concept of untouchability and trace the origin of the untouchables. To Ambedkar, the Shudras and Ati Shudras, who constituted the lowest caste in the ritual hierarchy of Hindu society, were distinct from the untouchables, who were outside the caste system altogether. The second, in 1948, *The Untouchables: Who Were They and Why*

---

[14] Ibid., p. 93.

[15] Keer, *Dr. Ambedkar*, p. 397.

[16] Vasant Moon (ed.), *Dr. Babasaheb Ambedkar: Writings and Speeches*, Vol. 7, Bombay Education Department: Government of Maharashtra, 1979.

They Became Untouchables, gave his version of the origins of untouchability. In the course of the book Ambedkar dismissed the Aryan invasion theory, which had been used to explain the origin of the caste system, a position that anticipated debates in Indian historiography that occurred half a century later. He also argued that the main dialectic of Indian history was an ideological conflict between Brahminism and Buddhism, with the former reforming itself in reaction to the latter. Untouchability was born from the struggle for supremacy between the two systems. 'Some closed the door,' he wrote, 'others found it closed against them.'[17] 'Brahminism,' Ambedkar declared, 'is the very negation of the spirit of Liberty, Equality and Fraternity.' Ambedkar's attempt at explaining a complicated issue for which little corroborative evidence was available on either side created predictable controversy, but as usual his analysis was marked by his talent for detailed reasoning and clarity of thought.

When Mahatma Gandhi was assassinated by a Hindu fanatic on 30 January 1948, Ambedkar remained uncharacteristically silent. As tributes and encomia flowed in from around the world, Ambedkar chose not to add his voice to them. He did not publicly utter a word on the monumental national tragedy of the Mahatma's killing, nor did he issue any statement of condolence. He joined the funeral procession for a while and retired to his study. But he did not write anything on the subject either.[18]

By 1948, the Drafting Committee revolved around his own person. A prominent member from Madras, T. T. Krishnamachari, told the Assembly in November 1948 that of the seven members of the committee, one had died and not been replaced; one was away on official duty in America; one was preoccupied with

---

[17] 'Castes in India: Their Mechanism, Genesis and Development', in Moon, *Dr. Babasaheb Ambedkar*, Vol. 1, pp. 5–22; as cited in Hirannya Sen, 'Advent and Evolution of the Caste System: A Close Reading of Ambedkar's "Castes in India"', *All About Ambedkar*.

[18] Keer, *Dr. Ambedkar*, p. 402.

other affairs of state; and two others were absent from Delhi for reasons of ill-health. The task of drafting the Constitution of the new country had essentially fallen on the chairman of the Drafting Committee, who with his characteristic single-mindedness had devoted himself day and night to the task. Ambedkar exhausted himself in the process, but prepared a document that would win admiration the world over.[19] (We will discuss its substantive content and political implications in the next section.)

In March 1948, Ambedkar returned to Bombay for medical consultations. He was chronically exhausted, suffered from neuropathic pain in his legs, was on elevated doses of insulin for diabetes, and could not sleep. Doctors advised him that he could not continue to neglect his health and drive himself this way; they urged him to settle down and find a companion who could care for him. It was in these circumstances that he met thirty-eight-year-old Dr Sharada Kabir, a Brahmin doctor who was also an admirer; he duly married her the day after his fifty-seventh birthday, on 15 April 1948, in a civil ceremony. Following traditional Maharashtrian practice, she took the name Savita Bhimrao Ambedkar and partnered him faithfully for the rest of his life as wife, doctor, companion, cook, care-provider, and helpmeet. She was revered as 'mai' or mother by many of his followers and lived to the age of ninety-three, surviving him by almost half a century.[20]

The work-obsessed Ambedkar, a widower for thirteen years, was an unlikely soulmate for any woman, as he confessed to his would-be mother-in-law in a letter:

I am a difficult man. Ordinarily I am quiet as water and humble as grass. But when I get into a temper I am

---

[19] Shahare, *Dr. Bhimrao Ambedkar*, p. 94.
[20] Ibid., p. 95; Pia Krishnakutty, 'Savita Ambedkar, a "social worker in her own right" who kept BR Ambedkar's legacy alive', *The Print*, 27 January 2021.

ungovernable and unmanageable. I am a man of silence. There is a charge against me that I don't speak to women. But I don't even speak to men unless they are my intimates. I am a man of moods. At times I talk endlessly, at other times I do not utter a word. At times I am very serious. At times I am full of humour. I am no gay person; pleasures of life do not attract me. My companions have to bear the burden of my austerity and asceticism. My books have become my companions. They are dearer to me than wife and children.[21]

This disarming confession offers an unusual personal insight into a man otherwise known almost entirely for his public utterances.

The draft Constitution underwent three readings by the Constituent Assembly and was extensively debated. Every article had to be discussed and debated in the Assembly, language amended and political compromises finessed. Some of Ambedkar's more radical suggestions, such as his advocacy of nationalizing agriculture and vital industries, were rejected. As many as 7,600 amendments were moved by members, which required consideration and response. Each article and amendment gave rise to a series of questions and comments to which Dr Ambedkar, as chairman, provided replies and clarifications. His performance in moderating and steering the discussion was so authoritative, reasoned, and impressive that the Constitution took shape in people's imaginations through his words. There was little doubt that Ambedkar's passionate commitment to social change had been infused into the ethos of the Constitution. Fulsome tributes poured forth in the Assembly from supporters and critics alike; many mentioned the evident toll his tireless work had had on his 'indifferent health', despite which he had carried on without rest. Several called him—in an

---

[21] Omvedt, *Ambedkar*, p. 108.

irony not lost on this 'untouchable'—a 'modern Manu' (Manu being the ancient lawgiver whose rules, among other things, codified untouchability).[22]

The Constitution of India, the longest in the world, was a remarkable document. In his speech on 4 November 1948 to the Constituent Assembly, Ambedkar declared:

> It is workable, it is flexible and it is strong enough to hold the country together both in peace time and in wartime. Indeed, if I may say so, if things go wrong under the new Constitution, the reason will not be that we had a bad Constitution. What we will have to say is that Man was vile.[23]

Ambedkar's text guaranteed constitutional protection for a large number of enumerated fundamental rights and freedoms for individual citizens, such as freedom of speech and assembly, and freedom of religion, including the freedom to propagate one's religion. It reconfirmed the abolition of untouchability, and outlawed all forms of discrimination. It was Ambedkar who ensured that it provided for extensive economic and social rights for women. But the provision that bore his distinctive stamp was the introduction of what has gone down in history as the world's oldest and farthest-reaching affirmative action programme, guaranteeing reservations of seats in educational institutions and legislature, and jobs in government institutions and the civil services, for members of the Scheduled Castes and Tribes.[24]

As the Dalit scholar K. Raju outlines it:

> The Constituent Assembly included several important rights in the Indian Constitution to ensure that principles of equality and social justice were the basis of all future developments in India. The fundamental rights, including

---

[22] Shahare, *Dr. Bhimrao Ambedkar*, p. 97.
[23] Keer, *Dr. Ambedkar*, p. 410.
[24] 'Scheduled Castes and Scheduled Tribes', United Nations in India.

Article 14, conferred equality before the law; Article 15 prohibited discrimination on the grounds of religion, race, caste, sex, place of birth and provided access to public spaces to all without discrimination; Article 16(4) served as a bedrock for the state to make provisions for the reservation of appointments or posts in favour of any backward class of citizens; and Article 17 prohibited untouchability. The directive principles, through Article 46, placed the responsibility on the state to make policies for the economic and educational progress of the scheduled castes, and to protect them from social injustices.[25]

Ambedkar resisted some of the Mahatma's ideas as advocated by the staunch Gandhians in the Assembly, in particular firmly rejecting their desire to make India's villages the bedrock of the state's overall constitutional architecture: 'Another criticism against the Draft Constitution,' he stated, 'is that no part of it represents the ancient polity of India. It is said that the new Constitution should have been drafted on the ancient Hindu model of a State and that instead of incorporating Western theories the new Constitution should have been raised and built on village panchayats and district panchayats. There are others who have taken a more extreme view. They do not want any Central or Provincial Governments. They just want India to contain so many village Governments. The love of the intellectual Indians for the village community is of course infinite if not pathetic…. What is the village but a sink of localism, a den of ignorance, narrow-mindedness and communalism? I am glad that the Draft Constitution has discarded the village and adopted the individual as its unit.'[26] Gandhians were furious at this slighting of their views, but Ambedkar's clear-eyed modernism prevailed.

---

[25] K. Raju, (ed.), Rethinking India Series, *The Dalit Truth: The Battles for Realizing Ambedkar's Vision*, New Delhi: Penguin Random House, 2022, p. xxvi.
[26] Jaffrelot, *Dr. Ambedkar and Untouchability*, p. 110.

Ambedkar did not get his way on every issue. He was unable to push through a uniform civil code, which instead was listed in the Constitution as a desirable objective. He was not in favour of Article 370, which granted a special constitutional status to Kashmir, but had to yield to the wishes of Nehru and Patel. He wanted the Constitution to grant ownership of agricultural land, education, health, and insurance to the state, based on his belief that fundamental rights emanated from economic structures in society, and that an unequal society dominated by rich upper castes would not guarantee fundamental rights to the Scheduled Castes. He preferred a presidential system for India,[27] but deferred to the strong preference of the majority for a parliamentary one. Indian nationalists wanted to adopt what the colonial rulers had denied them—the Westminster system the British enjoyed for themselves. Still, once a consensus had been reached on each contentious issue, Ambedkar served as an articulate and eloquent advocate of its adoption.

On 25 November 1949, Ambedkar delivered a powerful speech for the unanimous adoption of the draft Constitution. Quoted to this day, his speech talked of the need to preserve India's hard-fought and recently won independence and democracy, to give up the 'grammar of anarchy', to avoid hero-worship, and to work towards a social—not just a political—democracy.[28] He repeatedly made it clear that for him democracy was not just a form of government but a form of social organization.

'Will history repeat itself?' he asked the Assembly. 'Will [India] maintain her independence or will she lose it again? This is the first thought that comes to my mind. It is not that India was never an independent country. The point is that she once lost the independence she had. Will she lose it a second

---

[27] Bhanu Dhamija, 'India's Constitution makers Nehru, Patel, Ambedkar were divided on Parliamentary system', *The Print*, 25 January, 2019.

[28] B. R. Ambedkar in the *Constituent Assembly Debates*, 25 November 1949, also available on 'Why BR Ambedkar's three warnings in his last speech to the Constituent Assembly resonate even today', *Scroll.in*, 26 January 2016.

time? It is this thought which makes me most anxious for the future,' Ambedkar declared at the start of his speech. 'What perturbs me greatly is the fact that not only India has once before lost her independence, but she lost it by the infidelity and treachery of some of her own people.'[29] Citing several historical examples of betrayal and duplicity, he warned: 'This much is certain—that if the parties place creed above country, our independence will be put in jeopardy a second time and probably be lost for ever. This eventuality we must all resolutely guard against. We must be determined to defend our independence with the last drop of our blood.'[30]

Insisting that India's democratic traditions went back to the ancient Buddhist sanghas but had fallen into disuse, he speculated about the risks of Indian democracy being overtaken by dictatorship. To prevent this, he said, three things were needed. The first was 'to hold fast to constitutional methods of achieving our social and economic objectives', abandoning the 'bloody methods of revolution' including 'civil disobedience, non-cooperation and satyagraha'. Ambedkar knew this statement would trouble the Gandhians as an implicit criticism of the Mahatma's methods, so he explained: 'When there was no way left for constitutional methods for achieving economic and social objectives, there was a great deal of justification for unconstitutional methods. But where constitutional methods are open, there can be no justification for these unconstitutional methods. These methods are nothing but the Grammar of Anarchy and the sooner they are abandoned, the better for us.'[31]

The second thing, Ambedkar added, was not to entrust the country's fate to any 'great man, or to trust him with power which enables him to subvert their institutions'. Many in India

---

[29] Keer, *Dr. Ambedkar*, p. 413.
[30] Ibid., p. 414.
[31] BR Ambedkar, 'Why BR Ambedkar's three warnings in his last speech to the Constituent Assembly resonate even today', *Scroll.in*, 26 January 2016.

were grateful to great men who had served the country, but gratitude should not mean supplication. Quoting the Irish patriot Daniel O'Connell, he said, 'No man can be grateful at the cost of his honour, no woman can be grateful at the cost of her chastity and no nation can be grateful at the cost of its liberty.'[32] For Ambedkar, 'this caution is far more necessary in the case of India than in the case of any other country. For in India, Bhakti or what may be called the path of devotion or hero-worship, plays a part in its politics unequalled in magnitude by the part it plays in the politics of any other country in the world. Bhakti in religion may be a road to the salvation of the soul. But in politics, Bhakti or hero-worship is a sure road to degradation and to eventual dictatorship.'[33] (He was right, of course, and it is a warning resonant with contemporary echoes in twenty-first-century India, but there is a certain irony in this, given the extent to which Ambedkar himself is now the object of uncritical bhakti from devotees.)

The third thing Ambedkar advocated was for India to go beyond 'mere political democracy' to 'social democracy', by which he meant 'a way of life which recognises liberty, equality and fraternity as the principles of life ... to divorce one from the other is to defeat the very purpose of democracy.'[34] This brought him to the subject about which he was most passionate, the entrenched inequalities in Indian society.

> On the 26th of January 1950 [the date on which the Constitution would go into effect], we are going to enter into a life of contradictions. In politics we will have equality and in social and economic life we will have inequality. In politics we will be recognising the principle of one man one vote and one vote one value. In our social

---

[32] Keer, *Dr. Ambedkar*, p. 414
[33] Ibid., pp. 414–15.
[34] 'Why BR Ambedkar's three warnings in his last speech to the Constituent Assembly resonate even today', *Scroll.in.*

and economic life, we shall, by reason of our social and economic structure, continue to deny the principle of one man one value. How long shall we continue to live this life of contradictions? How long shall we continue to deny equality in our social and economic life? If we continue to deny it for long, we will do so only by putting our political democracy in peril. We must remove this contradiction at the earliest possible moment or else those who suffer from inequality will blow up the structure of political democracy which this Assembly has so laboriously built up.[35]

Calling the entire structure of caste 'anti-national', Ambedkar urged that true fraternity be established among India's peoples if India were to truly succeed as a nation. The 'down-trodden classes are tired of being governed. They are impatient to govern themselves. This urge for self-realisation in the down-trodden classes must not be allowed to devolve into a class struggle or class war.... [T]he sooner room is made for the realisation of their aspiration ... the better for the country, the better for the maintenance for its independence and the better for the continuance of its democratic structure.'[36]

It was a magisterial performance, tying the Constitution whose adoption he had just proposed to principles no delegate could disagree with, while insisting they could only be upheld by achieving the social reformation he had devoted his life's work to. The Assembly listened to Ambedkar in rapt attention, and when he finished, the silence was broken by thunderous applause.

*

While focusing principally on the making of the Constitution, Ambedkar also had responsibilities as India's first law minister,

---

[35] Ibid.

[36] Entire speech reproduced in 'Ambedkar's last words of wisdom', *The Tribune*, 14 April 2017.

and in this capacity, in October 1948, he introduced before the
Assembly, which served simultaneously as India's parliament,
the draft of a Hindu Code Bill.[37] The bill was the product of
seven years' work by a committee constituted by the British
to revise and codify Hindu Law; the British had allowed each
Indian community to be governed by its own personal law and
not by a common civil code, but because of multiple versions
of Hindu law in different parts of the country, some quite
retrograde, a single 'modern' code for Hindus was considered
necessary. As minister, Ambedkar received and significantly
modified the committee's draft submitted to him by its chairman,
Sir Benegal Narsing Rau. Among his amendments was to grant
Hindu women the right to inherit property, to initiate divorce,
and to manage their own finances. Ambedkar's approach was
anchored in his profound commitment to equality and to
women's rights as part of his faith in gender equity. Controversy
erupted over this and other provisions deemed too radical by the
traditionalists. The nation was divided and the government did
not rush to bring the bill forward for debate and passage.

Ambedkar took the criticism head on, and in a speech at
Siddharth College in 1950,[38] stated that there was nothing
revolutionary about the bill; it was merely intended to rationalize
and streamline elements that were unclear in the existing laws
and create a single code. Ambedkar made it a point to quote
extensively from the ancient Hindu texts, the shastras and the
smritis, in support of his arguments for specific provisions in
the bill. Nonetheless, Ambedkar redrafted certain elements in
the bill to take his critics on board, and in November 1950,
circulated in parliament a brochure explaining its provisions,
in the hope that this would encourage members to discuss and
pass the bill without further delay. The government, however,
proved reluctant to press parliament to take the bill up for

---

[37] Keer, *Dr. Ambedkar*, p. 417.
[38] Shahare, *Dr. Bhimrao Ambedkar*, p. 98.

consideration; the ferocity of opposition by traditionalists within the ruling party and outside had made even Prime Minister Nehru, a staunch reformer himself, less than keen on going into battle on the matter at a time when there were so many other issues to attend to.

Finally, in February 1951, Ambedkar was able to bring the bill before parliament. In the stormy nine-hour debate that followed, the critics of the bill outnumbered the supporters. While various provisions were objected to, four principal objections were voiced. One, predictably, raised the sacred nature of Hindu marriage and said the bill would introduce all the failings of Western society to Indian family life. A second, by Sardar Hukum Singh, later to be speaker of the house, saw the bill as an objectionable attempt to subsume the Sikh faith within Hinduism. Another, voiced by several, was that to pass such a bill was violative of the secular nature of the Constitution and the country's pluralist system. A fourth, which was widely echoed, was that the bill was too far-reaching to be passed by an indirectly elected body like the Assembly, which had originally been elected by the provincial assemblies to frame a Constitution, and should ideally await the election of a new parliament by the public at large.[39]

Ambedkar took the floor to respond patiently to these and other objections, but it was clear the majority was not with him and a vote was deferred. He put the bill aside for a few months and devoted his energies to the passage of the Representation of the People Act, which laid down the terms and conditions for the qualification of candidates to parliament. (Were political prisoners disqualified from membership of the British House of Commons?, one member wanted to know. No, 'only Lords and lunatics' were, Ambedkar responded to general laughter.[40]) His bill passed without any problem.

---

[39] Shahare, *Dr. Bhimrao Ambedkar*, p. 100.
[40] Ibid., p. 101.

In August 1951, with his health once again suffering, Ambedkar wrote to the prime minister requesting that the Hindu Code Bill be passed without further delay. Nehru asked for time till the following month, September, and then raised the issue in the Congress Parliamentary Party, to which Ambedkar did not belong, urging that the bill be quickly passed. Congressmen, however, did not prove quite as enthusiastic about this reform as Nehru had hoped. This 'winter session' of 1951 was to be the last session of parliament before the general elections of 1952, and Congress MPs argued strongly that the time was not propitious for such a major piece of legislation to be brought before the house. Nehru realized he would not easily get his way on this matter. In the end, Ambedkar reluctantly agreed to bring just the marriage and divorce clause of the bill to parliament for debate and passage, with other provisions held in abeyance, subject to the availability of time for their consideration.[41]

The debate on 17 September on the marriage and divorce clause turned unpleasant. The Congress Party had not issued a whip to its members to support the bill, and MPs were free to speak their own minds; they did so overwhelmingly against the reform of which this clause was a part. Syama Prasad Mookerjee, who had resigned from the cabinet and founded the Bharatiya Jana Sangh to advocate Hindu interests, declared that the bill was an assault on the very foundations of Hindu society. Ambedkar in turn responded testily to some of the points made, and the exchanges became so acrimonious that the prime minister himself intervened to suggest that the marriage and divorce clause be treated as a separate bill altogether, and its merits considered independently from the larger controversy over the rest of the Hindu Code Bill. Ambedkar gave in to this compromise and moved the truncated bill, expecting that its

---

[41] Ibid., pp. 101–102.

relatively non-controversial provisions would receive enough support for passage. He had underestimated the hostility of the house, however, and in the face of the implacable opposition of a majority of MPs, the resistance of President Rajendra Prasad (who made clear his lack of enthusiasm for the bill, which he would have to sign to pass into law), Hindu sadhus laying siege to parliament, and leading industrialists and businessmen warning they would withdraw their support for Congress in the 1952 elections, Prime Minister Nehru asked Ambedkar to drop the bill altogether.[42]

On 5 September, a minor provision of the marriage and divorce clause—and not the entire clause itself—was passed, with the rest of the Hindu Code Bill, for all practical purposes, jettisoned. Shredded by the experience, and physically and mentally exhausted by the ordeal, as well as feeling betrayed by the prime minister and his colleagues, Ambedkar resigned from the cabinet on 27 September 1951.[43] He had already been disappointed by being passed over to head the major new economic body, the Planning Commission; on top of that he felt the Scheduled Castes had continued to be neglected by the government. He also disagreed with the government on foreign policy, arguing that relations with a democratic USA should not be allowed to be undermined by India's friendship with China. He had advocated that Kashmir be resolved by a further partition, which was anathema to his cabinet colleagues. With frustrations building up on all these issues, the Hindu Code Bill was the last straw for the ailing Ambedkar. 'To leave inequality between class and class, between sex and sex, which is the soul of Hindu society, and to go on passing legislation relating to economic problems is to make a farce of our Constitution and to build a palace on a dung heap,' he declared.[44] He had no

---

[42] Ibid., p. 103.
[43] Ibid.
[44] Omvedt, *Ambedkar*, p. 121.

wish to be complicit in a process of passing economic laws without introducing social equality in Hindu society.

There was an unsavoury aftermath to this episode that forever poisoned Ambedkar's relations with Nehru and his government. Parliamentary traditions permit a minister, upon resignation, to address the house to give his reasons for leaving the government. Nehru, in his letter thanking Ambedkar for his outstanding service and regretting that he was leaving the government over a bill that he (Nehru) himself strongly supported, also asked Ambedkar for a copy of the resignation speech he intended to deliver. In his reply on 4 October, Ambedkar assured him that, should he have the time to prepare a text, he would share it with the prime minister, adding that he had been granted permission anyway to speak on 11 October after disposing of other business in his name.[45]

When Ambedkar duly rose on 11 October to speak, he was disallowed by the deputy speaker, who was presiding, on the grounds that Ambedkar had not given a copy of his speech to the speaker in advance, as required by the rules. He informed Ambedkar that once he did so, he could address the house at 6 p.m. that day. When a couple of MPs interjected to ask if this was not 'pre-censorship', the deputy speaker somewhat crassly replied that he was simply trying to ensure that the statement Dr Ambedkar would deliver contained nothing that was 'irrelevant or libellous'. At this, a furious Ambedkar stormed out of the house and refused to speak on such terms. From the next day he sat on the Opposition benches.[46]

Addressing the media on his resignation, Ambedkar spoke of 'major differences with the Prime Minister'. His bitterness at the circumstances of his departure, and his sense of betrayal were apparent, and to Nehru's mind, quite unjust, since the prime minister felt he had done everything possible to support

---

[45] Shahare, *Dr. Bhimrao Ambedkar*, p. 103.
[46] Ibid., pp. 103–104.

his law minister. But the two men would never be close again.

～

The general elections of 1952 did not go well for Ambedkar. Partly this was because he underestimated the hold of the Congress Party, the political embodiment of the country's nationalist movement, on the imaginations of the electorate, and partly because Ambedkar did not realize how unpopular some of his positions were in the eyes of the general public. When he contested the Bombay North seat, he was the principal draftsman of the Constitution, and the pre-eminent leader of the working class and the Scheduled Castes; yet he lost to his former assistant, the Congress Party candidate Narayan Sadoba Kajrolkar. The Congress nonetheless appointed Ambedkar a member of the upper house, the Rajya Sabha. Ambedkar did not relish that position, resenting his dependence on his old enemies, and sought to enter the Lok Sabha again, in a 1954 by-election from a constituency called Bhandara. This time he fared even worse, placing third. Once again, it was the Congress Party that won the seat.[47] A sullen Ambedkar remained in the Rajya Sabha.

Still, Ambedkar remained a significant presence in India's public life, his every utterance a major contribution to the national conversation. At a library function in Poona in 1952 he gave the world a remarkable definition of democracy: he said that democracy was 'a form and a method of government whereby revolutionary changes in the economic and social life of the people are brought about without bloodshed'.[48] In June 1952, the international acclaim for his work on the Constitution of India found Columbia University honouring him with an honorary degree of doctor of law, calling him 'one of India's leading citizens, a great social reformer and a

[47] Keer, *Dr. Ambedkar*, p. 440.
[48] Ibid., p. 445.

valiant upholder of human rights'.[49] Ambedkar was particularly looking forward to meeting John Dewey at Columbia, but while he was en route to the US, Dewey passed away on 2 June 1952. Ambedkar wrote a moving letter to his widow, saying, 'I am so sorry. I owe all my intellectual life to him. He was a wonderful man.'[50] And indeed Ambedkar did owe much to Dewey. As one scholar has pointed out:

> Ambedkar not only borrowed concepts and ideas from Dewey, his methodological approach and ways of argumentation also show Dewey's influence. The two thinkers share a predilection for examining the past to reflect upon its traces on the concerns and problems of the present and to determine how beneficial or detrimental these residues of the past are to the present moment. Both believe that change is fundamental to life and that the thought of any age is often circumscribed by the conditions of life operant at the time. Both therefore are suspicious of tradition worship and eternal truths. ... Their human is not the atomistic, isolated individual of Enlightenment thought, but the individual always already embedded in the social. And, finally, for both, democracy is the ideal social order for the sustenance and growth of the socialized individual.[51]

In 1953, Ambedkar occasioned a controversy by seemingly repudiating the Constitution he had himself prepared, in an ill-tempered and emotional speech in the Rajya Sabha in which he called himself a 'hack' in its drafting.[52] 'We lawyers defend many things,' he declared in a testy exchange with other MPs, implying

---

[49] Kaoukab Chebaro, 'Dr. Ambedkar and Columbia University: A Legacy to celebrate', Columbia University Libraries, 15 April 2019.

[50] Nanak Chand Rattu, *Last Few Years of Dr. Ambedkar*, New Delhi: Amrit Publishing House, 1997, p. 35.

[51] Arun P. Mukherjee, 'B. R. Ambedkar, John Dewey, and the Meaning of Democracy', *New Literary History*, Vol. 40, No. 2, 2009, pp. 345–70.

[52] Keer, *Dr. Ambedkar*, p. 449.

he had merely executed a brief given to him. 'People always keep on saying to me, "Oh! you are the maker of the Constitution." My answer is I was a hack. What I was asked to do, I did much against my will.' Then he burst out: 'Sir, my friends tell me that I made the Constitution. But I am quite prepared to say that I shall be the first person to burn it out. I do not want it. It does not suit anybody.'[53]

His impulsive outburst reflected more his state of mind and health than any considered rejection of a document he had so eloquently commended to the nation, in such thoughtful detail, just four years previously. Indeed, his health was his principal impediment: he was bedridden from June to October 1954 with complications of diabetes, and though he was back in action after that, he was a visibly ill man for much of the time. And he remained convinced the Constitution could be worked better, telling the Rajya Sabha in March 1955: 'The Constitution was a wonderful temple we built for the gods, but before they could be installed, the devils have taken possession.'[54]

Freed by his ministerial resignation from the burdens of government office, Ambedkar turned again to writing, publishing in 1955 his *Thoughts for Linguistic States*. 'The British who ruled India for more than 150 years never thought of creating linguistic States, although the problem was always there,' he observed. 'They were more interested in creating a stable administration and maintaining law and order throughout the country than in catering to the cultural craving of people in multilingual areas.' A year before such states were created in India, he argued in favour of their establishment; but he also argued that while linguistic states should be created, large states, including the three largest Hindi-speaking ones (Uttar

---

[53] Bhanu Dhamija, 'Why Ambedkar didn't Like India's Constitution', *The Quint*, 14 April 2018.
[54] Hira Singh, 'Raising the Bar or a Missed Opportunity', *Economic & Political Weekly*, Vol. I, No. 45, 7 November 2015.

Pradesh, Madhya Pradesh, and Bihar) should be broken up. 'One state, one language', did not, he argued, imply 'one language, one state'. Smaller states would promote more efficient administration and attention to specific regions, he explained, while also giving local Scheduled Caste communities a more level playing field to hold their own against numerically more powerful communities.[55] In this, too, he was right.

He did take a somewhat more complicated stand on the question of official languages, averring that his support for linguistic states was predicated on the understanding that 'the official language of every Province shall be the same as the official language of the Central Government'. If the language of each province were to serve as its official language, Ambedkar argued, this 'would lead to the creation of Provincial nationalities. For the use of the Provincial languages as official languages would lead Provincial cultures to be isolated, crystallised, hardened and solidified.' On the issue of language, Ambedkar expressed the view that the utility of a single language nationwide in the administration and the justice system required the continuation of English as a matter of practical convenience.[56] This implied that all the provinces (later states) and the central government would continue to function and deal with each other in English—which is exactly what has occurred in practice, though not without debates, agitations, riots, and fitful attempts by Hindi zealots to impose their language on the rest.

Ambedkar went on to stress that the Indian Union would be built on a foundation of important diversities: 'There is a vast difference between the North and the South. The North is conservative. The South is progressive. The North is superstitious, the South is rational. The South is educationally forward, the North is educationally backward. The culture of the South is

---

[55] B. R. Ambedkar, 'Article on Linguistic States', *Times of India*, 23 April 1953.
[56] Swarajya Archives, 'Rajaji in 1968: "Hindi is, at Best, the Language of a Large Minority"', *Swarajya*, 14 September 2016.

modern. The culture of the North is ancient.'[57] Little could he have imagined that the North–South issue would resurface in Indian politics more than six decades after he wrote these words.

This prescient work out of the way, Ambedkar embarked on another book he had long wanted to write, about the Buddha and his disciples. He also began studying religion with a more personal reason in mind.

Ambedkar had been long convinced that he would have to leave Hinduism in quest of a fair deal for his people, and the unsavoury behaviour of Hindu traditionalists over the Hindu Code Bill convinced him that there was no hope of meaningful social reform from that quarter. He therefore began exploring other faiths, with the intellectual curiosity and rigour that had marked his life, reading extensively and conducting conversations with religious leaders of various faiths. On a visit to Trivandrum, Ambedkar was taken around some of the temples in the city and after observing their practices and rituals minutely, he exclaimed: 'O what a waste of wealth and food!'[58]

Islam seemed to him ruled out because it was a 'closed corporation' and he objected to the 'alienating distinction' it made between Muslims and non-Muslims, a feeling that was underscored after Partition by the conduct of Pakistani Muslims at the time. Partition did not leave the Scheduled Castes unaffected. In the newly created Pakistan, members of the community came under severe pressure to convert, sometimes forcibly, or die. With reports streaming in of numerous atrocities in Pakistan in 1947–48, Ambedkar, who was a cabinet minister at the time, issued a bitter statement of condemnation, telling the Scheduled Castes that the Pakistani Muslims were not their friends, and urging them to flee to India for their safety. He publicly urged Nehru to facilitate their exodus to India. After this episode, the prospects of Ambedkar converting to Islam were nil.

---

[57] A. G. Noorani, 'Linguism Trap', *Frontline*, 23 April 2010.
[58] Keer, *Dr. Ambedkar*, p. 423.

Christianity did not appeal to Ambedkar because, he said, it was incapable of fighting injustice: it had failed to lift America's Negroes from slavery and oppression.[59] 'A civil war was necessary to give the Negro the freedom which was denied to him by the Christians.' He had earlier opposed conversion to Christianity on the grounds that it would only 'strengthen the hold of Britain upon our country'.

Sikhism, with its egalitarianism, seemed more tempting. As far back as 1935, when he had first publicly threatened conversion, he had mused aloud about what would be the best faith for the Depressed Classes to convert to. If they embraced Islam or Christianity, he said, 'They not only go out of Hindu religion, but also go out of Hindu culture. On the other hand, if they become Sikhs they remain within Hindu culture. This is by no means a small advantage to the Hindus. Conversion to Islam or Christianity will denationalize the Depressed Classes. If they go to Islam the number of Muslims would be doubled, and the danger of Muslim domination also becomes real. If they go over to Christianity it would help strengthen the hold of Britain on the country.' But in the intervening period, Ambedkar's conversations with Sikh leaders raised doubts in his mind. Untouchability was still practised in Punjab, he found, even among the Sikhs, and he did not want to convert and find himself a 'second-rate Sikh'.[60]

That left him with the faith that he had long been attracted to, Buddhism. When Ambedkar determined that his people would never be treated as equals within the Hindu system, he sought an alternative that incorporated religious and spiritual values, and bore within it the notion of a moral social order which would not sanctify discrimination or exploitation, or

---

[59] Anand Teltumbde and Chakradhar Hadke (eds.), *Dr. B.R Ambedkar's Complete Works*, Archive.org.
[60] Meena Bardia, 'Dr. B. R. Ambedkar: His Ideas About Religion and Conversion to Buddhism', *Indian Journal of Political Science*, Vol. 70, No. 3, 2009, pp. 737–49.

even hierarchy, on the basis of birth. Thus emerged his interest in the Buddhist faith, which had drawn him to involve himself in a number of activities already. He attended the second and third conferences of the World Fellowship of Buddhists, in 1950 in Ceylon, and in 1954 in Burma. In 1955, he founded the Bharatiya Bauddha Mahasabha, or the Buddhist Society of India. The more he made progress with his monumental work, *The Buddha and His Dhamma*, the more he found to like in the faith. As he explained his decision: 'My conversion is not for any material gain. There is nothing which I cannot achieve by remaining an Untouchable. My conversion is purely out of my spiritual attitude. The Hindu religion does not appeal to my conscience. It does not appeal to my self-respect.'[61] In May 1956, he announced that, together with his family and followers, he would embrace Buddhism in October that year.

On the eve of his conversion, Ambedkar addressed the press, telling them that he had specifically chosen Buddhism because it was a faith born on Indian soil that was an authentic part of Indian culture. He intended to follow the original principles laid down by the Buddha and had no intention of involving himself in disputes over either of the two contending schools of Buddhism, the Hinayana and the Mahayana.[62] He expressed the hope that in another ten to fifteen years, India would become a Buddhist nation.

On 14 October 1956, at Nagpur, once a historic centre of

---

[61] Speech delivered by Dr. Ambedkar to the Bombay Presidency Mahar Conference, 31 May 1936, Bombay, translated from the Marathi by Vasant W. Moon, 25 January 1988, available at 'What Path to Salvation?', Columbia.edu.
[62] In a recent critical edition of Ambedkar's *The Buddha and His Dhamma*, 2011, the editors (Singh, Rathore, and Verma) dedicate their whole introduction to a discussion of Ambedkar's exclusion from academic Buddhist discourse in India, on the grounds that his writings deliver a 'political message' ('theologizing his own political view and politicizing Buddha's views'—p. xi), thus assuming that 'religion' is inherently apolitical. The authors denounce the sarcasm of some—who derisively label Ambedkar's *The Buddha and His Dhamma* a 'liberation theology' (Shourie 1997)—and condemn others for their silence.

Buddhism, Ambedkar was formally initiated into the Buddhist faith by the oldest living monk in India, Bhikkhu Chandramani, a monk from Uttar Pradesh. Hundreds of thousands of his followers came to Nagpur for the occasion, which also coincided with the Dussehra festival, marking Lord Ram's victory and the triumph of good over evil. Ambedkar, dressed in a white silk dhoti and a white coat, repeated the 'three refuges and five precepts', administered to him by the monk, prostrated himself before a statue of the Buddha, and placed white lotus flowers at its feet. He had 'taken diksha'. He then addressed the half-million strong crowd that had assembled to witness his conversion. Reciting twenty-two pledges of his own devising, Ambedkar formally uttered the words, 'I renounce Hinduism'.[63]

It was an emotional moment. Observers noted that Ambedkar himself was overcome by the intensity of the moment and that his voice choked as he uttered his renunciation of the faith of his ancestors. He then collected himself, and asked those in the audience who wished to follow him into the Buddhist faith to rise. Everyone in attendance, including a former chief justice of the Nagpur High Court, did so. Ambedkar administered a mass initiation of Buddhist vows to all. 'By discarding my ancient religion, which stood for inequality and oppression, today I am reborn,' he declared. 'I will discard the caste system and spread equality among human beings. I will strictly follow the eightfold path of the Buddha. Buddhism is a true religion and I will be guided by the three principles of knowledge, right path and compassion.'[64] It was a moment of high drama for all those present. The media referred to the event as the Great Conversion.

The public reaction was a good deal more sympathetic than might have been expected. Much commentary focused on the fact that Ambedkar had chosen an Indian faith to

---

[63] Shahare, *Dr. Bhimrao Ambedkar*, p. 106.
[64] Sudarshan Agarwal, *B. R. Ambedkar, The Man and His Message: A Commemorative Volume*, Introduction, Rajya Sabha Secretariat, 1991, p. 2.

convert to, rather than opt for Christianity or Islam, with their foreign origins. The Hindutva ideologue, V. D. Savarkar, praised Ambedkar for reiterating his faith in the mother religion, since all he had done, according to Savarkar, was to adopt a non-Vedic form of Hinduism itself.[65]

Ambedkar himself saw Hinduism and Buddhism as branches of the same tree, rather like the Catholic and Protestant churches in Christianity; Buddhism was, he suggested, a kind of Hindu Protestantism. He once cited the words of the Welsh Indologist T. W. Rhys-Davids, who observed: 'We should never forget that Gautama was born and brought up as a Hindu and lived and died as a Hindu. His teaching, far-reaching and original as it was, and really subversive of the religion of the day, was Indian throughout. He was the greatest and wisest and the best of the Hindus.'[66] By endorsing such a comment, Ambedkar was in effect conveying to his critics that in adopting Buddhism he had not in fact strayed from the broader Hindu fold. Ambedkar envisioned an enlightened India, Prabuddha Bharat, that would combine the best of Hindu traditions with ideas of the European Enlightenment, both infused with Buddhist thought. *Prabuddha Bharat* was, indeed, the name he bestowed on the last of the four newspapers he edited in his prolific career.

On 15 November 1956,[67] Ambedkar travelled to Kathmandu, Nepal, to address the Fourth Conference of the World Fellowship of Buddhists. Ambedkar emotionally declared Buddhism to be the greatest of the world's religions and a great social system in itself. Five days later, he surprised many with a speech in which he found an affinity between the Buddha and Karl Marx, stating that both had the same desire to wipe sorrow and suffering

[65] Shahare, *Dr. Bhimrao Ambedkar*, p. 106.
[66] T. W. Rhys-Davids, *Buddhism*, pp. 116–17, quoted in Keer, *Dr. Ambedkar*, pp. 5–22. Quoted from Koenraad Elst, *Who is a Hindu? Hindu Revivalist Views of Animism, Buddhism, Sikhism, and Other Offshoots of Hinduism*, New Delhi: Voice of India, 2002.
[67] Shahare, *Dr. Bhimrao Ambedkar*, p. 106.

from the face of the earth. But Buddhism and Communism differed on the vital question of means; the Communists did not hesitate to resort to violence, whereas the Buddhists exalted non-violence and ahimsa as the cardinal principle. This was because Buddhism exemplified the highest moral values. It was true that there was no God in Buddhism, but that was only because Buddhism replaced God with morality.[68] Ambedkar continued on this theme on his way back from Nepal, making speeches at Banaras Hindu University and Kashi Vidyapith on the essence of Buddhism. In these centres of learning at the heart of Hinduism's holiest city, Ambedkar argued that whereas the Vedas focused on prayer, praise, and worship, Buddhism directed man to look inwards for self-realization.[69]

At Nagpur, Ambedkar had stressed that 'the fundamental principle of Buddhism is equality. O Bhikkhus, you belong to different castes, and have come from various lands. Just as the great rivers, when they have fallen into the great ocean, lose their identity; just so, O brethren, do these four castes, Kshatriyas, Brahmins, Vaisyas and Shudras, when they begin to follow the doctrine and discipline as propounded by the Tathagatha (Lord Buddha), they renounce different names of castes and rank and become members of one and the same society. These are the words of Buddha.'[70] Equality and fraternity were at the heart of Buddhism's appeal for Ambedkar.

With his usual restless energy, Ambedkar had also announced in Nagpur his intention to start yet another political party before the next general elections, which were due the following year. As he explained:

Before I die, I must establish a definite political direction for my people. They have remained poor, oppressed and

---

[68] Ibid., p. 107.
[69] Ibid.
[70] Ibid.

deprived, and because of that, now, a new consciousness and a new anger are growing among them. That is natural. But it is also natural that this type of community becomes attracted to Communism. I do not want my people to fall under the sway of the Communists.[71]

The Republican Party of India—named for the party that had ended slavery in America and would, Ambedkar believed, end the 'enslavement' of the Scheduled Castes in India—would be open to all Indians who believed in liberty, equality, and fraternity.

But Ambedkar's health, most frequently described as 'indifferent', was worsening noticeably during his exertions. His punishing schedule of travel and speeches, his relentless launching of new projects, and his insatiable appetite for work, writing late into the night, all took their toll. He had suffered for years from diabetes, rheumatism, high blood pressure, and chronically severe leg pain. By the time he had returned to New Delhi after Kathmandu and Banaras, he was visibly ailing, ate little, and complained of deep fatigue. His wife and he booked air tickets to return to their home in Bombay on 14 December. But in the early hours of 6 December 1956, three days after completing the manuscript of his monumental work, *The Buddha and His Dhamma*, Bhimrao Ramji Ambedkar passed away at night, slumped over the papers he had been working on at his desk. He was only sixty-five.[72]

As the news spread, a large crowd assembled at Ambedkar's official residence, 26 Alipur Road. The prime minister and senior members of the cabinet came personally to pay their last respects. The funeral procession wound its way from the house to Delhi airport through throngs of admirers, taking five hours for the forty-minute journey. Ambedkar's body was flown to Bombay and taken to the home he had built in Dadar. Workers

---

[71] Jaffrelot, *Dr. Ambedkar and Untouchability*, p. 86.
[72] Shahare, *Dr. Bhimrao Ambedkar*, p. 108.

in factories, textile mills, docks, and railway workshops across Bombay and beyond spontaneously laid down their tools in homage. Half a million people showed up at the crematorium where Ambedkar was consigned to the flames following Buddhist rituals. A police band played the Last Post, an honour normally reserved for serving officials of the government.

Moving speeches were made throughout the country in the days and weeks that followed. Prime Minister Nehru spoke feelingly in parliament of Ambedkar's great contributions to the nation and the government; posterity would remember him, he said, as a symbol of revolt against the oppressive features of Hindu society. He moved that parliament be adjourned for the day as a mark of respect. The Bombay government declared Ambedkar's birthday a public holiday and handed over to the Buddhist Society 11 acres of land on the site where Ambedkar had embraced Buddhism.

Two months before his death, Ambedkar had met his 'only dear friend' Naval Bhathena for the last time in October 1956. Bhathena, who had supported Ambedkar since their days as roommates at Columbia in 1913, recalled their last meeting:

> Our longest meeting was at his house two months before he died. We were together from three o'clock in the afternoon till six in the evening and no other person was allowed in the room. That day Ambedkar spoke from his heart. He criticized his son and also his nephew and I left the house, saddened [that] my friend was at journey's end. Even now, I can hardly believe that he [just] lived a couple of months more.[73]

People had become so accustomed to seeing Ambedkar go on, despite ill health, that his succumbing to illness came as a genuine shock. But the monumental scale of his accomplishments was already evident in the tributes paid upon his death.

---

[73] Dr. Savita Bhimrao Ambedkar, *Ambedkarachya Sahavasat*, Mumbai: Dr. Babasaheb Ambedkar Foundation, 2013, p. 354.

Almost typical of the man was that death did not stop his output. *The Buddha and His Dhamma* was published posthumously, but so too were *Waiting for a Visa*, an autobiographical work culled from papers found on his desk, and *Riddles of Hinduism*, an assault on the religion he had chosen to abandon. His ideas continued to generate debate and attract controversy for years after his passing.

They spanned a remarkable range of topics and themes— the origin and nature of the caste system; the eradication of untouchability and the uplift of the downtrodden; currency and exchange rate policy and high finance; agriculture and the viability of small holdings; religion and moral philosophy; the role of minorities; Partition and the creation of Pakistan; constitutional arrangements including centre–state relations and the feasibility of dividing India into linguistic states, to name some but not all of his principal preoccupations. The quality of his writings and speeches on this vast range of topics reflected his fertile intellect, the breadth and depth of his erudition and research, his diligent industriousness, his workaholism, and his fluency and rapidity as a writer. Ambedkar left behind a corpus of work so monumental that if he had done nothing else, he would have been remembered as one of the foremost public intellectuals of his age.

It must be said that he was not universally liked. He had a sharp tongue that he did not hesitate to deploy when he disagreed with someone; he had the brilliant mind's impatience with mediocrity, hypocrisy, and sycophancy, and he did not always make the effort to conceal his disdain. As someone who had had to struggle every inch of the way up, and who had had to endure humiliations and privations at every stage for no fault of his own, he was less than indulgent of those who challenged him or questioned his beliefs. He had earned the right to refuse to consider himself inferior to anyone, and his manner was that of one who would put up with no nonsense.

Everything had to be built on an edifice of reason and logic; he was impatient with the irrational, the emotional, and the superstitious. As a result, many at the receiving end saw him as imperious and intolerant. Human relationships did not seem to matter enough to him; only ideas did. He neglected his wife and children even while he worried about them. He had a legion of admirers but very few friends.

To some degree, therefore, he was a misfit in politics. None of the organizations or political parties he founded lasted very long or achieved great success. He lost more elections than he won, including his last, as a Scheduled Castes Federation candidate in 1954. He described himself, with some self-pity, in *Annihilation of Caste*, as 'one, almost the whole of whose public exertion has been one continuous struggle for liberty for the poor and for the oppressed, and whose only reward has been a continuous shower of calumny and abuse from national journals and national leaders'.[74] His own accomplishments and distinctions were legion, but his politics did not outlast him. Nor did he groom a second line of leadership to continue his work. As an admiring biographer, Dhananjay Keer, admitted:

> Ambedkar did not try to organize his political party on modern lines. He had no taste for individual organization. There were no regular annual conferences or general meetings of the organizations with which he was connected. Where and when he sat was the venue of conference and the time for decision. The President or the Secretary or the Working Committee had to fall in line with his arrangement. [...] When he wanted his people to assemble under his banner, he simply gave them a clarion call, and the organization sprang up like the crop in the rainy season.[75]

---

[74] B. R. Ambedkar, 'Annihilation of Caste', in Moon, *Babasaheb Ambedkar*, Vol. 1, p. 80.
[75] Keer, *Dr. Ambedkar*, p. 480.

A perceptive commentator in the *Times of India* on 23 May 1954 put it well:

> Dr Ambedkar's political life is the tragedy of a man who thinks that rationality is applicable to politics. A thing, he affirms, is right because it is rational. Untouchability is wrong because it is irrational. Ambedkar, being an essentially rational man, argues from premises to conclusions. But the vast herd of politicians is not rational. They argue backwards. They adjust their premises to support their conclusions.

Remarkably, however, Ambedkar has continued to grow in stature since his death. Today he is arguably amongst the most revered of Indians, his birthday the occasion of a five-night vigil by his devoted followers, his statues across the country second only in number to those of Mahatma Gandhi (and conceivably even more than the latter). Every village and every junction appears to have one, a stocky balding figure in a suit and tie clutching a law book meant to represent the Constitution. (A measure of his stature is that his and Gandhi's are the only two statues on the grounds in front of Parliament.) The salutation 'Jai Bhim' is widely used by his admirers and sympathizers and has become a slogan of the deprived and dispossessed underclass. A 'Bhim Army' seeks to organize Dalit resistance in parts of northern India. His official residence in Delhi has been converted to a memorial that attracts thousands of admirers annually. The Maharashtra government has acquired the house in London where Ambedkar lived during his student days in the 1920s and converted it to a memorial as well.[76] When India's highest civilian award, the Bharat Ratna, was conferred upon him posthumously in 1990, the only criticism was of why it had taken so long.

'Life,' he once observed, 'should be great rather than long.'

---

[76] Times Network, 'Maharashtra government buys Ambedkar's London house', *Times of India*, 26 September 2015.

Sixty-five years is not a long lifespan; but of its greatness, there can be no doubt. In 2012, Ambedkar was voted the 'Greatest Indian', ahead of Gandhi, Nehru, and Patel, in a poll conducted by two respected television channels, in which over 20 million votes were cast.[77] Every political party in India— from the Congress he opposed to the Hindutva warriors who denounced him—feels obliged to express their admiration for him; he has entered the rare pantheon of the unchallengeable. Ambedkar today is larger than life, and nearly seven decades after his death, he keeps on growing.

---

[77] Meenakshi Verma Ambwani, 'Dr. B.R Ambedkar voted as Greatest Indian', *Hindu Business Line*, 14 August 2012.

BOOK TWO

LEGACY

SIX

A Life Well-lived

One afternoon in 1959, the great African American preacher and civil rights leader Martin Luther King and his wife, on their month-long visit to India, journeyed to the Kerala capital of Trivandrum and visited Dalit high school students there. According to the award-winning American journalist Isabel Wilkerson, in whose book *Caste: The Lies That Divide Us* the incident is recounted, the school principal, introducing King, said: 'Young people, I would like to present to you a fellow untouchable from the United States of America.' The visiting dignitary, says Wilkerson, was 'floored':

> He had not expected that term to be applied to him. He was, in fact, put off by it at first. He had flown in from another continent, had dined with the prime minister. He did not see the connection, did not see what the Indian caste system had to do directly with him, did not immediately see why the lowest caste people in India would view him, an American Negro and a distinguished visitor, as low-caste like themselves, see him as one of them.
>
> 'For a moment,' he wrote, 'I was a bit shocked and peeved that I would be referred to as an untouchable.' Then he began to think about the reality of the lives of the people he was fighting for—20 million people, consigned to the lowest rank in America for centuries, 'still smothering in an airtight cage of poverty,' quarantined in isolated ghettoes, exiled in their own country. And he said to himself, 'Yes, I

am an untouchable, and every Negro in the United States of America is an untouchable.'

In that moment, he realized that the Land of the Free had imposed a caste system not unlike the caste system of India and that he had lived under that system all of his life. It was what lay beneath the forces he was fighting in America.[1]

Ambedkar's impact on King is one example of the widespread reach of his legacy. It is difficult today to imagine the scale of what Babasaheb Dr Bhimji Rao Ambedkar accomplished. To be born into an 'untouchable' family in 1891, and that too as the fourteenth and last child of a poor Mahar subedar in an army cantonment, would normally have guaranteed a life of neglect, poverty, and discrimination. Not only did Ambedkar rise above the circumstances of his birth, but he achieved a level of success that would have been spectacular for a child of privilege. One of the first Dalits ever to enter an Indian college, he became a professor (at the prestigious Sydenham College) and a principal (of no less an institution than Bombay's Government Law College). One of the earliest Indian students in the United States, he earned multiple doctorates from Columbia University and the University of London, in economics, politics, and law. An heir to millennia of discrimination, he was admitted to the bar in London and became 'India's James Madison', as the chair of the Constitution Drafting Committee. The son of illiterates, he wrote a remarkable number of books, whose content and range testify to an eclectic mind and a sharp, if provocative, intellect. An insignificant infant scrabbling in the dust of Mhow in 1891 became the first law minister of a free India, in the most impressive cabinet ever assembled in New Delhi. When he died, aged only sixty-five, he had accumulated a set of distinctions few

---

[1] Isabel Wilkerson, *Caste: The Lies That Divide Us*, New York: Penguin Random House, 2020, pp. 21–22.

have matched; only one remained, the Bharat Ratna, and that was awarded posthumously before his centenary.

Dr Ambedkar's greatness cannot be reduced to any one of these accomplishments, because all were equally extraordinary. Think of what he was born into, what he endured, and who he became, and even this bare outline of his life should take one's breath away. And yet many feel posterity has yet to get the measure of the man. 'History,' wrote the novelist Arundhati Roy, 'has been unkind to Ambedkar. First, it contained him, and then it glorified him. It has made him India's Leader of the Untouchables, the King of the Ghetto. It has hidden away his writings. It has stripped away the radical intellect and the searing insolence.'[2]

Whereas some of those who seek to stand on Ambedkar's shoulders today acknowledge his role in fighting discrimination against Dalits, and others honour his Constitution-making, they do not engage with the totality of his political and economic vision. Ambedkar's concerns and doubts about Indian democracy, his contempt for Hindu majoritarianism, and his leftist view of political economy and labour rights are usually conveniently overlooked by his professed admirers. They prefer instead to do exactly what he warned against—to worship him as an idol, an act of 'bhakti' rather than the critical engagement he might have welcomed.

Reviewing Ambedkar's colossal achievements requires us to neither restrict him to his role as the great emancipator of India's Dalits, nor to glorify him as a saint above criticism, but rather to embrace his life and his ideas as a whole (including some 17,500-odd pages of Ambedkar's writings and speeches), the activism and the politics, the triumphs and the failures that marked his extraordinary impact on India's public consciousness. Much of this has to do with the words he used, the ideas he

---

[2] Roy, *The Doctor and the Saint*, p. 52.

expressed in his written and spoken work, and the passion with which he pursued them. This was in keeping with the memorable teaching of Sant Tukaram: 'We possess the wealth of words. With weapons of words we will fight; words are the breath of our life, we will distribute the wealth of words among the people. Tukaram says that the words themselves are gods, our pride, only those we choose to worship.'[3]

Tukaram's devotee, Ambedkar, imbibed this lesson well. 'Men are mortal and so are ideas,' he argued. 'An idea needs propagation as much as a plant needs watering. Otherwise both will wither and die.' One of his key ideas was the importance of self-respect and human dignity. A perceptive scholar, Aakash Singh Rathore, has noticed that the word 'dignity' recurs some 150 times in Ambedkar's writings and speeches;[4] it is a concept that rarely seems to receive comparable attention from other nationalists of India's founding generation. In Rathore's words:

> Dignity, for Ambedkar, is precluded by caste. Brahminism, with its principle of graded inequality, prescribes graded dignity—different status and rank for different castes. But even more so than the concept of equality, the concept of dignity will brook no gradation; every gradation of dignity is degradation of dignity. Its absoluteness is its hallmark. Not so for Gandhi.... Ambedkar argues that the social and moral consequences of caste separation espoused by Gandhi in his ideal theory of varna ... are degrading to those condemned hereditarily, in that ideal system, to serve the other varnas: 'It educates them into slaves and creates all the psychological complex which follows from a slave mentality.... There is, on the one hand, tyranny, vanity, pride, arrogance, greed, selfishness' in the varnas

---

[3] Bhalchandra Nemade, *Tukaram*, Sahitya Akademi, Delhi, 1997.
[4] Aakash Singh Rathore, *Ambedkar's Preamble: A Secret History of the Constitution of India*, New Delhi: Penguin Random House, 2020, p. 122.

hereditarily entitled to service from others; 'and, on the other hand, insecurity, poverty, degradation, loss of liberty' as well as loss of self-reliance, loss of independence, and loss of 'dignity and self-respect' for those condemned merely to serve.[5]

The dignity of his people mattered enormously to Ambedkar, as did their capacity for self-respect. 'Learn to live in this world with self-respect,' Ambedkar had told young Dalits in Bombay, and he embodied that dictum in his own life.

AMBEDKAR THE CONSTITUTIONALIST

Ambedkar was principally known in his lifetime as a fighter for Dalit empowerment, but his first and foremost legacy to the nation was as a constitutionalist, the principal author of the founding document of the republic and the pre-eminent articulator of the meaning and import of its provisions.

In the course of his astonishing oeuvre, Ambedkar, more than any other Indian thinker or political activist, studied, thought through, and analysed in detail ideas relating to what kind of society India was and what a transformed modern India ought to become—and why. As a lawyer by profession and a moralist by instinct, he also developed his own ideas on the values and principles, spiritual as well as political, on which Indian society should be based. Interrogating himself on the essentials of a free social order, Ambedkar finds a twofold answer:

The first is that the individual is an end in himself and that the aim and object of society is the growth of the individual and the development of his personality. Society is not above the individual and if the individual has to subordinate himself to society, it is because such subordination is for his betterment and only to the extent necessary. The

---

[5] Aakash Singh Rathore in Begari, *B.R. Ambedkar and Social Transformation*, p. 35.

second essential is that the terms of associated life between members of society must be regarded by consideration founded on liberty, equality, fraternity.[6]

Ambedkar argued that unlike a drop of water which loses its identity when it joins the ocean, an individual human being does not lose his individuality as part of society. Man was not born merely to develop society, but above all to develop himself. The constitutional system must protect and facilitate such individual development.

The 'first essential' was a core conviction: Ambedkar felt he was living in a society that had failed to recognize and honour his worth as an individual, that subjected him to disabilities for the accident of his birth into a particular caste, and that failed to grant him enforceable rights against these disabilities. This infused his basic approach to Constitution-making: he sought to ensure the Indian state was founded on a recognition of individual rights and that those rights would transcend any of the timeless disabilities visited upon Indians by a discriminatory and hierarchical society. While the 'second essential' was a matter of the spirit and constituted a philosophy that would underpin his constitutional project, the first required the firmness and majesty of the law.

The idea of India as a modern nation based on a certain conception of human rights and citizenship, vigorously backed by due process of law, and equality before law, is a relatively recent and strikingly modern idea. Earlier conceptions of India drew their inspiration from mythology and theology. The modern idea of India, despite the mystical influence of Tagore, and the spiritual and moral influences of Gandhi, is a robustly secular and legal construct based upon the vision and intellect of the republic's founding fathers, notably (in alphabetical order!) Ambedkar, Nehru, and Patel. The Preamble of the Constitution

---

[6] Moon, *Babasaheb Ambedkar, Writings and Speeches*, Vol. 3, p. 95.

itself is the most eloquent enumeration of this vision. In its description of the defining traits of the Indian republic, and its conception of justice, of liberty, of equality, and fraternity, it firmly proclaims that the law will be the bedrock of the national project.

Ambedkar's concluding remarks to the Constituent Assembly in the 'The Grammar of Anarchy' speech he gave on 25 November 1949 remains the great statement of his credo as a constitutionalist and the clearest depiction of the paradoxes inherent in the 'life of contradictions' that a democratic India had embarked upon.

Ambedkar's eloquent assault on discrimination and untouchability had, over the years, cogently expanded the reach of the Indian idea to incorporate the nation's vast, neglected underclass. 'What a degradation,' he once observed, 'for these unfortunate souls who have been turned by this Hindu Civilization into social lepers.'[7]

As Ambedkar stressed in the Constituent Assembly, the working instrument of our democracy is the Constitution of India. It is the basic framework of our democracy. Under the scheme of our Constitution, the three main organs of the state are the legislature, the executive, and the judiciary. The Constitution defines their powers, delimits their jurisdictions, demarcates their responsibilities, and regulates their relationships with one another, and with the people. But the most important contribution of the Constitution to Indian civic nationalism was that of representation centred on *individuals*. As the scholar Madhav Khosla explains in his impressive book of legal history, *India's Founding Moment: The Constitution of a Most Surprising Democracy,* the political apparatus of establishing a constitutional democracy in postcolonial India—a land that was 'poor and literate; divided by caste, religion, and

---

[7] Moon, *Babasaheb Ambedkar, Writings and Speeches*, Vol. 5, p. 142.

languages; and burdened by centuries of tradition',[8] involved an attempt to free Indians from prevailing types of knowledge and understanding, to place citizens in a realm of individual agency and deliberation that was appropriate to self-rule and to alter the relationship that they shared with one another.

The founders of the republic chose—as Ambedkar recognized—to impose a liberal Constitution upon a society which was not liberal, hidebound as it was by traditional customs and entrenched prejudices relating to caste, religion, and social hierarchies. They saw the principles of liberal constitutionalism—the centrality of the state, non-communal political representation, and so on—as responsive to the challenges posed by the burden of democracy. In keeping with contemporary liberal thought, they committed India to a common language of the rule of law, constructed a centralized state, rejected localism, and instituted a model of representation whose units were individuals rather than groups. The key objective, according to Khosla, was to 'allow Indians to arrive at outcomes agreeable to free and equal individuals'.[9] That was not easy.

Constitutions are (and Ambedkar explicitly made this point) tools to control and restrain state power. The challenge lies in reconciling restrictions on state power with popular rule—to prevent temporary majorities (since in a democracy, a majority is always temporary, though some governments forget that) from completely undoing what the Constitution has provided. Khosla suggests that the founders of the Indian republic held a conception of democracy that went beyond majority rule and rejected, in the American philosopher Ronald Dworkin's notable phrase, 'the majoritarian premise'.[10] They subordinated

---

[8] Madhav Khosla, 'Introduction: The Indian Problem', *India's Founding Moment: The Constitution of a Most Surprising Democracy*, Cambridge, MA: Harvard University Press, 2019, p. 6.
[9] Ibid., p. 21.
[10] Ronald Dworkin, *Freedom's Law: The Moral Reading of the American Constitution*, Cambridge, MA: Harvard University Press, 1997, pp. 1–38.

politics to law. As Ambedkar put it, the rights of Indian citizens could not 'be taken away by any legislature merely because it happens to have a majority'.[11]

The struggle for Indian independence was, after all, not simply a struggle for freedom from alien rule. It was a shift away from an administration of law and order centred on imperial despotism. Thus was born the idea of 'constitutional morality', a term he advocated in his address to the Constituent Assembly on 4 November 1948, and which has been made fashionable of late by India's Supreme Court. The term 'constitutional morality' was defined by the English historian George Grote as 'a paramount reverence for the forms of the constitution, enforcing obedience to authority and acting under and within these forms, yet combined with the habit of open speech, of action subject only to definite legal control, and unrestrained censure of those very authorities as to all their public acts combined, too, with a perfect confidence in the bosom of every citizen amidst the bitterness of party contest that the forms of the constitution will not be less sacred in the eyes of his opponents than his own.'[12] Ambedkar's concern was to privilege and legalize 'constitutional morality' over the traditional religiously derived morality of Indian society, which embraced the caste system, and to replace it with a 'commitment to constitutional means, to its processes and structures, alongside a commitment to free speech, scrutiny of public action [and] legal limitations on the exercise of power'. In his view, constitutional morality could only be realized through an administration which is in sync with the spirit of the Constitution, and through the cultivation of constitutional values among the masses, by defeating the forces of feudalism, casteism, bigotry, and parochialism.

---

[11] This was later reaffirmed in the landmark judgment *I. C. Golaknath and Others vs State of Punjab* and Anr. AIR 1967 SC 1643.
[12] Snehil Kunwar Singh, 'Are we still where Ambedkar left us?', *Deccan Herald*, 12 August 2020. For Grote, see *History of Greece* (Vol. 1-12), complete edition, Chicago: IPG, e-artnow, 2022.

This was how Ambedkar intended freedom to flourish in India. Of course, Ambedkar realized it is perfectly possible to pervert the Constitution, without changing its form, by merely changing the form of the administration to make it inconsistent and opposed to the spirit of the Constitution. Ambedkar argued that constitutional morality 'is not a natural sentiment. It has to be cultivated. We must realize that our people have yet to learn it. Democracy in India is only a top dressing on an Indian soil which is essentially undemocratic.' He insisted that the Directive Principles—an unusual feature of the Indian Constitution not found elsewhere—were necessary because although the rules of democracy mandated that the people must elect those who will hold power, the principles confirmed that 'whoever captures power will not be free to do what he likes with it'.[13]

The historian Sunil Khilnani described Ambedkar as 'a public emblem both of how far we've come in addressing the blight of caste, and how central the state and politics are to that rectification'.[14] Indeed, Ambedkar saw in the institutions of Indian democracy that he was helping to create the best guarantee for the future development and welfare of his own people, the oppressed and marginalized of India. He fought hard to introduce into the Constitution fundamental protections and guarantees of civil liberties for individual citizens. Ambedkar also convinced the Constituent Assembly that it was not enough to abolish untouchability: what was needed to undo millennia of discrimination and exploitation was the world's first and farthest-reaching affirmative action programme to uplift the oppressed, including reservations of jobs in the civil services, schools, and universities.

One of the aims of the Constitution of India is to secure justice for all its citizens. The Preamble identifies three essential

---

[13] 'Directive principles of State Policy', *Legal Service India Journal*.
[14] Khilnani, 'Ambedkar: Building Palaces on Dung Heaps', *Incarnations*, p. 471.

components of justice—social, economic, and political. The three are interrelated; they are of the same fundamental substance, but manifest themselves in different distinct forms without a prescribed hierarchy. One may view this as a constitutional trinity. Otto Kirchheimer, the jurist and advocate of the Frankfurt School of philosophy, saw 'political justice' as obtaining political power through the use of legal institutions. However, the Indian constitutional understanding of political justice is much wider in scope, as it is the embodiment of principles regarding the rights of the people, especially the rights in relation to a democratic form of government and in the participation of political affairs.[15]

Ambedkar, as one of the principal makers of modern India, and one of the leading icons for the oppressed and impoverished sections of society, played a seminal role in the development of political justice through his emphasis on constitutional ethos and rights in his role as an advocate for liberties and freedom during the British Raj, and later in his position as chairman of the Drafting Committee of the Constitution. Ambedkar is one of the few Indian leaders who participated in all the deliberations to provide a constitutional framework for India, right from the Southborough Committee in 1919 till the Cabinet Mission Plan in 1946. In 1928, when many countries were still unsure of granting universal adult franchise, Ambedkar made a strong case in favour of it before the Simon Commission. For him, the right to vote was fundamental to all citizens, not merely to the landed and educated classes to whom the British were prepared to grant it. He stressed the importance of allowing impoverished sections of society to participate in political affairs, in order for them to use political power for social empowerment. He furthered this principle with the incorporation of reservations for the Scheduled Castes and Scheduled Tribes, in the legislature and public services, in the

---

[15] *Raghunathrao Ganpatrao and Ors. vs. Union of India,* 1993 AIR 1267.

Constitution of India, thereby providing them an opportunity to break from the shackles of centuries of exploitation. (True, the final provision for reservations fell short of the more far-reaching proposals Ambedkar had outlined in a memorandum that he had submitted in 1947, but in accepting them he showed a talent for pragmatic compromise that had not always been apparent earlier—and this provision inaugurated a lasting change.)

Ambedkar shared the profound conviction that political democracy cannot exist in the absence of a social democracy. He viewed social democracy as 'a way of life which recognizes liberty, equality, and fraternity as the principles of life. These principles of liberty, equality, and fraternity are not to be treated as separate items in a trinity. They form a union of trinity in the sense that to divorce one from the other is to defeat the very purpose of democracy.'[16] Therefore, the development of a social democracy is a sine qua non for the realization of the constitutional trinity, and especially for political justice.

But fraternity had a special place in Ambedkar's vision; the word was, in a sense, his distinctive contribution to India's constitutional discourse. The sociologist Dipankar Gupta argues that Ambedkar's distinctive emphasis on fraternity, with the implicit idea that the assets of the better off would be used to uplift the untouchables and other unfortunates, was his vital contribution. (In later life, he would link it to the Buddhist idea of maitri, which is inconsistent with hereditary hierarchy.) In contrast, the extension of reservations (which Ambedkar had restricted to the Scheduled Castes and Tribes) in 1990 to the 'Other Backward Classes' by the Mandal Commission[17]

---

[16] *Constituent Assembly Debates*, Vol. xi, 25 November 1949.

[17] The Socially and Educationally Backward Classes Commission (SEBC), established in India in 1979 and headed by B. P. Mandal, submitted a report in 1980 which was not implemented by prime ministers Charan Singh, Indira Gandhi, and Rajiv Gandhi. However, the V. P. Singh government decided in 1990 to accept its recommendation that members of Other Backward Classes (OBC,

saw caste as 'an important political resource to be plumbed in perpetuity'. Gupta avers that 'the Mandal programme, therefore, is not in the spirit of enlarging fraternity, as the Ambedkar proposals are'.[18] He goes on to argue that 'while Ambedkar campaigned for SC quota he was clear that his final aim was to uproot this unjust hierarchical order from public life. Mandal, on the other hand, had no such ambitions. For him caste was not to be "removed", as with Ambedkar, but to be "represented".' It entrenched caste rather than, as Ambedkar would have wished, annihilating it.[19]

But Ambedkar had almost anticipated such a development, saying himself that fraternity could not be a constitutional principle; it was more of an ethical and social imagination. In his classic book *Annihilation of Caste* Ambedkar explained fraternity as 'essentially an attitude of respect and reverence towards fellow men'. As one scholar has observed, 'the limits of representational politics in forging larger solidarities are, yet again, born from the same social hierarchies'.[20] Fraternity would both result from and lead to the erosion of such hierarchies.

Ambedkar was conscious that one of the most powerful institutions created by the Constitution is the judiciary. He contributed the notion of 'constitutional morality', which has been invoked by the judiciary to strike down laws which violate fundamental rights, such as the criminalization of same-sex relations through Section 377 of the IPC or laws which treat

---

a euphemism for 'lower' and intermediate castes) be granted reservations for 27 per cent of jobs under the central government and public sector undertakings, on top of the 22 per cent reservation for Scheduled Castes & Tribes.

[18] Dipankar Gupta, 'Positive Discrimination and the Question of Fraternity-Contrasting Ambedkar and Mandal on Reservations', *Economic & Political Weekly*, Vol. 32, Issue 31, 2 August 1997.

[19] Dipankar Gupta, 'A Tale of Two Reservations', *Times of India*, 29 February 2016.

[20] Ajay Gudavarthy, 'The Paradoxes of Indian Democracy That Babasaheb Ambedkar Predicted Are Coming True in Unexpected Ways', *The Wire*, 13 August 2021.

women as the chattel of men. The judiciary plays an important role in furthering political justice through the cultivation of constitutional morality and by acting as a vanguard of the fundamental rights that Ambedkar and other framers of the Constitution established in Part III of the Constitution. In Ambedkar's view, one of the most important fundamental rights in the Constitution is embedded in Article 32, which allows any citizen to approach the Supreme Court of India to enforce his or her rights. This was described by Ambedkar as the heart and soul of the Constitution, and has gone a long way in holding the instrumentalities of the state accountable and in remedying gross violations of fundamental rights.

Ambedkar had warned of the consequences of allowing forces which do not believe in the ideals of the Constitution to form the administration. In an atmosphere of growing contempt towards cherished values and foundational principles of the Constitution, including secularism, freedom of expression, and equality, Ambedkar's writings and body of thought could not be more relevant to our times.

AMBEDKAR'S DEMOCRATIC NATIONALISM

In the Constitution, Ambedkar, despite his public and private misgivings, took a more optimistic view of the prospects of democracy in India by asking Indians to have a new understanding of authority. They would be liberated through submission to an impersonal force that saw them as equal agents, and that liberated spirit would make possible socio-economic transformation. Both were equally important. India's Independence Day was not meant to be just a ritual of song and dance, the hoisting of the flag, and the singing of the anthem. The real significance of Independence lay in the freedom of the mind. Indians were meant to be able to recognize and overcome, in Tagore's immortal phrase, a world that had been 'been broken up into fragments by narrow domestic walls'.[21] In order to further the goals of the Constitution, India requires strong and credible institutions to maintain checks and balances, not power centralized around one figure. The strengthening of institutions is essential to prevent the creation of an authoritative regime, one which feeds off bhakti or hero worship, which, as has been noted, Ambedkar strongly and presciently warned against in his last address to the Constituent Assembly—words that have a fresh resonance today, in an age of growing centralization of power. Equally, adherence to the Constitution meant that revolutionary and extra-judicial methods need to be discarded, as they represent the 'grammar of anarchy'.

Ambedkar's distaste for 'bhakti' in politics extended to his mistrust of any and all leaders: 'Over regard for leaders saps self-confidence of the masses, leaving them helpless when left leaderless in the hour of trial or when led by unscrupulous leaders.'[22] Equally it emerged from his understanding of Hindu religious practice:

> One great reason for the downfall of the Hindu society and the perpetuation of its degraded position is the injunction of 'Krishna' that whenever in difficulties the people should look out for his 'Avatar' to redeem them from the slouch of despondency. That has made the Hindu community helpless in the face of calamity.... I don't want you to follow such a ruinous teaching. I don't want you to be dependent on any single personality for your salvation. Your salvation must lie in your own hands through your own efforts.[23]

Many nationalists who argued passionately outside the Constituent Assembly for a united India (including, many would

---

[21] Rabindranath Tagore, *Gitanjali: Song Offerings* (1912), Keighley: Pomona Press, 2007.
[22] Moon, *Babasaheb Ambedkar, Writings and Speeches*, Vol. 17, Part III, p. 236.
[23] Ibid.

argue, both Azad and Gandhi), nonetheless thought that India was indeed a collection of distinct communities, who could flourish together in amicable coexistence. But the Constituent Assembly, led by Nehru and Ambedkar, went in the opposite direction, consciously opting for individual citizenship as the root of nationhood, transcending the limitations that India's communities imposed on their members.

Ambedkar made this clear in his speech to the assembly: 'I do not believe there is any place in this country for any particular culture, whether it is a Hindu culture or a Muhammadan culture or a Kanarese culture or a Gujarati culture. There are things we cannot deny, but they are not to be cultivated as advantages, they are to be treated as disadvantages, as something which divides our loyalty and takes away from us our common goal,' he argued. 'That common goal is the building up of the feeling that we are all Indians. I do not like what some people say, that we are Indians first and Hindus afterwards or Muslims afterwards. I am not satisfied with that.... I do not want that our loyalty as Indians should be in the slightest way affected by any competitive loyalty, whether that loyalty arises out of our religion, out of our culture or out of our language. *I want all people to be Indians first, Indians last and nothing else but Indians*....'[24] Ambedkar took an uncompromising stand on the fundamental difference of opinion—whether people are Hindus or Muslims first, or Indians first—that continues to haunt our politics today.

In a controversial radio address in 1942, he had expressed the view, on behalf of his fledgling Labour Party, that nationalism 'is only a means to an end. It is not an end in itself to which Labour can agree to sacrifice the essential principles of life.'[25]

---

[24] Speech to the Bombay Assembly, quoted in S. Irfan Habib (ed.), *Indian Nationalism: The Essential Writings*, New Delhi: Aleph Book Company, 2017, p. 27. Emphasis added.
[25] Ambedkar's 1942 Bombay radio address, quoted in Luis Cabrera, *The Humble Cosmopolitan: Rights, Diversity, and Trans-state Democracy*, New York: Oxford

National belonging, in other words, had no moral significance in itself; nationalism could unite Indians, but only to serve the fulfilment of 'essential principles'. As the political theorist Bhikhu Parekh explains Ambedkar's thinking: 'A nation is not a primordial entity but a political project, not given by nature but a collective creation of the moral imagination of its members, and has claims on them only to the extent that it includes them fully in its self-understanding.'[26] Ambedkar's nationalism was real, but it did not rest on the same understanding as that of his critics.

'In a world where nationality and nationalism were deemed to be special virtues in a people,' Ambedkar observed somewhat tartly in 1940, 'it was quite natural for the Hindus to feel, to use the language of Mr H. G. Wells, that it would be as improper for India to be without a nationality as it would be for a man to be without his clothes in a crowded assembly.'[27] That sardonic comment, by the man who would chair the Drafting Committee of India's Constitution, was not intended to be taken as a dismissal of the idea of Indian nationalism. Rather it was his way of questioning the existing underpinnings of that idea, especially in the context of the challenge that had arisen to it with the demand of the Muslim League for the partition of the country.

Ambedkar was deeply troubled by the iniquities of the caste system and the fear of many Dalits that national independence would merely lead to the social and political dominance of the upper castes. As an opponent of caste, and a nationalist, he believed that the Dalits must support India's freedom from British rule but they must pursue their struggle for equal rights within the framework of the new Constitution that he had a major hand

University Press, 2019, p. 277; Moon, *Dr. Babasaheb Ambedkar*, Vol. 10, p. 41.
[26] Bhikhu Parekh, 'The Intellectual and Political Legacy of B. R. Ambedkar', in Aakash Singh Rathore (ed.), *B.R. Ambedkar: The Quest for Justice*, New Delhi: Oxford University Press, 2021, p. 25.
[27] Moon, *Dr. Babasaheb Ambedkar: Writings and Speeches*, Vol. 8, pp. 29–30.

in drafting. Ambedkar realized that he could not confront two powerful enemies at the same time—the British and the Hindu upper castes whose exactions weighed upon his people. He had to choose which would be his priority, and he had no doubt where his duty lay: with the social reforms that were vital for the survival and development of his people. This led him to tactical alliances with the British in an attempt to balance and hold in check the oppressions of upper-caste Hindu society.

Critics are troubled by Ambedkar's willingness to cooperate with the British rulers, since he saw in the British Raj an instrument of liberation for his own community. The former editor and BJP minister Arun Shourie has authored a mammoth critique of Ambedkar, *Worshipping False Gods: Ambedkar and the Facts That Have Been Erased,* principally indicting him as a collaborator with the imperial oppressor.[28] It is true that Ambedkar—despite his searing articulation of the famines, misgovernance, and iniquities of British rule to both Indian and international audiences, including at the Round Table Conferences—saw in the prolongation of British rule better opportunities for his own community to overcome the imposed handicaps of untouchability and caste discrimination. If foreign rule could be used to achieve that end, Ambedkar believed, it could be preserved until such emancipation had been achieved. This did not endear him to nationalists, who saw him as betraying their sacred passion for freedom from foreign oppression, but Ambedkar argued that for his community, freedom from domestic oppression was even more urgent and important.

In *Worshipping False Gods,* Shourie argues that the glorification of Ambedkar is based on a continuing misrepresentation of facts, which he then proceeds to excavate at considerable length. Shourie excoriates Ambedkar as consistently opposed to the national struggle for freedom: 'At every possible turn he opposed

---

[28] Arun Shourie, *Worshipping False Gods: Ambedkar and the Facts That Have Been Erased,* New Delhi: HarperCollins Publishers, 1997, p. 229.

the campaigns of the National Movement, at every setback to
the Movement he was among those cheering the failure.'[29] In
Shourie's telling, Ambedkar saw Gandhi and the Congress as
merely seeking a shift in rule from the British to the Hindu
majority in India, which in practice meant the upper castes or
'the Brahmin and the Bania'. As Ambedkar wrote:

> The Brahmin enslaves the mind and the Bania enslaves the
> body. Between them they divide the spoils which belong to
> the governing classes. Can anyone who realizes what the
> outlook, tradition and social philosophy of the governing
> class in India is, believe that under the Congress regime, a
> sovereign and independent India will be different from the
> India we have today?[30]

However, this was indeed Ambedkar's deeply thought-through
position; from the perspective of an untouchable, he argued,
to support the Congress is to let tyranny have freedom to
enslave.[31] 'The Swaraj wherein there were no fundamental
rights guaranteed for the Depressed Classes,' he wrote, 'would
not be a Swaraj to them. It would be a new slavery for them.'[32]
Ambedkar's is a rational position, even if one's political views
may disagree vehemently with it: 'It is foolish to take solace in
the fact that because the Congress is fighting for the freedom of
India, it is, therefore, fighting for the freedom of the people of
India and of the lowest of the low,' Ambedkar said. 'The question
whether the Congress is fighting for freedom has very little
importance as compared to the question for whose freedom is
the Congress fighting.'[33] His conceptual contribution, one scholar

[29] Ibid., p. 3.
[30] Moon, *Babasaheb Ambedkar: Writings and Speeches*, Vol. 9, pp. 216–17.
[31] Shourie, *Worshipping False Gods*, p. 13.
[32] Roy, 'Is Unbridled Capitalism a Threat to Constitutional Democracy in India?',
Dr. Ambedkar Memorial Lecture, 2015, p. 6.
[33] Ambedkar, *What Congress & Gandhi Have Done to the Untouchables*, p.
193; Moon, *Dr. Babasaheb Ambedkar*, Vol. 9, p. 202.

has argued, was to make a distinction between 'the freedom of the country' and 'the freedom of the people'.[34]

This was a fair position for a member of an oppressed community to take, and indeed had been prefigured by Mahatma Phule in the previous century: 'There can not be a "Nation" worth the name until and unless all the people ... such as Shudras, Ati-Shudras [Untouchables], Bhils [tribals] and fishermen etc., become truly educated, are able to think independently for themselves and are uniformly unified and emotionally integrated. If [a tiny proportion of the population such as] the upstart Aryan Brahmins alone were to found the "National Congress", who will take any notice of it?'[35] But Shourie sees such a view as essentially anti-nationalist. As a result of his perception, Shourie notes, Ambedkar had even compared the Sanatana or upper-caste Hindus with bloodthirsty Nazis, waiting to eliminate the untouchables:

> When Nazism is at its height and the West is engaged in a mighty war against it, Ambedkar takes great care to characterize the Indian social system as being nothing but another version of the Nazism of Hitler with which the West had perforce become familiar, and of characterizing those who were fighting for freedom from the British as those who were fighting for the perpetuation of this brand of Nazism at home.[36]

Shourie piles up considerable evidence (his book is over 700 pages long) for Ambedkar having sought the perpetuation of British rule till the very end, citing his own statements as well as notes, letters, and minutes of the high British officials to whom he spoke. In the last quarter-century of British rule,

---

[34] Bidyut Chakrabarty, *Politics, Ideology and Nationalism: Jinnah, Savarkar and Ambedkar versus Gandhi*, New Delhi: SAGE Publications, pp. 160–61.
[35] Jotirao Phule, *Slavery: Collected Works of Mahatma Jotirao Phule*, Vol. 1, Bombay: Government of Maharashtra, 1991, p. 29.
[36] Shourie, *Worshipping False Gods*, p. 15.

Shourie argues, Ambedkar 'took positions which were ever so convenient for the British', including attacking the Mahatma and the Congress, voicing 'the exact notions that the British wanted voiced to counter the nationalist movement ... not only in coordination with them but at their express "suggestion"'.[37] Shourie goes on: 'This pattern continued: Council members like Ambedkar continued to endorse and speak up for what the British wanted done, and the British continued to cite their statements and the fact that these Indians had been associated with taking the decision ... as justification of what was being done.'[38]

According to Shourie, Ambedkar even supported a hare-brained scheme that would have given Britain treaty rights to supervise the Indian government and intervene in Indian affairs even after Independence.[39] Netaji Subhas Chandra Bose, no less, remarked that 'Ambedkar had had his leadership thrust upon him by the benign British government because his services were necessary to embarrass the nationalist leaders.'[40]

But Ambedkar's reasons for his conduct were clear. In his own words:

> It is difficult to expect that in a country like India, where most persons are communally minded, those in authority will give equal treatment to those who do not belong to their community. Unequal treatment has been the inescapable fate of the Untouchables in India.... [T]he Hindus in the administration have the same positive[ly] anti-social and inimical attitude to the Untouchables which the Hindus outside the administration have. Their one aim is to discriminate against the Untouchables and to deny and deprive them not only of the benefits of Law, but also of

---

[37] Ibid., p. 64.
[38] Ibid., p. 93.
[39] Ibid., p. 49.
[40] Keer, *Dr. Ambedkar*, p. 146.

the protection of the Law against tyranny and oppression. The result is that the Untouchables are placed between the Hindu population and the Hindu-ridden administration, the one committing wrong against them and the other protecting the wrong-doer, instead of helping the victims.... [S]uch a Swaraj would aggravate the sufferings of the Untouchables.[41]

In a 1927 article he remarked, 'If Tilak had been born among the untouchables, he would not have raised the slogan "Swaraj is my birthright", but [rather] the slogan "Annihilation of untouchability is my birthright".'[42] And as Ambedkar put it with characteristic sharpness, as if anticipating the charge that his stand was anti-national and even treasonous: 'Any claim for the sharing of power by the minority is called communalism while the monopolizing of the whole power by the majority is called Nationalism.'[43]

Ambedkar was aware of the contemporary criticism, writing that people like him were portrayed in the press 'as the showboys of the British, with no record of service to or sacrifice for the country, agents of British imperialism, enemies of the country, job hunters, fellows out to sell the interests of the country for a mess of pottage and so on'.[44] He was first dubbed a British stooge, along with other attendees to the first Round Table Conference in 1930, because he accepted the British government's invitation at a time when Congressmen were being imprisoned for breaking the salt laws after Gandhi's Salt March. Similarly, others at the time called him an opportunist for agreeing to serve as labour member of the

---

[41] Moon, *Babasaheb Ambedkar: Writings and Speeches*, Vol. 1, pp. 406–10.
[42] Editorial, *Bahishkrut Bharat*, 29 July 1927, quoted in Keer, *Ambedkar: Life and Mission*, p. 81.
[43] Moon, *Babasaheb Ambedkar: Writings and Speeches*, Vol. 1, p. 427.
[44] Babasaheb Ambedkar, 'What Congress and Gandhi have done to the Untouchables?', in Moon, *Babasaheb Ambedkar: Writings and Speeches*, Vol. 9, p. 149.

British viceroy's Executive Council during 1942–46, when Congress leaders were in jail during the 'Quit India' movement. His demand for separate electorates for untouchables (which he conceded in the Poona Pact) and his support for the Muslim League's case for Pakistan also earned him the sobriquet of 'anti-national'. (His suggestion that Jammu and Kashmir be trifurcated was similarly dubbed at the time, though subsequent developments appear to be taking us to a point where that suggestion might only make Ambedkar again appear prescient.)

To those who, like Shourie, thus dismiss Ambedkar as an 'anti-national' agent of British imperialism, one can only offer Ambedkar's own words of proud nationalism in response: 'The point is that nationality is not primarily a matter of geography, culture or language.... Nation on the contrary is a spiritual reality binding people into a deep comradeship.'[45] Ambedkar went on: 'This country of ours is the true land of promise. This race of ours is the chosen race.' Speaking of his criticism of the two most prominent leaders, he said: 'I insist that if I hate Mr. Gandhi and Mr. Jinnah—I dislike them—I do not hate them—it is because I love India more. That is the true faith of a nationalist. I have hopes that my countrymen will some day learn that the country is greater than men.'[46] In his speech to the Bombay Assembly, he had laid out his all-inclusive nationalism in the memorable words: 'I want all people to be Indians first, Indians last and nothing else but Indians.'[47]

It is true that in his 1940 book on the subject, Ambedkar conceded the case for Pakistan, arguing that, though their religion did not necessarily justify the argument for a separate nationality, if 'the Musalmans' wanted separation there was not much that the others could do about it. Ambedkar, discussing

---

[45] Sukhadeo Thorat, 'Foreword', in Christophe Jaffrelot and Narender Kumar (eds.), *Dr. Ambedkar and Democracy*, New Delhi: Oxford University Press, 2018, p. xviii.
[46] Moon, *Babasaheb Ambedkar: Writings and Speeches*, Vol. 1, p. 209.
[47] Speech to the Bombay Assembly, quoted in Habib, *Indian Nationalism*, p. 27.

the differences between Hindus and Muslims in pre-Partition India, wrote:

> The things that divide are far more vital than the things which unite. In depending upon certain common features of Hindu and Mahomedan social life, in relying upon common language, common race and common country, the Hindu is mistaking what is accidental and superficial for what is essential and fundamental. The political and religious antagonisms divide the Hindus and the Musalmans far more deeply than the so-called common things are able to bind them together.[48]

He was being realistic in the circumstances of that time, and, in light of the Partition that did occur seven years later, prescient. He did concede, 'The prospects might perhaps be different if the past of the two communities can be forgotten by both'[49] (though his book argued that such forgetting was unlikely).[50] Yet today too many believe in the divisive notion of totalizing Hindu or Muslim identity—even though such monolithic religious identities did not exist conceptually in India, a land of myriad localisms and particularisms, before the nineteenth century.

Nationalism in the Congress sense, of an all-encompassing nature harking back to ancient glories, did not appeal unconditionally to Ambedkar. As he had stated on 1 January 1943, 'Labour [his party] is not prepared to make a fetish of nationalism.... If nationalism means the worship of the ancient past—the discarding of everything that is not local in origin and colour—then [we] cannot accept nationalism as [our] creed. [We] *cannot allow the living faith of the dead to become the dead faith of the living*. Labour will not allow the

---

[48] Moon, *Babasaheb Ambedkar: Writings and Speeches*, Vol. 8, p. 36.
[49] K. R. Phanda and Prafull Goradia, 'Jinnah Proposed, Gandhi Disposed... Thus India Divided', Center for Advanced Research, Reference, Information & Enhanced Documentation, a unit of SAMARTH, 2014, p. 53.
[50] Moon, *Babasaheb Ambedkar: Writings and Speeches*, Vol. 10, p. 40.

ever-expanding spirit of man to be strangled by the hand of the past which has no meaning for the present and no hope for the future....'[51]

As for other forms of nationalist expression, notably those pursued by the Hindu Mahasabha and the Muslim League, Ambedkar was even more wary. He understood that the idea of Hindu or Muslim nationalism conflates ideas of religion and culture with those of nation and state. Nationhood is by definition indivisible, whereas religion and culture take on multiple manifestations; an Indian national can be a Christian from Kerala or a Buddhist from Arunachal Pradesh, with distinct religious and cultural practices from those of a Hindu from Madhya Pradesh or a Sikh from Punjab. All these cultures, of course, contribute to national identity; yet no singular understanding of culture can define the nationalism of a plural land like India.

This was the idea of India that Ambedkar, in common with Jawaharlal Nehru and the Congress liberals, sought to enshrine in the Constitution. With the adoption of Articles 25, 26, 27, and 28 of the Constitution, guaranteeing freedom of conscience and the right to profess, practise, and propagate one's religion, to manage one's own religious affairs and to enjoy the freedom of religious worship, India wrote itself a secular Constitution. But was it necessary to include the word 'secular' itself in the Constitution? Ambedkar thought not. He said: 'What should be the policy of the State, how the Society should be organised in its social and economic side are matters which must be decided by the people themselves according to time and circumstances. It cannot be laid down in the Constitution itself because that is destroying democracy altogether.'[52]

Though the concept of secularism was unarguably implicit

---

[51] Ibid., p. 41.
[52] Jayita Mukhopadhyay, 'Ambedkar's vision of a secular Constitution', *The Statesman*, 6 April 2018.

in India's constitutional philosophy, it wasn't Western-style secularism, which meant irreligiousness, which even avowedly atheist parties like the Communists or the various manifestations of the southern DMK movement found unpopular amongst their voters. Rather, secularism meant, in the Indian tradition, a profusion of religions, none of which was privileged by the state, which (in Amartya Sen's words) preserved an 'equidistance' from, and an 'equal symmetry' of treatment of, all religions.[53]

Ambedkar had addressed the subject of majoritarianism in a famous speech on 4 November 1948:

> To diehards who have developed a kind of fanaticism against minority protection, I would like to say two things. One is that minorities are an explosive force which, if it erupts, can blow up the whole fabric of the State. The history of Europe bears ample and appalling testimony to this fact. The other is that the minorities in India have agreed to place their existence in the hands of the majority.... They have loyally accepted the rule of the majority, which is basically a communal majority and not a political majority. It is for the majority to realise its duty not to discriminate against minorities.[54]

The 'communal majority' Ambedkar referred to is of the community as a whole, which includes all Hindus, and not only the political majority of those Hindus today voting for the BJP. (The distinction between a 'communal majority' and a 'political majority' was well made by Ambedkar: 'A political majority is changeable in its class composition. A political majority grows. A communal majority is born. The admission to a political majority is open. The door to a communal majority is closed. The politics

---

[53] Amartya Sen as quoted in Keerthik Sasidharan, 'Whose Secularism is it Anyway?', *The Hindu*, 10 September 2017.

[54] Dr B. R. Ambedkar, *Constituent Assembly Debates*, Vol. 7, 4 November 1948, M. V. Pylee, *India's Constitution*, 16th edition, New Delhi: S. Chand & Company Limited, 2017, p. 10.

of a political majority are free to all to make and unmake. The politics of a communal majority are made by its own members born in it.'[55])

Today, India is in the grip of the very majoritarianism that Ambedkar had so presciently warned against, and this communal majority must resist the persistent efforts of the BJP and its supporters to polarize the country. To take a not isolated example, Praveen Kumar, a former IPS officer and a Dalit, joined the Bahujan Samaj Party in Telangana and exhorted Dalit-Bahujans to realize Ambedkar's dream of gaining political power.[56] He attracted a large turnout at a public meeting he organized to launch himself. But when he administered an oath to students that was similar to the one Ambedkar did in his conversion to Buddhism, cases were filed against him for hurting Hindu sentiments. This is no longer the India in which Ambedkar flourished.

Ambedkar was not the only great Indian who warned of the dangers of majoritarianism. Sardar Patel, the hero of the BJP prime minister Narendra Modi (during whose rule there have been many infamous instances of majoritarian misbehaviour), urged in the Constituent Assembly on 25 May 1949: 'It is for us who happen to be in a majority to think about what the minorities feel, and how we in their position would feel if we are treated in the manner they are treated.'[57] Given the Modi government's oft-expressed admiration for the likes of Ambedkar and Sardar Patel, it is disappointing that their current approach reduces individuals to their religious affiliations and denies them their agency as free citizens of our democratic republic. The suggestion that only a Hindu, and only a certain kind of

---

[55] Moon, *Babasaheb Ambedkar: Writings and Speeches*, Vol. 1, p. 169.
[56] Ajay Gudavarthy, 'The Paradoxes of Indian Democracy That Babasaheb Ambedkar Predicted Are Coming True in Unexpected Ways', *The Wire*, 13 August 2021.
[57] Sardar Vallabhbhai Patel, *Constituent Assembly Debates*, Vol. 8, 26 May 1949.

Hindu, can be an authentic Indian is, as Ambedkar understood, an affront to the very premise of Indian nationalism.

Indeed, Ambedkar's notorious 1953 speech publicly disowning his own Constitution in the Rajya Sabha reflects the fact that in the last years of his life Ambedkar was troubled about the majoritarianism inherent in the Constitution. 'It was clear,' he had said before becoming chairman of the Drafting Committee, 'that if the British system was copied it would result in permanently vesting executive power in a communal majority.'[58] As a member of the Constituent Assembly, he went along with its majority view in favour of accepting the British parliamentary system, but in a 1953 interview to the BBC, he reiterated in more negative terms something he had already warned against in that assembly: 'Democracy will not work,' he declared gloomily, 'for the simple reason [that] we have got a social structure which is totally incompatible with parliamentary democracy.'[59] This gloominess about the workings of Indian democracy reflected both his own frustrations as a Scheduled Caste leader and the inherent radicalism that had animated so many of his iconoclastic statements and actions throughout his life. It remains a striking feature of the Ambedkar story that the Father of the Indian Constitution was also its most restless son.

The Constitution allowed each Indian to create their individual political identity and thus collectively to fashion the nation's destiny. But, as Ambedkar warned, a Constitution is only as good as those who work it. That is where, sadly, India seems today to be falling short.

AMBEDKARISM ABROAD

Ambedkar said with characteristic prescience that 'if Hindus

---

[58] Teltumbde and Yengde (eds.), *The Radical in Ambedkar*.
[59] 'Transcript of Dr Ambedkar's 1953 Interview with the BBC—When Dr Ambedkar Said Democracy Won't Work in India', Velivada.

migrate to other regions on earth, Indian caste would become a world problem'.[60] Many Hindus carry their caste with them when they leave India. But awareness of, and resistance to, caste practices has also been growing abroad, even if Dalits outside India have not faced the kind of atrocities still tragically familiar in India. For over two decades, Dalit organizations in Britain have actively lobbied for a law to address the impact of caste discrimination in that country. British Dalits have been seeking to be protected under the provisions of the Equality Act 2010, though debate still continues on whether such inclusion will outlaw 'caste consciousness' or promote it. In 2015, the first caste discrimination case to capture public attention in Britain, *Tirkey vs Chandok*, has been followed by other lawsuits alleging casteism in employment practice. The 2019 BBC television documentary 'Hindus: Do We Have a Caste Problem?' has already confirmed that caste awareness is widespread in the Indian diaspora in Britain. The register of charities for England and Wales lists a number of organizations that have caste names in their descriptions. Surprisingly, casteism extends to the Sikh community as well. The Sikh Report 2018 (an annual study of the UK's Sikhs, tabled in Parliament every year) found nearly 50 per cent of British Sikh respondents believed in the caste system. There are gurdwaras and temples in the UK serving specific castes, matrimonial websites reinforcing caste selection, and occasional examples of casteist diatribes on social media.[61] However, in 2022, Mohinder K. Midha of the Labour Party made history by becoming the first woman mayor from the Dalit community in Britain, when she was elected mayor of West London's Ealing Council.[62]

In the US on 2 June 2022, a US-based Dalit civil rights

---

[60] Moon, *Dr. Babasaheb Ambedkar: Writings and Speeches*, Vol. 1, pp. 5–22.

[61] Santosh Dass, 'Caste in the UK, and why Ambedkar matters', *Indian Express*, 8 August 2021.

[62] 'UK elects first Dalit woman mayor to London council: Who is Mohinder K Midha?' , *Firstpost*, 25 May 2022.

organization, Equality Labs, accused Google of having casteist and hostile workplace practices after the cancellation of a talk by its executive director to Google News staff as part of April's Dalit History Month. Equality Labs alleged that Google management 'endangered its employees as they allowed caste bigotry and harassment to run rampant'.[63] A senior manager resigned in protest over the incident. Other minorities have found inspiration in Ambedkar's fight against discrimination. In the late 1990s, some Hungarian Romani people drew parallels between their own situation and that of the downtrodden Dalits in India. Inspired by Ambedkar, they started to convert to Buddhism.[64]

Attempts by Dalit activists to internationalize the issue of caste discrimination by comparing it to racism and even to apartheid have attracted global attention, even though they have not yet succeeded. The issue arose at the 2001 World Conference against Racism in Durban,[65] where it was effectively headed off by Indian diplomats who pointed out that untouchability is outlawed in the Indian Constitution and did not require international involvement to sanction it. Arundhati Roy argues that 'though caste is not the same as race, casteism and racism are indeed comparable. Both are forms of discrimination that target people because of their descent.'[66] She recalls a public meeting in Washington D.C. in 2014 commemorating Martin Luther King Jr. which issued an African–American 'Declaration of Empathy' calling for 'an end to the oppression of Dalits in India'.[67] Awareness of

---

[63] PTI, 'Dalit civil rights activist accuses Google of casteist, hostile workplace practices', *Hindustan Times*, 4 June 2022.

[64] Pradeep Attri, 'Ambedkar in Hungary', *The Hindu*, 22 November 2009.

[65] World Conference against Racism, Racial Discrimination, Xenophobia and Related Intolerance, 31 August to 8 September 2001.

[66] Arundhati Roy, 'The Doctor and the Saint', *My Seditious Heart*, New Delhi: Penguin Random House India, 2019, pp. 673–74.

[67] From Arundhati Roy's introduction to Ambedkar's *The Annihilation of Caste*, extracted in *Prospect*.

caste issues has grown since then. California State University, the largest public university system in the United States, and Carleton University in Ottawa have specifically added caste to their official lists of non-discrimination policies.[68]

Caste consciousness has percolated into other areas as well, this time in a desire to promote justice. Environmental scholars are arguing that the untouchables in India are being deprived of 'environmental justice' through the denial of equitable access to natural resources and unequal implementation of the right to health because of their lower status in the caste hierarchy.[69] The analysis of environmental injustice towards scheduled castes and tribes and other backward communities has emerged as another branch of the study of 'environmental racism', first pioneered in the US. In India, 'environmental casteism' includes, but is not restricted to, manual scavenging, which though largely outlawed in India still persists, as Dalits in many places are required to clear and transport night soil by hand; illegal encroachments upon Dalit premises; and disproportionate evictions of Dalit slum dwellers for development projects like dams. There is even discrimination in disaster relief after ecological disasters like floods and earthquakes, though this is partially attributable to Dalits and other poorer individuals living in less accessible areas.[70]

It is not too ambitious to suggest that all these developments vindicate Ambedkar's pioneering role as a thinker about issues of caste discrimination, and point to the ways in which he opened the doors for Dalits everywhere to fight for their rights. His legacy, in other words, lives on not just in India, but everywhere that the struggle against any form of discrimination is waged.

---

[68] Sakshi Venkatraman, 'All Cal State universities add caste to anti-discrimination policy', *NBC News*, 19 January 2022.
[69] Bhimraj M., 'A Dalit Critique of Environmental Justice in India', Faculty of Legal Studies, South Asian University.
[70] 'Environmental Casteism: An Overdue Apology We Owe to Ecology and Victims of Caste', *Nickeled and Dimed*, 9 April 2021.

AMBEDKAR'S FOUR FLAWS

But this is not a hagiography, and an honest and complete survey of Ambedkar's life and impact must look at the flaws in his record as well. The criticisms directed at Ambedkar for his role in working with the British to emancipate the Dalits have lost their sting. What then can he still be reproached for?

An unworthy charge we can quickly dispose of is that of Shourie, who accuses Ambedkar and his admirers of exaggerating the hardships that Ambedkar had to put up with, to de-emphasize the help he received from persons belonging to higher castes. Shourie's charge is that 'by exaggerating the hardships the apologists seek to explain away Ambedkar's collaborating with the British, his hankering for office'. Shourie argues that 'these hardships were the sort that are commonplace in India'—but whereas others endured such hardships and became resolute nationalists, 'it is only in Ambedkar's case that his followers and apologists think that those hardships justify his collaborating with the British against the National Movement'.[71] No one who has read of Ambedkar's privations, and the indignities that Dalits had to endure, can disagree that these were substantially worse than any inflicted upon Hindus of higher castes, so the objection fails to carry any weight. And while one may disagree with Ambedkar's choice, to suggest that his efforts to use the British as an instrument to redeem his people were inherently illegitimate is blinkered in the extreme. It was a valid option for one in his situation. Faced with the resistance of a powerful Hindu society thwarting his community's rise, it was entirely logical for Ambedkar to try and make common cause with the even more powerful alternative available to him—that of the British colonial government.

There are, however, four areas on which Ambedkar can legitimately be faulted. The first was his blind spot about

---

[71] Shourie, *Worshipping False Gods*, pp. 61–62.

the Adivasis—India's aboriginals, now officially classified as Scheduled Tribes—who deserved his support as others ostracized by Indian society as Dalits were, but whom he tended to regard dismissively as 'savages' in need of 'civilizing'. He refers to them leading the life of 'hereditary animals', and even warns 'the Hindus' that the 'aborigines are a source of potential danger'. Later, in his address to the All-India Scheduled Castes Federation conference in Bombay on 6 May 1945,[72] while discussing the issue of proportionate representation, Ambedkar is patronizing at best, and offensive at worst:

> My proposals do not cover the Aboriginal Tribes although they are larger in number than the Sikhs, Anglo-Indians, Indian Christians and Parsees.... [T]he Aboriginal Tribes have not as yet developed any political sense to make the best use of their political opportunities and they may easily become mere instruments in the hands either of a majority or a minority and thereby disturb the balance without doing any good to themselves.... The proper thing to do for these backward communities is to establish a Statutory Commission to administer what are now called the 'excluded areas' on the same basis as was done in the case of the South African Constitution.[73]

The very idea of a Dalit leader prescribing the confinement of other deprived Indian citizens to Bantustans is cringeworthy; but it is made worse by Ambedkar echoing the very language he objected to in Gandhi, when the Mahatma argued that the untouchables had not yet developed the political sense to use the vote, let alone make use of separate electorates that Ambedkar had demanded. It is dismaying to see Ambedkar echoing

---

[72] B. R. Ambedkar, 'The Communal Deadlock and a Way to Solve It', in Moon, *Dr. Babasaheb Ambedkar: Writings and Speeches*, Vol. 1, p. 375.

[73] Ambedkar as quoted in 'Communal deadlock and a way to solve it', *Modern Rationalist*, 1 January 2022.

colonialist language and prejudice towards the Adivasis, whose own representative in the Constituent Assembly from Jharkhand, Jaipal Singh, had argued on 19 December 1946: 'What my people require, Sir, is not adequate safeguards.... We do not ask for any special protection. We want to be treated like every other Indian.' Addressing the assembly on the Objectives Resolution moved by Jawaharlal Nehru in 1946, Jaipal Singh proudly said:

> Sir, I am proud to be a *Jungli*, that is the name by which we are known in my part of the country. As a *jungli*, as an *Adibasi*, I am not expected to understand the legal intricacies of the Resolution. But my common sense tells me, the common sense of my people tells me that every one of us should march in that road of freedom and fight together. Sir, if there is any group of Indian people that has been shabbily treated it is my people. They have been disgracefully treated, neglected for the last 6,000 years. This Resolution is not going to teach *Adibasis* democracy. You cannot teach democracy to the tribal people; you have to learn democratic ways from them. They are the most democratic people on earth.[74]

It demeans Ambedkar to have spoken with language bordering on prejudice and racism about the Adivasi people.

A second criticism of Ambedkar relates to what Bhikhu Parekh calls his 'quasi-Manichaean' view of Hinduism and Hindu society.[75] Whereas Christophe Jaffrelot sees Ambedkar 'wavering between the aspiration to rise within Hindu society and the urge to sever his links with it',[76] Ambedkar's language about Hindus and Hinduism is too sweepingly scathing to admit any realistic possibility of his having sought the former:

---

[74] Anurag Bhaskar, 'When It Comes to Dalit and Tribal Rights, the Judiciary in India Just Does Not Get It', *The Wire*, 3 May 2020.
[75] Parekh, 'The Intellectual and Political Legacy of B. R. Ambedkar', in Rathore, *B.R. Ambedkar: The Quest for Justice*, p. 27.
[76] Jaffrelot, *Dr. Ambedkar and Untouchability*, pp. 88–89.

Hindus are a ... race of pygmies and dwarfs, stunted in stature and wanting in stamina. It is a nation 9/10ths of which is declared to be unfit for military service. This shows that the Caste System does not embody the eugenics of modern scientists. It is a social system which embodies the arrogance and selfishness of a perverse section of the Hindus who were superior enough in social status to set it in fashion and who had authority to force it on their inferiors.[77]

Equally savage was his declaration that 'Hindu civilization is a diabolical contrivance to enslave humanity. Its proper name would be infamy.' And on occasion he could be devastating: 'There can be a better or a worse Hindu. But a good Hindu there cannot be.'[78] In a 1942 speech he confessed, 'I thought for long that we could rid the Hindu society of its evils and get the Depressed classes incorporated into it in terms of equality.... Experience has taught me better ... we no longer want to be part of the Hindu society.'[79] But there were many Hindus whose lives, beliefs, and conduct did not conform to the Ambedkar stereotype; several who rejected caste and refused to respect caste rules in their personal lives; and many others who reached across caste divides to support Ambedkar and the Dalit cause. His sweeping denunciations of Hinduism left no room to admit such Hindus, nor the Hinduism of spiritual enquiry and philosophical debate, nor the Hinduism of the Bhakti movement, of Chokhamela and Kabir and Ramdas. The philosophy of 'acceptance of difference' preached by Vivekananda; Adi Shankara's acknowledgement that the Atman

---

[77] B. R. Ambedkar, 'Annihilation of Caste', in Moon, *Dr. Babasaheb Ambedkar: Writings and Speeches*, Vol. 1, p. 50.
[78] Ibid., p. 89.
[79] B. G. Kunte (ed.), *Source Material on Dr Babasaheb Ambedkar and the Movement of Untouchables*, Vol. 1, Bombay: Education Department, Government of Maharashtra, 1970, p. 382.

in a Chandala (a Dalit) is no different from the Atman in a Brahmin; the eclectic, pluralist Hinduism practised differently in millions of Hindu homes—all these have no place in Ambedkar's blanket denunciations of Hinduism. It can be argued that he was denouncing Hindu society, not the Hindu faith, but in fact Ambedkar conflated the two, attributing the ills of Hindu society (hierarchical discrimination in particular) to the religion that in his view sanctified these ills, and thereby damning the entire faith in the process. One can understand and forgive Ambedkar his bitterness, as Mahatma Gandhi did, because of what he had suffered and watched other Dalits endure; but such a black-and-white dismissal of a great religion and the complexities of its adherents, while politically pardonable, was intellectually unworthy. This simplistic, homogenizing denigration of a great religion was emotionally entirely comprehensible but too unsubtle for a man of otherwise rigorous intellect, and undermined the credibility of his analysis.

The third criticism relates to his clash with Gandhi—not his disagreement with the Mahatma, which he was perfectly entitled to have, but the ungraciousness of his manner of expressing it, including even after Gandhi's death. Ambedkar cannot be faulted for honestly disagreeing with Gandhi on varnashrama in Hinduism, the political representation of the Depressed Classes, incompatible economic philosophies, 'village India', and the role of the state in empowering the underclass, all of which were issues on which the two stood poles apart. His surrender to the Mahatma's 'emotional blackmail' over the 1932 Poona Pact also long rankled with Ambedkar. All these are legitimate grounds for disagreement and debate. But Ambedkar's ungracious and conspicuous silence on the Mahatma's death was unworthy of a man of education and sensitivity, who would normally have been expected to acknowledge those intentions and contributions for which most Indians were grateful. He spoke of Gandhi with bitterness and acrimony for nearly a quarter of a century afterwards, denouncing him in two books—with the titles *Mr Gandhi and the Emancipation of the Untouchables* and *What Congress and Gandhi have Done to the Untouchables*—spurning the older man's entreaties, refusing to acknowledge Gandhi's role in ensuring Ambedkar a place in independent India's first cabinet and in being awarded the chairmanship of the Drafting Committee of the Constitution, and uttering personal remarks that should have been beneath a man of his stature. A BBC interview Ambedkar gave in 1955 was especially churlish: 'I know Gandhi better than his disciples [do]. They came to him as devotees and saw only the Mahatma. I was an opponent, and saw the bare man in him. He showed me his fangs.'[80] Ambedkar was almost alone in mistrusting Gandhi's sincerity: 'He was absolutely an orthodox Hindu. He was never a reformer. He has no dynamics in him, you see.... [H]e wanted that the untouchables would not oppose his movement of Swaraj. I don't think beyond that, he had any motive of uplift.'[81]

The undeniable fact is that Gandhi made great personal efforts against untouchability. As Bhikhu Parekh describes it:

> Gandhi ... insisted that the Hindus must put their house in order. Untouchability was a Hindu practice, and it was their duty to 'repent', 'do penance', express regrets, and fight it.... They owed it to 'Hinduism and themselves'.... [Gandhi] appealed to Hindu pride, guilt, shame, self-interest, and the good name of their religion, and generated enormous moral and political energy in support of his reformist cause. He set a personal example by adopting an untouchable girl, cleaning latrines, living and sharing meals with untouchables, attending marriages only when one

---

[80] Ambedkar interview on the BBC, broadcast 31 December 1955, available on YouTube.
[81] Ibid.

of the parties belonged to them—all in themselves trivial but symbolically significant and subversive of deeply held taboos.[82]

Ambedkar's hostility stands in contrast to Gandhi's extensive record of striving for the abolition of untouchability and his overt expressions of respect for the Dalit leader. In a letter to Ambedkar dated 6 August 1944, Gandhi acknowledged their 'different views' and the fact that 'we see things from different angles', but sought engagement nonetheless; 'I would love to find a meeting ground between us.... I know your great ability and I would love to own you as a colleague and a co-worker.' With great humility the Mahatma went on: 'I must admit my failure to come nearer to you. If you can show me a way to a common meeting ground between us, I would like to see it.'[83] But Ambedkar could not rise above his antagonism, quoting Gandhi's view on caste with what even an admirer admits was 'venomous disdain and contempt'.[84] Ambedkar concluded his scathing appraisal of the social, political, and psychological consequences of Gandhi's faith in the Hindu varna system with the devastating words: 'Democratic society cannot be indifferent to such consequences. But Gandhism does not mind these consequences in the least.'[85]

This criticism from the present writer comes from one who, on the key question of the Mahatma's romanticized idealism about self-reliant village republics in India versus the enlightened urban modernism of Ambedkar, comes down firmly on the latter's side. Gandhi called modern cities an 'excrescence' that

---

[82] Parekh, 'The Intellectual and Political Legacy of B. R. Ambedkar', in Rathore, *B.R. Ambedkar: The Quest for Justice*, pp. 25–26.

[83] *The Collected Works of Mahatma Gandhi*, Vol. 84, New Delhi: Publications Division, Government of India, 1999, p. 272.

[84] Aakash Singh Rathore, *Ambedkar's Preamble: A Secret History of the Constitution of India*, New Delhi: Penguin Random House, 2020, p. 18.

[85] Aakash Singh Rathore in Begari, *B. R. Ambedkar and Social Transformation*, p. 35.

'served at the present moment the evil purpose of draining the life-blood of the villages'. Ambedkar disagreed: he considered, as we have seen from a Dalit point of view, Gandhi's ideal village to be 'a sink of localism, a den of ignorance, narrow-mindedness and communalism'. As he explained it:

> Indian villages represent a kind of colonialism of the Hindus designed to exploit the Untouchables. The Untouchables have no rights. They are there only to wait, serve and submit. They are there to do or to die. They have no rights because they are outside the village republic and because they are outside the so-called republic, they are outside the Hindu fold. This is a vicious circle. But this is a fact which cannot be gainsaid.[86]

In his focus on social justice, Ambedkar preferred to rest his hopes not on the village but the city. Ambedkar argued that 'strange though it may seem, [the] industrialisation of India is the soundest remedy for the agricultural problems of India'. In Ambedkar's view, industrialization was the best means of weaning surplus agricultural labour into employment outside of agriculture, thus taking the pressure off land and preventing its fragmentation, while developing the necessary technology and processes of mechanization to increase agricultural productivity and incomes. His emphasis was accordingly on urbanism, modernism, and industrialization as the way forward for India, a far cry from the self-governing village republics that Gandhi envisaged in *Hind Swaraj*. On this, in my view, Ambedkar was right and Gandhi was wrong, and it was the former's point of view that prevailed; but that made it all the more incumbent on the winner to show magnanimity to the great man whose ideas he had vanquished in the Constituent Assembly. As an admirer of Ambedkar, I find it disappointing that he could not rise above

---

[86] Rodrigues, 'Outside the Fold', in *The Essential Writings of B. R. Ambedkar*, p. 331.

his own bitterness to show any generosity of spirit towards the Mahatma.

The fourth and final criticism that must be aired is of Ambedkar's statism—his absolute faith in the institutions and mechanisms of a strong central government to bring about the empowerment of the Dalits, to the exclusion of the moral and spiritual reforms that Gandhi had sought, and without heed to the need to bring people along with him in the adventure of changing time-old traditions and practices. Ambedkar saw the state as an instrument to transform society, using the coercive instrument of the law; the state, for him, was the agent of enlightenment, whereas Indian society was regressive and backward. His disdain for village India made him a centralizer, directing top-down transformation to overcome the prejudices and hidebound ways of the ossified villages. His omission of local self-government from the provisions of the Constitution was pointed out at the time, by Gandhians in the Constituent Assembly, but the lacuna was only effectively addressed with the Seventy-third and Seventy-fourth Constitutional Amendments in the early 1990s. Greater empowerment of elected village councils is surely the right way to achieve emancipation in a liberal democracy, whereas, as a perceptive scholar has pointed out, 'to turn to the Westernized social and political elite as the sole agent of social transformation was not only to condemn the vast majority of Indians to the status of passive objects but also to alienate them from the State and weaken its legitimacy in their eyes'. [87]

The image of Ambedkar, in his suit and tie, issuing 'progressive' modern diktats to ignorant dhoti-clad bigots covered in the dust and grime of their rural backwardness is not a reassuring one, evoking the authoritarian fantasies of other modernizing autocracies, rather than the evolutionary change,

---

[87] Rathore, *Ambedkar's Preamble*, p. 18.

anchored in local realities, that a democracy requires for its development. Ambedkar once even suggested that the best way to summarily eradicate the caste system and untouchability was if India could produce an Atatürk or a Mussolini.[88] It was this kind of thinking that lay behind his proposals to get the state to regulate the theology and practice of the Hindu religion, an appalling idea that reveals the extent to which he allowed his obsession with annihilating caste to erode his better judgement.

And yet none of these criticisms can vitiate the scale of his achievements described in this book. They are the human flaws of a driven human being, animated by passion and outrage, who overcame overwhelming odds to expand the realm of the possible for his people. This also required a pragmatism that, as Jaffrelot points out,[89] was part of the secret to his political resilience: every time that he seemed outflanked or isolated, he found a way back into the national discourse. Sidelined in the elections of 1946, he was in the cabinet the following year; seemingly bypassed by history when his opponents in the Congress won Independence, he led the drafting of the Constitution; thwarted on the Hindu Code Bill and out of government, he changed the conversation about Dalits with his conversion to Buddhism. Even death neither stopped his prolific output nor ended his influence; he has grown ever larger in the national imagination since.

AMBEDKAR TODAY

As the social scientist Badri Narayan has observed, 'If Babasaheb Ambedkar were alive today, he would probably have been quite amazed to see how political parties with completely different ideologies are vying with each other to associate themselves with

---

[88] Parekh, 'The Intellectual and Political Legacy of B. R. Ambedkar', in Rathore, *B.R. Ambedkar: The Quest for Justice*, p. 28.
[89] Jaffrelot, *Dr. Ambedkar and Untouchability*, p. 159.

his persona.'[90] For Narayan, Ambedkar's life and work have been reinvented and reimagined 'to occupy a larger space in the public imagination' than ever before. Narayan attributes this to Dalits becoming more politically aware than in the past and political parties using their proclaimed commitment to Ambedkar's vision as their instrument of political outreach to Dalit voters. Yashica Dutt, echoing Ananya Vajpeyi, argues that it is precisely because he opposed them: 'his blunt analyses about complex power structures were too dangerous for the upper-caste establishment', and it was safer to neutralize Ambedkar by appropriating him:

> The BJP, known for its astute political strategy, discovered that Ambedkar was a clear and direct path to Dalits and their votes. But they couldn't possibly risk engaging with his ideas, which directly attack their foundational principles and would not be palatable to the powerful upper-caste vote bank. So they appropriated Ambedkar but did not discuss his philosophy or his criticism of the established power structure. By aligning with Ambedkar's image, which has been a symbol for Dalit rights, they would like to project themselves as a political party that stands for equality. But most political parties want nothing to do with his ideas.[91]

The decision of the Aam Aadmi Party government elected in Punjab in 2022 to display portraits of Dr Ambedkar (as well as of the freedom fighter Bhagat Singh) in government offices was one more example of the iconic status he has now attained in India. It can, of course, be suggested that the decision was merely a cynical ploy for the Dalit vote, which is estimated at some 16.6 per cent of the electorate. But that too represents a significant change from Ambedkar's day, when Dalits found themselves

---

[90] Badri Narayan, 'BR buzz: How Ambedkar Jayanti celebrations became a political contest', *Times of India*, 10 April 2022.
[91] Dutt, *Coming Out As Dalit*, pp. 125–26.

being taken for granted, especially since they were outnumbered by caste Hindu voters even in the constituencies reserved for Dalit candidates. Today, the Left parties, the right-wing BJP, the centrist Congress, and the non-ideological AAP have all expressed their admiration for Ambedkar, decades after mainstream politicians doing so might have made a difference in his own life.

Strikingly, Ambedkar might well have derived greater satisfaction from the birth of the Bahujan Samaj Party (BSP), led by Kanshi Ram and later Mayawati, which established the principle that Dalits would be better off representing themselves through a party dedicated principally to their own advancement, rather than by seeking benefits from mainstream political parties vying for their votes. Indeed, the BSP formula has resulted in Mayawati being elected three times as chief minister of India's most populous state, Uttar Pradesh—a Dalit woman in command of the government of India's Hindi heartland, something unthinkable for perhaps 3,000 years before her ascent to power in Aryavrata at the cusp of the twenty-first century. It was a vindication of Ambedkar's conviction that Dalits needed to assert themselves politically, rather than depend on the grace and favour of the 'upper' castes. But he himself was never able, through any of the parties he established, to achieve meaningful political power—except as a parliamentarian appointed by the larger nationalist party, the Congress.

Similarly, in his own lifetime, the combative Ambedkar had never been regarded as a contender for high national honours; yet in 1990, thirty-four years after his death, the minority government of Prime Minister V. P. Singh, anxious to shore up its levels of political support, awarded him the country's highest honour, the Bharat Ratna.

Ambedkar statues continue to proliferate around the country, but they are getting bigger and more majestic as the competitive adulation of Ambedkar in statuary proceeds apace. The 'Statue of Knowledge', a 70-foot-tall statue of Ambedkar, was unveiled in Latur city, Maharashtra, in April 2022.[92] Soon followed an announcement from the state of Telangana that a 125-foot-tall statue of Ambedkar would soon be installed at NTR Gardens near Hussain Sagar Lake in Hyderabad.[93] Maharashtra, not to be outdone, declared that work on a memorial to Ambedkar in his native Mumbai was 'progressing smoothly and the world-class monument is expected to be completed by March 2024'.[94] With a budget of ₹1,000 crore and made of bronze and steel, it will be the tallest Ambedkar statue in the world at 450 feet, standing as high as a fifty-storey building and weighing 80 tons. The site will feature other Ambedkar memorabilia and a replica of Chawdar Lake, the site of his first agitation.[95] (There is already a more modest memorial in Airoli in Navi Mumbai, which also features a library dedicated to Ambedkar's life and works.)[96]

On 19 May 2022, the state government of Andhra Pradesh went one better and announced it wished to rename its Konaseema district as the Dr B. R. Ambedkar Konaseema district.[97] The government has issued a notification inviting objections and suggestions from the people residing within Konaseema on the proposal to rename the district. It is considered highly unlikely that anyone would object. It is only a matter of time before another state government decides to take the next step and name an entire city after Ambedkar.

---

[92] PTI, 'Maharashtra: "Statue of Knowledge" Dedicated to Dr Ambedkar to Be Unveiled in Latur on April', *News 18*, 8 April 2022.
[93] '125-ft-tall B.R. Ambedkar statue in Hyderabad by December', *Deccan Chronicle*, 14 April 2022.
[94] 'Ambedkar memorial in Mumbai to be ready by March 2024', *daijiworld. com*, 12 May 2022.
[95] 'Work starts in city on 125 feet tall Ambedkar statue', *Deccan Chronicle*, 9 September 2021.
[96] Amit Srivastava, 'Navi Mumbai: "Keep Dr. Babasaheb Ambedkar's memorial big for future generations", says Atomic scientist Dr. Anil Kakodkar', *Free Press Journal*, 5 May 2022.
[97] Express News Service, 'Move to rename Konaseema district after Ambedkar', *New Indian Express*, 19 May 2022.

All this would been greeted with incredulity in India just fifty years ago, but it is a measure of how much Ambedkar's stature has grown. The attitude of India's newly dominant Hindutva movement towards Ambedkar has also evolved. Initially dismissive of him for his savage remarks on Hinduism and his mobilization of the Dalits—which went against the Rashtriya Swayamsevak Sangh (RSS)'s emphasis on Hindu unity—the Hindutva movement was relieved when he chose to convert to Buddhism, an Indic faith, rather than to Islam or Christianity, and began speaking of him with respect after his death. Two prominent RSS ideologues, Dattopant Thengadi and Dr Krishna Gopal, even authored books on Ambedkar. The RSS duly celebrated Ambedkar's birth centenary, and Mahatma Jyotiba Phule's death centenary, in 1990, praising them for their efforts to reform Hindu society and rid it of discriminatory practices and injustices. By the time of his 125th birthday, the BJP was in full celebration mode, and their attempts to appropriate him have proceeded apace, with Prime Minister Modi frequently invoking Ambedkar in his speeches and BJP grandees conspicuous by their presence at local 'Ambedkar Jayanti' celebrations on his birth anniversary each year. In 2022, the BJP extended the observance to an entire 'social justice week' commencing on Ambedkar's birthday.

Many public institutions in India are named in his honour, including such diverse entities as the Dr Babasaheb Ambedkar International Airport in Nagpur,[98] the Dr B. R. Ambedkar National Institute of Technology, Jalandhar,[99] and Ambedkar University in Delhi.[100] In June 2022, the Delhi government announced its decision to replace the word 'Harijan' in the names of the capital's streets and colonies with the name 'Dr

---

[98] 'Nagpur Airport being renamed', *The Hindu*, 15 October 2005.
[99] Official website of NITJ.
[100] Delhi Gazette notification, available on the official website of Government of National Capital Territory of Delhi.

Ambedkar' instead.[101] India Post issued special postage stamps dedicated to his birthday in 1966, 1973, 1991, 2001, and 2013, and featured him on other stamps in 2009, 2015, 2016, and 2017. But even here there was a perception that they had acted much later than they should have. 'The growth of Ambedkar stamps is more an outcome of people's aspiration and public pressure from the ground up rather than the government's own initiative,' one critic commented.[102]

The adulation of Ambedkar has now crossed borders. Bhikhu Parekh has remarked on the contrast between the global image of Martin Luther King and that of Ambedkar, whom he considers the 'deeper thinker' with 'a greater impact on his community and country than Martin Luther King had on his'. On 30 June 2021, Gray's Inn inaugurated a room named after its former alumnus, Ambedkar, and unveiled a radical portrait of him by artist David Newens, based on a photograph by the legendary Margaret Bourke-White. In 2022, Ambedkar's 131st birthday on 14 April was celebrated across the globe, sometimes along with memorializing his forerunner, the other anti-caste icon, Mahatma Jyotiba Phule. Thus, Canada's British Columbia province has declared April as 'Dalit History Month'.[103] Nepal's first president presided over that country's commemoration of Ambedkar's life.[104] Nepal and India jointly decided to establish a Dr Bhimrao Ambedkar Chair for Buddhist Studies in Lumbini Buddhist University.[105] Celebrations occurred in Dubai[106] and

---

[101] 'Delhi to replace word "Harijan" with "Dr Ambedkar" in names of colonies, streets: Minister Gautam', *Economic Times*, 2 June 2022.

[102] Nidhima Taneja, 'Ambedkar was latecomer in world of stamps where Nehru's and Gandhi's "could fill floors"', *The Print*, 8 June 2022.

[103] 'Canada: Province of British Columbia: A Proclamation', available on British Columbia official website.

[104] Shirish B. Pradhan, 'Ambedkar's birth anniversary observed in Nepal', *The Print*, 13 April 2022.

[105] 'India, Nepal agree to set up Dr Bhimrao Ambedkar Chair at Lumbini Buddhist University', *edexlive.com*, 16 May 2022.

[106] 'Dr BR Ambedkar Jayanti celebrated with fervor in Dubai', *ANI*, 25 April 2022.

in the United Kingdom.[107] In Jamaica, visiting Indian president Ram Nath Kovind inaugurated Dr Ambedkar Avenue in downtown Kingston. 'Let us always remember that icons like Dr Ambedkar and Marcus Garvey cannot be limited to just one nation or community,' Kovind, a Dalit himself, said on the occasion. 'Their message of equality for all and their appeal to end all forms of discrimination has universal resonance. Therefore, Dr Ambedkar's message is as relevant to Indians as it is to Jamaicans and to people in every part of the world.'[108] The Dalit scholar Bhalchandra Mungekar hails Ambedkar as 'one of the greatest thinkers of renewal worldwide'.[109] In the United States, where Isabel Wilkerson had referred to Ambedkar as 'the Martin Luther King of India',[110] the states of Colorado and Michigan in the US declared a 'Dr B.R. Ambedkar Equity Day', echoed in India by the state of Tamil Nadu calling it a 'Day of Equality' while the state of Uttar Pradesh preferred to proclaim his birthday the 'Day of Social Harmony'.

Such commemorations are proliferating by the year in India, though it is clearly open for debate as to what extent they represent any genuine commitment to his vision and ideals rather than mere tokenism for political gain. In the Dalit community, he is revered as a legendary hero, the subject of folk tales, dramas, and ballads; Dalit writers like Suraj Yengde have recounted how grandmothers told stories of Ambedkar to inspire little Dalit children.[111] For other communities, however, he is a less significant figure. Still, the historian Sunil Khilnani considers Ambedkar 'the founding father most meaningful to

---

[107]'Indian High Commissioner to the UK pays tribute to B R Ambedkar and Lord Basaveshwara in London', *The Print*, 3 May 2022.

[108]'President Kovind inaugurates street named after Ambedkar in Jamaican capital', *The Print*, 17 May 2022.

[109]Bhalchandra Mungekar (ed.), *The Essential Ambedkar*, New Delhi: Rupa Publications, 2017, p. xii.

[110]Wilkerson, *Caste*, p. 32

[111]Yengde, *Caste Matters*, pp. 123–24.

ordinary Indians today'.[112] Student bodies like the Ambedkarite
Students' Association (ASA), which was formed on the Hyderabad
University campus in 1994, the Birsa-Ambedkar-Phule Students'
Association (BAPSA) at Jawaharlal Nehru University in New
Delhi, and the Ambedkar–Periyar Study Circle at IIT Madras
have helped disseminate Ambedkar's ideas on campus, fight
student union elections, and win new adherents to his vision.
Almost in confirmation of his resonance with a new generation,
a new genre of 'Dalit rap' has emerged on India's music scene,
as young Dalit rappers like Mahi Ghane, Sumeet Samos, and
Rekoil Chafe belt out numbers extolling the life and work
of Ambedkar.[113] An ambitious young rapper from Odisha's
poverty-stricken rural district of Kalahandi who calls himself
Dule Rocker, after being exposed to the writings of Ambedkar,
has declared that he wants to further celebrate the vision of
the constitutional stalwart through his music, and plans a new
album 'to take forward Ambedkar's legacy'.[114] Meanwhile,
Dalit literature has acquired significant standing, starting with
Marathi where writers like Namdeo Dhasal, Raja Dhale, and
J. V. Pawar have acquired considerable eminence and popular
success, which has spread into other Indian languages and,
increasingly, in translation into English as well.

LOOKING BACK ON A LIFE: A CODA

Ambedkar's complex life and monumental achievements, as
summarized in this book, lend themselves to no easy distillation.
Still, at the risk of repetition, it may be useful to pull together,
in this concluding section, the principal themes and strands we
have discussed.

---

[112] Khilnani, 'Ambedkar: Building Palaces on Dung Heaps', *Incarnations*,
p. 468.
[113] Rishabh Jain, 'Anti-caste rap: A hip-hop revolution in the making in India',
TRT World, 17 May 2022.
[114] Akanksha Mishra, 'Annihilation of Caste, Kalahandi rapper Dule Rocker
plans album "to take forward Ambedkar's legacy"', *Scroll.in*, 4 July 2021.

Dr Bhimrao Ambedkar was a self-made man in the profoundest sense of that term. Even his name was his own creation, for he was born a Sakpal, but took a name based on that of his village (Ambavade) as Maharashtrian Brahmins did. He was born a Hindu Mahar, but died a Buddhist. He wore Western suits in rejection of the traditional trappings of a society that had for so long enslaved his people. It was he who forced India to confront the reality of discrimination by facing up to the reality of caste oppression. And he did so bluntly, in a manner which youngsters today would call 'in your face'. Not for him the mealy-mouthed platitudes of the well-meaning: he was prepared to rage against the injustice of social discrimination, and to do so in every forum available to him. It was an attitude that Indian society was not prepared for, but at a time when Indians were fighting for their freedom from foreign rule, it was both appropriate and necessary that Indians should fight equally against domestic oppression.

Ambedkar rejected what he saw as the patronizing indulgence of the Gandhian approach to untouchability. Infuriated by what he saw as Mahatma Gandhi's condescension towards the untouchables and his presumption in claiming to speak for them without having ever experienced what they daily endured, Ambedkar had little patience for the Father of the Nation. The Mahatma called them 'Harijans'—children of God. Arrant nonsense, said Ambedkar—aren't we all children of God? He used, instead, Marathi and Hindi words for the 'excluded' (Bahishkrit), the 'oppressed' (Dalit), and the 'silent' (mook). He publicly burned the *Manusmriti*, the ancient lawbook of caste Hindus. He was an equal opportunity offender, condemning caste-consciousness in the Muslim community with as much vehemence as he savaged the Hindus. Ambedkar was an enemy of cant and superstition, an iconoclast who had contempt for traditions that he felt deserved no sanctity.

None of his battles were easy. As a nationalist, he was

sensitive to the charge that he was dividing Indians at a time when they needed to be united against the British. When he demanded separate electorates for his people, Mahatma Gandhi undertook a fast unto death until, as we have seen, an unconvinced Ambedkar, fearing mass reprisals if the Mahatma died, caved in. Gandhi, who abhorred untouchability, believed that the answer lay in the social awakening of caste Hindus rather than in building walls of separation. Partition may well have helped the Dalits by making the Constituent Assembly more receptive to the protection of individual rights, especially of people belonging to minority groups, giving Ambedkar the chance to shape the Constitution India enjoys today, with extensive built-in protections for the rights of citizens, and especially for his own community. Yet Ambedkar, who lived with the daily reality of caste discrimination, was still not convinced that the entrenched practices of traditional Hinduism could ever disappear. In the end he opted out of the religion altogether, embracing the ethics of equality that Buddhism embodied.

Buddhism also inspired his faith in democracy, which infused his role as the Father of India's Constitution. Whereas some saw Ambedkar, with his three-piece suit and formal English, as a Westernized exponent of Occidental constitutional systems, he was inspired far more by the democratic practices of ancient India, in particular the Buddhist sanghas. As chairman of the Drafting Committee of the Constituent Assembly, Ambedkar argued that the constitutional roots of Indian republicanism ran deep. He remarked that some ancient Indian states were republics, notably those of the Licchavis who ruled northern Bihar and lower Nepal in the sixth and fifth centuries BCE (around the Buddha's time), the Mallas, centred in the city of Kushinagara, and the Vajji (or Vriji) confederation, based in the city of Vaishali. Early Indian republicanism can be traced back to the independent gana sanghas, which appear to have existed between the sixth and fourth centuries BCE. The Greek historian Diodorus Siculus, describing India at the time of Alexander the Great's invasion in 326 BCE (though he was writing two centuries later), recorded that independent and democratic republics existed in India.[115] They seemed, however, to include a monarch or a raja, and a deliberative assembly that met regularly and discussed all major state decisions. The gana sanghas had full financial, administrative, and judicial authority and elected the raja, who therefore was not a hereditary monarch. The raja reported to the assembly and, in some states, was assisted by a council of other nobles. Ambedkar was inspired by such precedents.

Ambedkar's life and career threw him into the maelstrom of two simultaneous freedom struggles, against British colonial rule and against untouchability and caste oppression. He did so by the unusual expedient for someone of his caste—acquiring a world-class education, arguably more impressive than any of his peers in Indian public life before or since, and using it to guide his work and positions. Rising from a background of poverty, he naturally identified with the downtrodden, but with his education he also aspired to standards and accomplishments different from most of his contemporaries. From finding inspiration in the Western ideals of 'liberty, equality and fraternity' that the French Revolution had bequeathed the world (rather than in the Hindu traditions and values that inspired Gandhi and others, but which Ambedkar identified with the subjugation of his people), to his obsession with acquiring books for his ever-expanding library (even spending money his family needed for food to buy books instead), Ambedkar was distinctively unlike most Indian politicians of the period. Still, his nationalism had Indian roots, and it was striking that, with growing conviction,

---

[115] Diodorus Siculus, *Bibliotheca Historica*, Vol. II., translated by C. H. Oldfather, Library of History: Loeb Classical Library, Cambridge, MA: Harvard University Press, 1935.

he located those Western Enlightenment ideas in an authentically Indian tradition, that of the Buddha and his message.

Ambedkar's early enquiry into the origins and evolution of the caste system made him something of a pioneering sociologist. His explanation of the reasons for the caste system surviving so much longer than other systems of hierarchy across the world remains a powerful and original insight. He argued that the caste system owed its durability to a unique structure of 'graded inequality'[116] that embraced the totality of society; since every caste and sub-caste had a defined place in the structure, no caste ever contemplated making common cause with a caste below it to overthrow the system, for fear of losing its own privileges. As a result, discrimination was internalized as much by its victims as its beneficiaries, on 'an ascending scale of reverence and a descending scale of contempt', to the point where it was accepted as the natural order of things, and required little or no physical coercion to enforce. This remains true decades after Ambedkar made his profound observation, since caste groups have shown no great capacity or inclination to unite against the assumptions of the existing social hierarchy. Instead, each group has tried to mobilize for itself, often flaunting its hierarchical disabilities as an argument for greater political clout. Caste, which Nehru had believed would disappear from Indian life, has become even more entrenched than ever. As one person sardonically observed to me, 'these days you can't go forward unless you're a backward'.

Inspired by Ambedkar's teachings, Isabel Wilkerson has explained the impact of caste in these terms:

> Caste is the granting or withholding of respect, status, honor, attention, privileges, resources, benefit of the doubt,

---

[116] Anup Hiwrale, 'Caste: Understanding the Nuances from Ambedkar's Expositions', *Journal of Social Inclusion Studies*, Vol. 6, Issue 1, 1 June 2020, pp. 78–96.

and human kindness to someone on the basis of their perceived rank or standing in the hierarchy.... Any action or structure that seeks to limit, hold back, or put someone in a defined ranking, seeks to keep someone in their place by elevating or denigrating that person on the basis of their perceived category, can be seen as casteism. Casteism is the investment in keeping the hierarchy as it is in order to maintain your own ranking, advantage, privilege, or to elevate yourself above others or keep others beneath you. For those in the marginalized castes, casteism can mean seeking to keep those on your disfavored rung from gaining on you, to curry the favor and remain in the good graces of the dominant caste, all of which serve to keep the structure intact.... Like the cast on a broken arm, like the cast in a play, a caste system holds everyone in a fixed place.[117]

Reading Ambedkar is essential for his insights into the sociology, the psychology, the economics, and the architecture of Indian democracy, but tracing his actions, as we have tried to do, is equally vital. Ambedkar's political activism included demanding access for his people to water from a public well, burning the *Manusmriti* to protest the justification for his community's oppression, and challenging the assumptions and methods of the greatest nationalist leader of that era, Mahatma Gandhi. He rejected Gandhi's Hindu reformism without being seduced by the alternative of Communist revolution; instead he sought liberation through law, social awakening through democratic debate, and nation-building through a Constitution. He rejected the Mahatma's millenarian vision of restoring 'Ram Rajya' in free India because he associated this mythical Golden Age with the sanctification of his people's humiliations.

As a result, Ambedkar remains the first and most important articulator of a non-Hindu conception of Indian nationalism,

---

[117] Wilkerson, *Caste*, pp. 70–71.

which makes current attempts by the Hindutva movement to appropriate him all the more hypocritical. Ambedkar deplored the religious sanctity accorded to caste discrimination, the lack of any record of shame or regret in Hindu literature over untouchability, the absence of any serious revolt against the practice by any major upper-caste figure and, by implication, Hindu society's undemocratic nature as reflected in its internalization of inequality and untouchability. 'If Hindu Raj does become a fact,' he bitterly exclaimed, 'it will, no doubt, be the greatest calamity for this country. No matter what the Hindus say, Hinduism is a menace to liberty, equality and fraternity. On that account it is incompatible with democracy. Hindu Raj must be prevented at any cost.'[118] The greatest Hindu of the age, Mahatma Gandhi, nonetheless, had expressed 'the highest regard' for Ambedkar, remarking: 'He has every right to be bitter. That he does not break our head is an act of self-restraint on his part.'[119](Interestingly enough, Ambedkar would have found himself on the same side as the Hindutva icon V. D. Savarkar on one issue today. Savarkar, as a rationalist reformer, would have had little patience for the cow vigilantism that those who swear by his doctrines have been practising in recent years, assaulting Muslims and Dalits for allegedly transporting or consuming the holy animal. Savarkar had urged Hindus to care for the cow because of its utility (upayuktavadi), rather than worship it. 'Why are cow's urine and dung purifying while even the shadow of a man like Ambedkar is defiling?'[120] Savarkar asked pointedly in terms that none of his admirers in the BJP would care to recall today.)

  At the same time, Ambedkar, as a lawyer and constitutionalist, was perhaps more of a conformist than his radical reputation

---

[118] Harish K. Puri, 'Ambedkar had warned about Indian democracy's fragility. He must be heeded', *Indian Express*, 15 April 2022.

[119] Ibid.

[120] Mukul Dube, 'Read what VD Savarkar wrote: Care for cows, do not worship them', *Scroll.in*, 20 October 2015.

suggests. He wanted to reform the disabilities built into Indian society precisely because he foresaw the distinct possibility of a counter-revolution by the oppressed, in reaction to the paradox of political equality coexisting with social inequality and centralization of economic power. 'We must remove this contradiction at the earliest possible moment or else those who suffer from inequality will blow up the structure of political democracy which this Assembly has so laboriously built up,' he ominously warned the Constituent Assembly. Suraj Yengde similarly echoes the same concern when he writes, 'Simply put, the hope of the state continues to function adjacent to Dalit hope, both intangible and virtuous. The day Dalit hope ends, the state's hope for Dalits will end. This end is to the peril of the Indian state and all who cohabit in it.'[121]

This was why Ambedkar constantly expressed fear that the democracy he had helped create in the Constitution could be undemocratically transformed: 'It is quite possible for this new-born democracy to retain its form, but give place to dictatorship in fact. If there was a landslide of popular support, the danger of that possibility becoming an actuality is much greater.'[122] These words have a haunting resonance in an India that, under Hindutva rule, is increasingly being described today as an 'electoral autocracy'.

As one who had first-hand experience of caste discrimination and who had suffered under its privations, Ambedkar knew how important it was to struggle for justice—but by education and temperament he wanted that struggle to be within the framework of the law and the Constitution. His work as a lawyer sought to establish a robust legal and constitutional framework—both for equality, with guaranteed rights for the dispossessed and marginalized, and also for the methods by

---

[121] Yengde, *Caste Matters*, p. 27.
[122] 'Why BR Ambedkar's three warnings in his last speech to the Constituent Assembly resonate even today', *Scroll.in*, 26 January 2016.

which the dispossessed and marginalized could fight for their rights. As a constitutionalist, Ambedkar viewed the law as a source of strength and support for those fighting for equality and justice; their rights, and their right to struggle for these rights, would be constitutionally protected. This made him more of a conciliator than a revolutionary, but it was in keeping with the spirit of accommodation that had often marked his political choices, most notably over the Poona Pact.

Ambedkar's surrender to Gandhi on the Poona Pact and the constitutional arrangement that reserves seats for Scheduled Castes and Tribes but requires a Dalit candidate to be elected by all voters—in practice a non-Dalit majority—is now being questioned by Dalit activists. Dalit scholar Raja Sekhar Vundru, for instance, argues that the current electoral system has failed to advance the interests of the Dalits in a majoritarian polity.[123] Gandhi placed Hindu unity above the Dalit interest in electing their own leaders. But the result is that since Dalits do not form a majority in any constituency, and in effect a majority of non-Dalits decides which Dalits will win, Dalit candidates and parties are forced to make compromises with non-Dalit interests, rather than articulating their own.

Though the Poona Pact and subsequently Ambedkar's affirmative action provisions in the Constitution provided new opportunities for Dalits in education and employment, Vundru and others argue that it has diluted effective Dalit political representation by placing their true leaders at the mercy of non-Dalit parties and voters, including the upper castes. After all, there could no greater proof of their argument than the fact that Ambedkar himself was twice defeated in the Lok Sabha elections as the candidate of a Dalit party and had to be elected to the Rajya Sabha with Congress support. How could Dalit leaders whose survival in politics requires them to

---

[123] Raja Sekhar Vundru, 'Expanding the Possibilities', in Raju, *The Dalit Truth*, pp. 21–38.

be beholden to 'ruling-class parties' effectively safeguard the interests of the most vulnerable? How could Dalits having to contest against candidates of non-Dalit parties with their immense financial resources and non-Dalit 'vote-banks', hold their own? Interestingly enough, the Executive Committee of the Scheduled Caste Federation had passed a resolution in August 1955 asking for the abolition of the system of reserved seats, because, in Jaffrelot's words, they 'tended to isolate the Untouchable electorate and hampered efforts to tap the votes of other social groups'.[124] While independent India has seen Dalit presidents, chief ministers, and ministers in the central and state governments, mainly but not solely from the Congress Party, the question is asked: 'Have the Dalit elected representatives been able to secure equity and justice for the Dalits?'[125]

Six decades after Ambedkar's death, the more heinous aspects of the caste system have mellowed considerably, thanks to the doors he pushed open, the affirmative action he instituted, and the social changes he made possible. Dalits have recorded various 'firsts'—the first Dalit president (and the second, now followed by the first from a Scheduled Tribe), the first Dalit deputy prime minister, the first Dalit chief justice, the first Dalit billionaire. And yet the condition of Dalits in India today has not improved nearly as much as Ambedkar might have hoped. This summary by K. Raju in 2022 says it all:

> The majority of Dalits lead troubled lives as landless labourers, small-scale farmers, artisans in villages, manual labourers and hawkers working in the informal sector and living in slums in urban areas. Seventy-four per cent of Dalit households live in rural areas, where the per-household land area they own on an average is less

---

[124] Jaffrelot, *Dr. Ambedkar and Untouchability*, p. 85.
[125] Raju, *The Dalit Truth*, pp. xxi–xxii.

than 0.3 hectares—most of them are landless according to the 2011 census. Untouchability continues to thrive. Atrocities against the Dalits are on the rise. Access to quality education is still a distant dream for the Dalits. Successful industrialists and entrepreneurs who are Dalits are, unsurprisingly, few and far between. Even after the implementation of agrarian land reforms, most of the Dalits continue to be landless agriculture labourers. Most of them continue to struggle on a day-to-day basis as unorganized workers. Educated Dalit youths face entry barriers to enter the private sector. Employment opportunities in the government sector are dwindling, and reservation in the private sector is a far cry. The Dalits' share of political power is very nominal, considering the portfolios allotted to them in the ministries of Central or state governments. Adequate budgetary resources are not being provided to bring the Dalits on a par with the rest of the society.... The Dalits' share of ownership of the nation's wealth is far lower than their share in the population.[126]

Or as Yashica Dutt put it graphically in her searing memoir *Coming Out As Dalit*: 'Our Dalitness is imprinted onto us through the burned bodies of our children, suicides of our PhD scholars and college students, rapes of young girls and women, asphyxiation of our manual scavengers and "honour killings" of lovers.'[127] Sexual assaults on Dalit women remain rife. Caste, wrote Yengde, 'is a measure of destruction, pillage, drudgery, servitude, bondage, unaccounted rape, massacre, arson, incarceration, police brutality and loss of moral virtuosity for 300 million Indian Untouchables.'[128]

---

[126] Ibid., pp. xxviii, xxxvii.

[127] Dutt, *Coming Out As Dalit*, p. xi.

[128] Yengde, *Caste Matters*, p. 7. There is a searing Twitter thread listing in detail Dalit massacres in independent India: https://twitter.com/lokeshbag67/status/1547534467866456064?s=20&t=vbFeAyraAKktBawxjVNu5Q

Indeed, stories of caste-discrimination-related horrors abound in the media. In 2006, forty-year-old Surekha Bhotmange and her seventeen-year-old daughter Priyanka, a twelfth-grade topper, were mercilessly raped, beaten, and killed by upper-caste assailants in a village not far from Nagpur, in broad daylight; Priyanka's brothers, aged nineteen and twenty-one, were also brutally beaten and killed. 'Had it not been for Dalit activists and a young American reporter who was then interning at the *Times of India*,' Yengde wrote, the story 'would have been completely buried.'[129] Other news stories abound: Shankar, a twenty-two-year-old Dalit from Tamil Nadu, was hacked to death in full public view by the parents of a 'higher' caste girl he married out of love. Dalit youth Pranay Kumar, twenty-three, was beheaded in broad daylight when he walked out of hospital with his twenty-one-year-old pregnant 'upper-caste' spouse in Telangana. Even as this book was being written in 2022, a seventeen-year-old girl was murdered by her father after the family found out that she was in love with a Dalit youth from a neighbouring village in Mysuru.[130]

Dalit portrayals in popular cinema are limited, marginal, and largely stereotyped. Under-representation of Dalits in mainstream journalism restricts the community's ability to bring its stories to national attention. 'Caste India is yet to democratize its institutions,' observes Yengde. 'The institutions of films, academia, theatre, business, religion and bureaucracy remain enamoured with caste pathology, imposing physical and mental harm upon the lower-caste subjects in the graded hierarchy. This affects the ability to understand the Indian problem, which is a caste problem—therefore, caste matters.'[131]

Caste matters, but it is often hidden behind a veil of denial.

[129] Ibid., p. 14.
[130] Ananth Shreyas, 'Father Kills 17-Year-Old Daughter for Relationship With Dalit Youth in Mysuru', *The Quint*, 8 June 2022.
[131] Yengde, *Caste Matters*, p. 24.

'For some of us being Dalit means a lifetime of discrimination and abuse,' Dutt writes:

> [T]o escape discrimination and become part of society, which is still mostly upper-caste, we have to leave some of our Dalitness behind. We leave behind our food, our songs, our culture and our last names, so we can be 'better' and 'purer', more upper caste and less Dalit. We don't leave our Dalitness behind just so that we can blend in more easily. We do it because sometimes that's our only option. We change our last names so we can get jobs and rent houses. We lie about our caste so our friends, classmates and teachers don't think we are lesser than them. We learn their habits so no one can use our Dalitness to make fun of us.[132]

It is instructive that the Scheduled Castes and Scheduled Tribes (Prevention of Atrocities) Act, 1989, lists in excruciating detail the types of atrocities against Dalits which would be considered crimes under the Act. These acts were commonly perpetrated against Dalits and their listing in the legislation, according to sociologist Meena Radhakrishna, 'is an acknowledgement by the state that very specific kinds of barbarities are [still] committed against the SC and ST people'.[133] In January 2016, the suicide of a bright Dalit university student, Rohith Vemula, after months of harassment on campus during which he was even denied his stipend for seven months, shook the nation. His suicide note still reverberates in the nation's conscience: 'The value of a man was reduced to his immediate identity and nearest possibility. To a vote. To a number. To a thing. Never was a man treated as a mind. As a glorious thing made up of stardust.... My birth is my fatal accident.'[134]

---

[132] Dutt, *Coming Out As Dalit*, pp. 180–81.
[133] Meena Radhakrishna, 'The Dark Realities of the SC/ST Atrocities Act: An Ethnographic Reading', *The Wire*, 4 April 2018.
[134] 'My Birth is my Fatal Accident: Rohith Vemula's Searing Letter is an Indictment of Social Prejudices', *The Wire*, 17 January 2017.

Strikingly, even areas where progress has been made have provoked a casteist backlash: in 2022, for instance, a woman hockey player was abused with casteist slurs outside her home after the Indian team, for which she was a star player (something unlikely half a century ago), lost a crucial match. Her presence as a Dalit star was only tolerable if she helped India win.[135]

Ambedkar authored two major books specifically on untouchability, *Who Were the Shudras? How They Came to Be the Fourth Varna in the Indo-Aryan Society* (published in 1947) and *Who Were the Untouchables?* (published in 1948; the two books were reprinted together as *Ambedkar 1990*, Vol. 7). In these works, he framed the struggle of the Dalits as not being for themselves alone, but as unifying agents of social change for the vulnerable and marginalized, including labourers and the working class, categories to which many Dalits belonged. At the same time, he had closely studied the question of why untouchability survived in India while institutions like slavery and serfdom had disappeared in other societies. He concluded that the composition of hierarchies in other countries was based on social and economic considerations of class, which were not sacrosanct and changed over time and depending on altered political and economic circumstances, whereas untouchability in India was anchored in the dominant religion and enjoyed divine sanction, making it much less vulnerable to change. Ambedkar realized that the abolition of untouchability and the inclusion of Dalits in public life required religious change and not merely social or economic progress. He tried to argue that Hindu society's own moral fibre and political dynamism would be enhanced by uplifting the morale of the lowest of its members, but ended up leaving Hinduism altogether, considering it to be unreformable.[136]

---

[135] 'Hockey player Vandana Katariya's family faces casteist slurs after Olympic loss', *Scroll.in*, 5 August 2021.
[136] Vundru, 'Expanding the Possibilities', in Raju, *The Dalit Truth*, p. xxx.

This complex vision was reflected in the political thrust of the first party he founded, the Independent Labour Party (ILP). Ambedkar argued that the socialists and communists who claimed to speak for the working class ignored the problems of untouchable workers, who suffered from the double disability of being both untouchable and labourers. Caste, he stressed, was as important as class in representing their interests; he would oppose both Brahminism and capitalism. His second political party, the Scheduled Castes Federation (SCF), though more explicitly formed in 1942 to represent the Dalits and seek recognition for them as prime actors in the debates over a future independent India, also reiterated the caste–class concerns that had animated its predecessor. Ironically, both parties failed to do well electorally, not just because upper-caste voters supported Congress Dalit candidates rather than ILP or SCF ones, but also because of sub-caste divisions within the Dalit community, many of whose members saw these parties as principally serving the interests of Ambedkar's Mahar community rather than other Dalit groups. It was to overcome this perception that Ambedkar created a third party shortly before his death, the Republican Party of India, seeking to represent all Dalit groups and both rural and agrarian outcastes, through a manifesto infused with Buddhist principles. When Ambedkar died, he had not transcended the image of a principally Mahar leader; this he was to do posthumously and triumphantly, becoming the unquestioned symbol of India's 200 million Dalits.

India's then president R. Venkatraman wrote in his introduction to *Ambedkar: The Man and his Message* (1991):

> I have no doubt that, whether we agreed with him or not in many matters, that perseverance, that persistence and that, if I may use the word, sometimes virulence of his opposition to all this did keep the people's mind awake and did not allow them to become complacent about matters which could not be forgotten, and helped in rousing up those

groups in our country which had suffered for so long in the past.... There can be no doubt that the day is not far off when Babasaheb Ambedkar's Dream of 'samata' [equality] will become a reality.[137]

The debate over whether Mahatma Gandhi was right to put the unity of Indians against British imperialism above everything else or whether Ambedkar was justified in his insistence that rectifying the injustice of untouchability took precedence is academic today. The claim of Mahatma Gandhi to represent the Depressed Classes and Ambedkar's demand for Dalit self-representation has been settled in favour of the latter. The Mahatma's view of the indispensability of varnashrama dharma to Hindu society is vindicated by the survival of the caste system in Hindu social practice, but his other ideas have largely passed into obsolescence, honoured only through lip service, whereas it is Ambedkar's legal vision that endures, codified in the Constitution of the republic.

And that vision is his finest legacy. In the perennial tension between communitarian privileges and individual rights, Ambedkar stood squarely on the side of the individual. In the battle between timeless traditions and modern conceptions of social justice, Ambedkar tilted the scales decisively towards the latter. In the contestation between the wielders of power and the drafters of law, Ambedkar carved a triumphant place for enabling change through democracy and legislation. In a fractured and divided Hindu society he gave the Dalits a sense of collective pride and individual self-respect. In so doing, he transformed the lives of millions yet unborn, heaving an ancient civilization into the modern era through the force of his intellect and the power of his pen.

---

[137] Agarwal, 'Introduction', *Dr. B.R. Ambedkar, The Man and His Message*, p. ix.

Acknowledgements

This book required an extensive amount of research and reading, both from Dr Ambedkar's own copious output, and from the vast amounts of diligent scholarship that has been undertaken on his life and work. The task of writing a short, accessible, and yet sufficiently thorough biography would have been impossible to undertake were it not for the invaluable assistance rendered to me by two friends who doubled as researchers, Katherine Abraham and Sheeba Thattil. Prof. Thattil dug up digital copies of many volumes by and on Ambedkar that I might not otherwise have been able to access. Katherine not only identified additional resources but undertook considerable research on her own, including into ancillary subjects ranging beyond the original scope of my own reading, and suggested specific lines of enquiry. Her diligent support in meticulously checking and revising my footnotes and endnotes, and helping me compile the bibliography, make hers an indispensable role in the preparation of this book for a worldwide readership. My vocabulary is inadequate to express the extent of my profound thanks to both of them.

My gratitude also goes, as always, to my brilliant publisher and editor at Aleph, David Davidar, to my diligent and meticulous editor, Aienla Ozukum, and Karishma Koshal, who stewarded this volume to publication. My thanks, too, to Bena Sareen for another terrific cover and Vasundhara Raj Baigra who, with her usual cheerful efficiency, is responsible for the book's marketing and publicity campaign.

Nonetheless, as the author, I remain solely responsible for the contents of the book, and any errors of fact or interpretation should be laid exclusively at my door.

Bibliography

BOOKS

Ambedkar, B. R., *The Annihilation of Caste*, New Delhi: General Press, 2020.

———, *The Evolution of Provincial Finance in British India: A Study in the Provincial Decentralization of Imperial Finance*, 1925.

———, *What Congress and Gandhi Have Done to the Untouchables*, New Delhi: Gautam Book Centre, 2009.

Ambedkar, Savita Bhimrao, *Ambedkarachya Sahavasat*, Mumbai: Dr. Babasaheb Ambedkar Foundation, 2013.

Anand, Mulk Raj, *Untouchable*, New Delhi: Penguin India, 2001.

Bagul, Baburao, *When I Hid My Caste: Stories,* translated by Jerry Pinto, New Delhi: Speaking Tiger, 2018.

Begari, Jagannatham, *B.R. Ambedkar and Social Transformation*: *Revisiting the Philosophy and Reclaiming Social Justice*, New Delhi: Routledge India, 2021.

Byapari, Manoranjan and Mukherjee, Sipra, *Interrogating My Chandal Life: An Autobiography of a Dalit*, New Delhi: SAGE Publications, 2017.

Cabrera, Luis, *The Humble Cosmopolitan: Rights, Diversity, and Trans-state Democracy*, Oxford: Oxford University Press, 2019.

Chadwick, Ruth, *Encyclopedia of Applied Ethics*, Amsterdam: Academic Press, 2012.

Dangle, Arjun (ed.), *Poisoned Bread: Translations from Modern Marathi Dalit Literature*, New Delhi: Orient Blackswan, 2009.

Dhasal, Namdeo, *A Current of Blood*, New Delhi: Navayana, 2019.

Diodorus Siculus, *Bibliotheca Historica, Vol. II.*, translated by C. H. Oldfather, Library of History: Loeb Classical Library, Cambridge, MA: Harvard University Press, 1935.

Dutt, Yashica, *Coming Out As Dalit*, New Delhi: Aleph Book Company, 2019.

Dworkin, Ronald, *Freedom's Law: The Moral Reading of the American Constitution*, Cambridge, MA: Harvard University Press, 1997.

Faustina, Bama, *Karukku*, New Delhi: Oxford University Press, 2014.

Habib, Irfan S. (ed.), *Indian Nationalism: The Essential Writings*, New Delhi: Aleph Book Company, 2017.

Heimsath, Charles Herman, *Indian and Hindu Social Reform Nationalism*, Princeton: Princeton University Press, 2015.

Jadhav, Narendra, *Untouchables: My Family's Triumphant Escape from India's Caste System*, Oakland: University of California Press, 2007.

Jaffrelot, Christophe, *Dr Ambedkar and Untouchability: Analysing and Fighting Caste*, London: Hurst & Company, 2005.

K., Raju (ed.), *The Dalit Truth: The Battles for Realizing Ambedkar's Vision*, New Delhi: Vintage Books, 2022.

Kadam, K. N., *Dr. Babasaheb Ambedkar and the Significance of His Movement: A Chronology*, London: Sangam Books, 1991.

Kandasamy, Meena, *The Gypsy Goddess*, New Delhi: HarperCollins Publishers India, 2014.

Keer, Dhananjay, *Dr. Ambedkar: Life & Mission*, 3rd edition, Bombay: Popular Prakashan, 1971 (repr.).

Khilnani, Sunil, *Incarnations: A History of India in 50 Lives*, New Delhi: Penguin Random House India, 2017.

Khosla, Madhav, *India's Founding Moment: The Constitution of a Most Surprising Democracy*, Cambridge, MA: Harvard University Press, 2019.

Kolge, Nishikant, *Gandhi Against Caste*, New Delhi: Oxford University Press, 2017.

Kunte, B. G. (ed.), *Source Material on Dr Babasaheb Ambedkar and the Movement of Untouchables*, Vol. 1, Bombay: Education Department, Government of Maharashtra, 1970.

McLeod, Jon, *Sovereignty, Power, Control: Politics in the States of Western India, 1916–1947*, Leiden: Brill, 1999, p. 136.

Mohanty, Gopinath, *Harijan: A Novel*, translated by Bikram Das, New Delhi: Aleph Book Company, 2021.

Moon, Vasant (ed.), *Dr. Babasaheb Ambedkar: Writings and Speeches*: Vol. 1, Bombay: Education Department, Government of Maharashtra, 1979.

———, *Dr. Babasaheb Ambedkar: Writings and Speeches*: Vol. 3, Bombay: Education Department, Government of Maharashtra, 1987.

———, *Dr. Babasaheb Ambedkar: Writings and Speeches*: Vol. 5, Bombay: Education Department, Government of Maharashtra, 1989.

———, *Dr. Babasaheb Ambedkar: Writings and Speeches*: Vol. 8, Bombay: Education Department, Government of Maharashtra, 1990.

———, *Dr. Babasaheb Ambedkar: Writings and Speeches*: Vol. 9, Bombay: Education Department, Government of Maharashtra, 1991.

———, *Dr. Babasaheb Ambedkar: Writings and Speeches*: Vol. 10, Bombay: Education Department, Government of Maharashtra, 1991.

———, *Dr. Babasaheb Ambedkar: Writings and Speeches*: Vol. 12, Bombay:

Education Department, Government of Maharashtra, 1993.

Mukherjee, Arun Prabha and Valmiki, Omprakash, *Joothan: An Untouchable's Life*, New York: Columbia University Press, 2008.

Mungekar, Bhalachandra (ed.), *The Essential Ambedkar*, New Delhi: Rupa Publications, 2017.

Narake, Hari, Kamble, N. G., Kasare, M. L., and Godghate, Ashok (eds.), *Dr. Babasaheb Ambedkar: Writings and Speeches:* Vol. 17: Part III: *Dr. B. R. Ambedkar and his Egalitarian Revolution*, Bombay: Education Department, Government of Maharashtra, 1979.

Nisar, M. and Kandasamy, Meena, *Ayyankali: A Dalit Leader of Organic Protest*, Kozhikode: Other Books, 2007.

Omvedt, Gail, *Ambedkar: Towards an Enlightened India*, New Delhi: Penguin, 2007.

———, *Buddhism in India: Challenging Brahmanism and Caste*, New Delhi: SAGE India, 2003.

———, *Dalits and the Democratic Revolution: Dr Ambedkar and the Dalit Movement in Colonial India*, New Delhi: SAGE India, 1994.

———, *Seeking Begumpura: The Social Vision of Anticaste Intellectuals*, New Delhi: Navayana Publishers, 2009.

Pawar, Daya, *Baluta*, translated by Jerry Pinto, New Delhi: Speaking Tiger, 2015.

Pawar, Urmila, *The Weave of My Life: A Dalit Woman's Memoirs*, New York: Columbia University Press, 2009.

Phule, Jotirao, *Slavery: Collected Works of Mahatma Jotirao Phule: Vol. 1*, Bombay: Government of Maharashtra, 1991.

Ramabadran, Sudarshan and Paswan, Guru Prakash, *Makers of Modern Dalit History: Profiles*, New Delhi: Penguin Random House India, 2021.

Ranjan, Ravi and Singh, M. K., *Dr. Bhimrao Ambedkar*, New Delhi: K. K. Publications, 2021.

Rathore, Aakash Singh (ed.), *Ambedkar's Preamble: A Secret History of the Constitution of India*, New Delhi: Vintage Books, 2020.

Roy, Arundhati, *My Seditious Heart: Collected Non-Fiction*, New Delhi: Penguin Random House India, 2019.

———, *The Doctor and the Saint: The Ambedkar-Gandhi Debate: Caste, Race and Annihilation of Caste*, New Delhi: Penguin Random House India, 2019.

Sarkar, Sumit and Sarkar, Tanika (eds.), *Caste in Modern India*, New Delhi: Orient Blackswan, 2015.

Satyanarayana, K. and Tharu, Susie, *The Exercise of Freedom: An Introduction to Dalit Writing*, New Delhi: Navayana, 2013.

Shah, Ghanshyam, *Caste and Democratic Politics in India*, New Delhi: Permanent Black, 2004.

Shahare, M. L., *Bhimrao Ambedkar: Life and Works*, New Delhi: NCERT, 1986.

Shahare, M. L. and Anil, Nalini, *Babasaheb Dr. Ambedkar Ki Sangharsh Yatra Evam Sandesh*, New Delhi: Samyak Prakashan, 2014.

Shourie, Arun, *Worshipping False Gods: Ambedkar and the Facts Which Have Been Erased*, New Delhi: ASA Publications, 1997.

Sowell, Thomas, *Affirmative Action Around the World: An Empirical Study (Nota Bene)*, New Haven, CT: Yale University Press, 2005.

Sundar, Unnamati Syama, *No Laughing Matter: The Ambedkar Cartoons: 1932–1936*, New Delhi: Navayana, 2019.

Tagore, Rabindranath, *Gitanjali: Song Offerings*, Keighley: Pomona Press, 2007.

Teltumbde, Anand, *Dalits: Past, Present and Future*, New Delhi: Taylor & Francis, 2016.

The Collected Works of Mahatma Gandhi, Vol. 84, New Delhi: Publications Division Government of India, 1999.

Wilkerson, Isabel, *Caste: The Origin of Our Discontents*, New York: Penguin Random House, 2020.

Yengde, Suraj, *Caste Matters*, New Delhi: Penguin Books, 2019.

Yusufji, Salim, *Ambedkar: The Attendant Details*, New Delhi: Navayana, 2017.

Zelliot, Eleanor, *Ambedkar's World: The Making of Babasaheb and the Dalit Movement*, New Delhi: Navayana, 2012.

Zene, Cosimo (ed.), *The Political Philosophies of Antonio Gramsci and B. R. Ambedkar: Itineraries of Dalits and Subalterns*, Abingdon, New York: Routledge, 2013.

JOURNAL ARTICLES, CHAPTERS IN BOOKS, AND SPEECHES

'Ambedkar's Last Word of Wisdom', *The Tribune*, 14 April 2017, available at https://www.tribuneindia.com/news/archive/comment/ambedkar-s-last-words-of-wisdom-391549 [accessed on 28 June 2022].

Agarwal, Sudarshan, 'Introduction', in *Dr. B. R. Ambedkar, the Man and his Message: A Commemorative Volume*, New Delhi: Rajya Sabha Secretariat, 1991.

Aiyar, Swaminathan and Anklesaria, S., 'Despite Modi, India Has Not Yet Become a Hindu Authoritarian State', Cato Institute, 2020, http://www.jstor.org/stable/resrep28731 [accessed on 28 June 2022].

Ambedkar, B. R., 'Castes in India: Their Mechanism, Genesis and Development', paper read at an anthropological seminar of Alexander Goldenweiser in New York on 9 May 1916 quoted in B. R. Ambedkar, 'Castes in India. Their Mechanism, Genesis and Development', *Indian Antiquary*, Vol. 61, 1917, reprinted in *Dr. Babasaheb Ambedkar, Writings and Speeches*, Vol. 1, Bombay,

Government of Maharashtra, 1979.

———, 'Federation versus Freedom', Kale memorial lecture, Gokhale Institute of Politics and Economics, 1939.

———, 'The Grammar of Anarchy', speech to the Constituent Assembly, 25 November 1949.

———, 'What Path to Salvation?', speech to the Bombay Presidency Mahar Conference, 31 May 1936, Bombay. Translated from Marathi by Vasant Moon, 25 January 1988.

Arya, Sunaina, 'Dalit or Brahmanical Patriarchy? Rethinking Indian Feminism', *CASTE: A Global Journal on Social Exclusion*, Vol. 1, No. 1, 2020, available at https://www.jstor.org/stable/48644572 [accessed on 28 June 2022].

———, 'Theorising Gender in South Asia: Dalit Feminist Perspective', *CASTE: A Global Journal on Social Exclusion*, Vol. 1, No. 2, 2020, available at https://www.jstor.org/stable/48643560 [accessed on 28 June 2022].

Bajpai, Rochana, 'Multiculturalism in India: An Exception?', *Multiculturalism in the British Commonwealth: Comparative Perspectives on Theory and Practice*, edited by Richard T. Ashcroft and Mark Bevir, 1st edition, Berkeley: University of California Press, 2019, available at http://www.jstor.org/stable/j.ctvr7fcvv.10 [accessed on 28 June 2022].

Bardia, Meena, 'Dr. B.R. Ambedkar: His Ideas About Religion and Conversion to Buddhism', *The Indian Journal of Political Science*, Vol. 70, No. 3, 2009.

Bhaskar, Anurag, '"Ambedkar's Constitution": A Radical Phenomenon in Anti-Caste Discourse?', *CASTE: A Global Journal on Social Exclusion*, Vol. 2, No. 1, 2021, available at https://www.jstor.org/stable/48643388 [accessed on 28 June 2022].

———, 'Ambedkar, Lohia, and the Segregations of Caste and Gender: Envisioning a Global Agenda for Social Justice', *CASTE: A Global Journal on Social Exclusion*, Vol. 1, No. 2, 2020, available at https://www.jstor.org/stable/48643565 [accessed on 28 June 2022].

Bhimraj, M., 'A Dalit Critique of Environmental Justice in India', *Contemporary Environmental Concerns: Multi-Disciplinary Aspects of Environmental Law*, Patiala: Rajiv Gandhi National University of Law, 2020, available at: https://www.researchgate.net/publication/344218629_A_Dalit_Critique_of_Environmental_Justice_in_India [accessed on 28 June 2022].

Chebaro, Kaoukab, 'Dr. Ambedkar and Columbia University: A Legacy to Celebrate', *Global Studies Blog*, Columbia University Libraries, 15 April 2019, available at https://blogs.cul.columbia.edu/global-studies/2019/04/15/speaking-truth-to-power-dr-ambedkar-and-columbia-university/ [accessed on 28 June 2022].

Constituent Assembly Debates, Vol. 11, 25 November 1949.

Elphinstone, John, 'Report on Education of Depressed Classes', in Vasant Moon (ed.), *Babasaheb Ambedkar Writings and Speeches*, Vol. 2, Bombay: Education Department, Government of Maharashtra, 1979.

Garalytè, Kristina, 'Dalit Counterpublic and Social Space on Indian Campuses', *CASTE: A Global Journal on Social Exclusion*, Vol. 1, No. 2, 2020, available at https://www.jstor.org/stable/48643570 [accessed on 28 June 2022].

Ghadage, Tushar, 'Ambedkarites in Making: The Process of Awakening and Conversion to Buddhism among Non-Mahar Communities in Maharashtra', *CASTE: A Global Journal on Social Exclusion*, Vol. 1, No. 2, 2020, available at https://www.jstor.org/stable/48643568 [accessed on 28 June 2022].

Gorringe, H., 'Out of the Cheris: Dalits Contesting and Creating Public Space in Tamil Nadu', *Space and Culture*, Vol. 19, No. 2, 2016.

Guru, Gopal, 'Dalit Women Talk Differently', *Economic and Political Weekly*, Vol. 30, No. 41/42, 1995, available at http://www.jstor.org/stable/4403327 [accessed on 28 June 2022].

Ingole, Prashant, 'Intersecting Dalit and Cultural Studies: De-Brahmanizing the Disciplinary Space', *CASTE: A Global Journal on Social Exclusion*, Vol. 1, No. 2, 2020, available at https://www.jstor.org/stable/48643567 [accessed on 28 June 2022].

Jayasankar, Krishnamurty, 'Ambedkar's Educational Odyssey: 1913–1927', *Journal of Social Inclusion Studies*, 2020.

Kapur, Devesh, 'Why Does the Indian State Both Fail and Succeed?', *The Journal of Economic Perspectives*, Vol. 34, No. 1, 2020, available at https://www.jstor.org/stable/26873528 [accessed on 28 June 2022].

Khilnani, Sunil, 'Ambedkar: Building Palaces on Dung Heaps', in *Incarnations: A History of India in 50 Lives*, New Delhi: Penguin Random House India, 2017.

Kumar, Raj (ed.), 'Dalit and Power Stucture', in *Essays on Dalits*, New Delhi: Discovery Publishing House, 2003.

Loftus, Timothy, 'Ambedkar and the Buddha's Saṅgha: A Ground for Buddhist Ethics', *CASTE: A Global Journal on Social Exclusion*, Vol. 2, No. 2, 2021, available at https://www.jstor.org/stable/48645681 [accessed on 28 June 2022].

Meadowcroft, Keith, 'The All-India Hindu Mahasabha, untouchable politics, and "denationalising" conversions: the Moonje–Ambedkar Pact', *Journal of South Asian Studies*, Vol. 29, No. 1, 2006.

Namala, Paul Divakar, 'Norm Entrepreneurship at the UN-Dalits and Communities Discriminated on Work and Descent', *CASTE: A Global Journal on Social Exclusion*, Vol. 2, No. 2, 2021, available at https://www.jstor.org/stable/48645680 [accessed on 28 June 2022].

Nasr, Vali, 'South Asia from 1919', in Francis Robin (ed.), *The New Cambridge*

History of Islam, Cambridge: Cambridge University Press, 2010.

Nigam, Aditya, 'Hindutva, Caste and the "National Unconscious"', in Vishwas Sagar (ed.), *Racism After Apartheid: Challenges for Marxism and Anti-Racism*, Johannesburg: Wits University Press, 2019, available at https://doi.org/10.18772/22019033061.10 [accessed on 28 June 2022].

Parekh, Bhiku, 'The Intellectual and Political Legacy of B. R. Ambedkar', in Aakash Singh Rathore (ed.), *B.R. Ambedkar: The Quest for Justice*, New Delhi: Oxford University Press, 2021.

Patel, Vallabhbhai, *Constituent Assembly Debates*, Vol. 8, 26 May 1949.

Phanda, K. R. and Goradia, Prafull, 'Jinnah Proposed, Gandhi Disposed...Thus India Divided', Centre for Advanced Research, Reference, Information & Enhanced Documentation, 2014.

Pramod, Maya, 'As a Dalit Woman: My Life in a Caste-Ghetto of Kerala', *CASTE: A Global Journal on Social Exclusion*, Vol. 1, No. 1, 2020, available at https://www.jstor.org/stable/48644567 [accessed on 28 June 2022].

Prasad, Indulata, 'Caste-Ing Space: Mapping the Dynamics of Untouchability in Rural Bihar, India', *CASTE: A Global Journal on Social Exclusion*, Vol. 2, No. 1, 2021, available at https://www.jstor.org/stable/48643389 [accessed on 28 June 2022].

Ray, Ishita Aditya and Ray, Sarbapriya, 'An Appraisal of Influence of Eminent Personalities on Ambedkar's Political Thought during Early Twentieth Century', *Historical Research Letter*, Vol. 2, 2012.

Responses to Information Requests—Immigration and Refugee Board of Canada, available at https://www.justice.gov/eoir/page/file/1243266/download [accessed on 28 June 2022].

Rodrigues, Valerian, 'Introduction', in Valerian Rodrigues (ed.), *The Essential Writings of B. R. Ambedkar*, New Delhi: Oxford University Press, 2002.

Roy, Ishita, 'A Critique of Sanskritization from Dalit/Caste-Subaltern Perspective', *CASTE: A Global Journal on Social Exclusion*, Vol. 2, No. 2, 2021, available at https://www.jstor.org/stable/48645684 [accessed on 28 June 2022].

Sawariya, Meena, 'Caste and Counselling Psychology in India: Dalit Perspectives in Theory and Practice', *CASTE: A Global Journal on Social Exclusion*, Vol. 2, No. 1, 2021, available at https://www.jstor.org/stable/48643392 [accessed on 28 June 2022].

Shankar, Shiva and Kanthi, Swaroop, 'Manual Scavenging in India: The Banality of an Everyday Crime', *CASTE: A Global Journal on Social Exclusion*, Vol. 2, No. 1, 2021, available at https://www.jstor.org/stable/48643385 [accessed on 28 June 2022].

Shyam Ratna, Gupta. 'New Light on the Cripps Mission', *India Quarterly*, Vol.

28, No. 1, 1972, available at Jstor, http://www.jstor.org/stable/45069909.

Simon, Laurence, '"I Can't Breathe": Perspectives on Emancipation from Caste', *CASTE: A Global Journal on Social Exclusion*, Vol. 2, No. 1, 2021, available at https://www.jstor.org/stable/48643380 [accessed on 28 June 2022].

Singh, Hira, 'Raising the Bar or Missed Opportunity', *Economic & Political Weekly*, Vol. 50, No. 45, 7 November 2015.

Sinha, Arvind and Sinha, Indu, 'State, Class and "Sena" Nexus: Bathani Tola Massacre', *Economic and Political Weekly*, Vol. 31, No. 44, 1996.

Stausberg, Michael, 'Leaving Hinduism: Deconversion as Liberation', *Handbook of Leaving Religion*, edited by Daniel Enstedt et al., Leiden: Brill, 2020, available at http://www.jstor.org/stable/10.1163/j.ctv2gjwshc.11 [accessed on 28 June 2022].

Thorat, Amit, et al., 'Persisting Prejudice: Measuring Attitudes and Outcomes by Caste and Gender in India', *CASTE: A Global Journal on Social Exclusion*, Vol. 1, No. 2, 2020, available at https://www.jstor.org/stable/4864356 [accessed on 28 June 2022].

Vundru, Raja Sekhar, 'Expanding the Possibilities', in K. Raju (ed.), *The Dalit Truth: The Battles for Realizing Ambedkar's Vision*, New Delhi: Vintage Books, 2022.

NEWSPAPERS, ARTICLES, AND ONLINE RESOURCES

'"Gandhi shedding clothes not revolutionary, but Ambedkar wearing three-piece suit is"', *The Hindu*, 25 April 2015.

'1942 Quit India Movement', *Making Britain*, The Open University.

'All Insults Don't Count as Offences Under SC/ST Act: Supreme Court', *The Wire*, 6 November 2020.

'B R Ambedkar's granddaughter Rama Ambedkar demands release of all political prisoners', *Scroll.in*, 8 July 2021.

'Communal deadlock and a way to solve it', *The Modern Rationalist*, 1 January 2022.

'Directive Principles of State Policy', *Legal Service India Journal*.

'Environmental Casteism: An Overdue Apology We Owe to Ecology and Victims of Caste', *Nickeled and Dimed*, 9 April 2021.

'His first struggle was to access his own education but he did not use it for self-advancement alone: Justice DY Chandrachud on Dr. BR Ambedkar', *Bar and Bench*, 18 July 2021.

'In the 1910's, Off to Columbia, On to London', Columbia University, available at https://bit.ly/3OTeI8P [accessed on 28 June 2022].

'Indian Army's Mahar regiment: Home to two army chiefs and a Param Vir

Chakra', *The Print*, 3 January 2018.

'Khairlanji massacre: 15 years on, FPJ revisits the killing of Bhotmange family which rocked Maharashtra', *Free Press Journal*, 29 September 2021.

'Maharashtra: "Statue of Knowledge" Dedicated to Dr Ambedkar to Be Unveiled in Latur on April', *News 18*, 8 April 2022.

'Massacre in Shankarbigha', *Frontline*, 13 February 1999.

'Move to rename Konaseema district after Ambedkar', *The New Indian Express*, 19 May 2022.

'Rajaji in 1968: "Hindi is, at Best, the Language of a Large Minority"', *Swarajya*, 14 September 2016.

'Round Table Conferences 1930–32', *Making Britain,* The Open University.

'Stafford Cripps', *Making Britain*, The Open University.

'Video of Dalit govt employee falling at caste Hindu's feet triggers protest in Coimbatore', *The Hindu*, 7 August 2021.

'Who Was Ramabai Ambedkar? Some Lesser-Known Facts About B. R. Ambedkar's Wife', *NDTV*, 27 May 2022.

'125-ft-tall B.R. Ambedkar statue in Hyderabad by December', *Deccan Chronicle*, April 14, 2022.

Aiyar, S. A., 'Ambedkar vs Gandhi: The risks of village empowerment', *The Times of India*, 9 February 2014.

Akhil, (@akhiles04984831), Twitter post, 23 July 2021, <https://twitter.com/akhiles04984831/status/1418409744453148672?s=19>.

Ambedkar International Centre, (@ambedkar_center), Twitter post, 20 July 2021, <https://twitter.com/ambedkar_center/status/1417471063307395079?s=19>.

Ambedkar interview on the BBC, broadcast 31 December 1955, available at https://www.youtube.com/watch?v=3dJETivg7nw [accessed on 28 June 2022].

Ambedkar, B. R., 'A Reply to the Mahatma', *Round Table India*, 30 September 2014.

———, 'Need for Checks and Balances: Articles on Linguistic States', *The Times of India*, 23 April 1953.

———, *Constituent Assembly Debates*, 25 November 1949.

Ambwani, Meenakshi Verma, 'Dr. B. R. Ambedkar voted as Greatest Indian', *The Hindu Businessline*, 14 August 2012.

ANI, 'Dr B R Ambedkar Jayanti celebrated with fervour in Dubai', *The Print*, 25 April 2022.

———, 'India, Nepal agree to set up Dr Bhimrao Ambedkar Chair at Lumbini Buddhist University, Nepal', *The Print*, 16 May 2022.

Babu, D. Shyam, 'Fault lines in a "landmark" judgment', *The Hindu*, 21 July 2018.

Bellwinkel-Schempp, Maren, 'Ambedkar Studies at Heidelberg', University of Columbia.

Bhaskar, Anurag, 'When It Comes to Dalit and Tribal Rights, the Judiciary in India Just Does Not Get It', *The Wire*, 3 May 2020.

Bose, Mrityunjay, 'Dr Ambedkar memorial in Mumbai to be ready by March 2024', *Deccan Herald*, 11 May 2022.

Chavan, Akshay, 'Against All Odds', *Live History India*, 6 December 2018.

Dass, Santosh, 'Caste in the UK, and why Ambedkar matters', *The Indian Express*, 8 August 2021.

Dhamija, Bhanu, 'India's Constitution makers Nehru, Patel, Ambedkar were divided on Parliamentary system', *The Print*, 25 January 2019.

————, 'Why Ambedkar didn't like India's Constitution', 14 April 2018.

Dhanraj, Christina, 'Red Earth and the Sky Dalit Blue', *Outlook*, 19 October 2020, pp. 23–24.

Dutta, Amrita, '"RSS detested Ambedkar in his lifetime but now must praise him": Ramachandra Guha', *The Indian Express*, 8 September 2018.

Elphinstone College official website, available at https://www.elphinstone.ac.in/disalumni.php [accessed on 28 June 2022].

Fernando, Antony, 'Fifty years after caste violence, Keezhvenmani village waiting for daylight', *New Indian Express*, 23 December 2018.

Gandhi, M. K., 'The curse of Untouchability', available at https://www.mkgandhi.org/about-us.html [accessed on 28 June 2022].

Government of India Act, 1935, Constitution of India.

Gowri, Madan, (@madan3), Twitter post, 23 July 2021, <https://twitter.com/madan3/status/1418441398064279553?s=19>.

Gupta, Sachin, (@sachingupta787), Twitter post, 22 July 2021, <https://twitter.com/sachingupta787/status/1418241605123796998?s=03>.

Hamsa, Dhwani (@HamsadhwaniA), Twitter post, 4 July 2021 <https://twitter.com/HamsadhwaniA/status/1411677803955638274?s=03>.

Henry, Nikhila, 'Caste Discrimination at IIT-Madras? Asst Professor Complains to OBC Commission', *The Quint*, 12 August 2021.

Human Rights Watch, 'Attacks on Dalit women: A pattern of impunity', available at https://www.hrw.org/reports/1999/india/India994-11.htm [accessed on 28 June 2022].

Indian National Congress, 'Dr. B. R. Ambedkar', available at https://inc.in/our-inspiration/dr-b-r-ambedkar [accessed on 28 June 2022].

Jain, Rishabh, 'Anti-caste rap: A hip-hop revolution in the making in India', *TRT World*, 17 May 2022.

Jeyarani, 'Media's Conspiracy of Silence', *Outlook*, 12 October 2020.

K., Malmarugan, (@Kodungolan737), Twitter post, 18 August 2021, <https://

twitter.com/Kodungolan737/status/1427956394473316359?s=03>.

Kamble, Dayanand, (@dayakamPR), Twitter post, 20 July 2021, <https://twitter.com/dayakamPR/status/1417315203872559105?s=19>.

———, (@dayakamPR), Twitter post, 21 July 2021, <https://twitter.com/dayakamPR/status/1417678779644710920?s=19>.

Kamble, Swati, 'Interjections, Intersections', *Outlook*, 19 October 2020.

Kancha Ilaiah, 'Why Ambedkar supported Sanskrit as national language: A response to Murli Manohar Joshi', *The News Minute*, 27 April 2016.

Khobragade, Uttam, 'Constitution Revolution engendered by Dr. Ambedkar', *The Times of India*, 4 May 2020.

Kolappan, B., 'Little-known facts about a well-known leader', *The Hindu*, 21 August 2012.

Kothari, Urvish, 'Parsis in Baroda berated Ambedkar for his caste. But Naval Bhathena changed everything', *The Print*, 6 December 2019.

Krishnan, Anjali, 'Chhatrapati Shahu Maharaj, the King Who Fought the Caste System & Shaped Dr Ambedkar's Education', *The Better India*, 24 April 2022.

Lawson, Alaistair, 'Indian maharajah's daring act of anti-colonial dissent', *BBC News*, 10 December 2011.

'Maharashtra government buys Ambedkar's London house', *Times Network*, 26 September 2015.

Maitreya, Yogesh, 'Ambedkar: A Spartan Warrior who Made Knowledge and Justice his Weapon', *Cultural Forum*, 14 April 2020.

———, 'In Chokamela's Bhakti, Past Transforms into Radical Present', *Newsclick*, 16 November 2019.

Mandal, Dilip, (@Profdilipmandal), Twitter post, 21 July 2021, <https://twitter.com/Profdilipmandal/status/1417707584081960965?s=19>.

———, (@Profdilipmandal), Twitter post, 22 July 2021, <https://twitter.com/Profdilipmandal/status/1418087246608015363?s=19>.

Meena, Ravi, (@RaviMeena4089), Twitter post, 23 July 2021, <https://twitter.com/RaviMeena4089/status/1418482625954476032?s=19>.

Meghwal, Arjun Ram, 'B R Ambedkar laid the foundation for workers' rights, social security in India', *The Indian Express*, 1 May 2020.

Mishra, Akanksha, 'Annihilation of Caste: Kalahandi rapper Dule Rocker plans album "to take forward Ambedkar's legacy"', *Scroll.in*, 4 July 2021.

Mission Ambedkar, (@MissionAmbedkar), Twitter post, 18 July 2021, <https://twitter.com/MissionAmbedkar/status/1416660774785671169?s=19>.

Mukhopadhyay, Jayita, 'Ambedkar's vision of a secular Constitution', *The Statesman*, 6 April 2018.

Nair, Supriya, 'The Ambedkar Suit and Dalit Identity', *The Voice of Fashion*,

22 April 2019.

Narayan, Badri, 'BR buzz: How Ambedkar Jayanti celebrations became a political contest', *Sunday Times of India*, 10 April 2022.

——, 'Why Dalit is no longer an empowering word for some marginalised communities in UP', *The Indian Express*, 10 August 2018.

Noorani, A. G., 'Linguism Trap', *Frontline*, 23 April 2010.

Pradhan, Shirish B., 'Ambedkar's birth anniversary observed in Nepal', *The Print*, 13 April 2022.

Priyesh, (@Priyesh_py29), Twitter post, 22 July 2021, <https://twitter.com/Priyesh_py29/status/1418036352491290625?s=19>.

PTI, 'Dalit civil rights activist accuses Google of casteist, hostile workplace practices', *The Hindu*, 4 June 2022.

——, 'Indian High Commissioner to the UK pays tribute to B R Ambedkar and Lord Basaveshwara in London', *The Print,* 3 May 2022.

——, 'President Kovind inaugurates street named after Ambedkar in Jamaican capital', *The Print*, 17 May 2022.

Pudur, Arun, (@arunpudur), Twitter post, 23 July 2021, <https://twitter.com/arunpudur/status/1418438977510469632?s=19>.

Puri, Harish K., 'Ambedkar had warned about Indian democracy's fragility. He must be heeded', *The Indian Express*, 15 April 2022.

Radhakrishna, Meena, 'The Dark Realities of the SC/ST Atrocities Act: An Ethnographic Reading', *The Wire*, 4 April 2018.

Rai, Piyush, (@Benarasiyaa), Twitter post, 23 July 2021, <https://twitter.com/Benarasiyaa/status/1418282467799093248?s=19>.

Ramachandran, Shreya, '18-hour study marathon commemorates Ambedkar's legacy', *The Hindu*, 10 April 2017.

Ramavarman, T., 'Dalit artist posted at Guruvayur temple', *The Times of India*, 26 August 2021.

Ramesh, Randeep, 'India reserves half of university places for lower castes', *The Guardian*, 10 April 2008.

Roy, Arundhati, 'India's shame: Democracy hasn't eradicated the country's caste system. It has entrenched and modernised it', *Prospect Magazine*, 12 November 2014.

Roy, Debayan, 'Insulting, abusing SC/ST person not an offense under SC/ST Act unless victim abused on account of caste: Supreme Court', *Bar and Bench*, 5 November 2020.

Roy, Nilanjana S., 'The Ambedkar letters', *Business Standard*, 14 June 2013.

Roy, Siddharth Swapan, 'The Lake of Liberation', *Outlook*, 8 April 2016.

Sasidharan, Keerthik, 'Whose secularism is it anyway?', *The Hindu*, 10 September 2017.

Seshadri, Badri, 'Breaking Caste Barriers in Temples: Tamil Nadu Has Dealt the First Blow But Many Divisive Walls Stand', *CNN-IBN News*, 20 August 2021.

Siddharth, (@Actor_Siddharth), Twitter post, https://twitter.com/Actor_Siddharth/status/1418448497708212225?s=19 >.

Siddharth College of Arts, Science and Commerce, Mumbai, Official Website, available at https://siddharthcollegeofasc.com/ [accessed on 28 June 2022].

Siddharth, '"Bahishkrit Bharat": Ambedkar's decisive challenge to Brahmanism', *Forward Press*, 30 January 2020.

Singh, Deepika, (@Deepika_opines), Twitter post, 23 July 2021, <https://twitter.com/Deepika_opines/status/1418296208003518466?s=19>.

Singh, Shashank Shekhar, 'Remembering Babasaheb Ambedkar the lawyer', *Bar and Bench*, 14 April 2020.

Singh, Snehil Kunwar, 'Are we still where Ambedkar left us?', *Deccan Herald*, 12 August 2020.

Sonowane, Sankul, (@Sankul333), Twitter post, 23 July 2021, <https://twitter.com/Sankul333/status/1418438775269511171?s=19>.

Srinivasan, Krithika, 'Love and harmony over caste, dowry: Ground rule for weddings in these Tamil Nadu tribal hamlets', *New Indian Express*, 11 August 2021.

Srivasatava, Amitabh, 'Caste census: Counting the castes', *India Today*, 6 August 2021.

Srivastava, Amit, 'Navi Mumbai: "Keep Dr. Babasaheb Ambedkar's memorial big for future generations", says Atomic scientist Dr. Anil Kakodkar', *Free Press Journal*, 5 May 2022.

Subramanian, Archana, 'Striking a deal', *The Hindu*, 3 March 2016.

Sud, Danish, 'The Fascinating story of B. R. Ambedkar', *The Times of India*, 17 October 2020.

Sultana, Ayesha, 'On the Participation of Women: A Reading of Ambedkar's "The Mahad Satyagraha"', *All About Ambedkar: A Journal of Theory and Praxis*, available at https://www.allaboutambedkaronline.com/post/an-overview-of-the-mahad-satyagraha [last accessed 28 June 2022].

Sumit, 'A jurist with no equals', *Forward Press*, 13 July 2017.

Talati, Shlok, 'How prejudice rooted in an ancient social system has migrated from India to Canada', *CBC News*, 16 May 2022.

Team Ambedkarite Today, *Bahishkrit Hitakarini Sabha*.

Vajpeyi, Ananya, 'BR Ambedkar: the life of the mind and a life in politics', *Indian Cultural Forum*, 14 April 2021.

Velayudhan, Meera, 'Politics as a Sedative', *Outlook*, 19 October 2020.

Venkatraman, Sakshi, 'All Cal State universities add caste to anti-discrimination policy', *NBC News*, 19 January 2022.

Verma, Mohit and Sharma, Sankalp, 'Women, Lower Caste Postgrad Students Have Higher Anxiety: Survey', *The Quint*, 10 August 2021.

Vij-Arora, Bhavna, 'Casteaways', *Outlook*, 19 October 2020.

Yadav, Shyamlal, 'Explained: The caste census debate, and the government stand over the years', *The Indian Express*, 27 July 2021.

LEGAL CITATIONS

Hitesh Verma vs The State Of Uttarakhand, 2020.

I. C. Golaknath & Ors vs State Of Punjab & Anrs., AIR (1967) SC 1643.

Indra Sawhney vs Union of India, 1992.

M. Nagaraj & Others vs Union Of India & Others, 2006.

Raghunathrao Ganpatrao Etc. vs Union Of India, AIR (1993) SC 58.

Writ Petition (Civil) 61 of 2002.

Index